Excel® Dashboards
& Reports

Excel® Dashboards & Reports

by Michael Alexander and John Walkenbach

WILEY

Wiley Publishing, Inc.

Excel® Dashboards & Reports

Published by
Wiley Publishing, Inc.
111 River Street
Hoboken, NJ 07030-5774
www.wiley.com

Copyright © 2010 by Wiley Publishing, Inc., Indianapolis, Indiana

Published by Wiley Publishing, Inc., Indianapolis, Indiana

Published simultaneously in Canada

For general information on our other products and services, please contact our Customer Care Department within the U.S. at 877-762-2974, outside the U.S. at 317-572-3993, or fax 317-572-4002.

For technical support, please visit www.wiley.com/techsupport.

Wiley also publishes its books in a variety of electronic formats. Some content that appears in print may not be available in electronic books.

Library of Congress Control Number: 2010932452

ISBN: 978-0-470-62012-0

Manufactured in the United States of America

10 9 8 7 6 5 4 3 2 1

WILEY

About the Author

Mike Alexander is a Microsoft Certified Application Developer (MCAD) and author of several books on advanced business analysis using Microsoft Access and Excel. He has more than 15 years experience consulting and developing Microsoft Office solutions. Michael has been named a Microsoft MVP for his ongoing contributions to the Excel community. In his spare time he runs a free tutorial site, www.datapigtechnologies.com, where he shares basic Access and Excel tips with the Office community.

John Walkenbach is a leading authority on spreadsheet software, and principal of J-Walk and Associates Inc., a one-person consulting firm based in southern Arizona. John has received a Microsoft MVP award every year since 2000. He's the author of more than 50 spreadsheet books, and has written more than 300 articles and reviews for a variety of publications, including *PC World, InfoWorld, PC Magazine, Windows,* and *PC/Computing*. John also maintains a popular Web site (*The Spreadsheet Page*, http://spreadsheetpage.com), and is the developer of several Excel utilities, including the Power Utility Pak, an award-winning add-in for Excel. John graduated from the University of Missouri, and earned a Masters and PhD from the University of Montana.

About the Technical Editor

Mike Talley works for K2 as a Program Manager. Prior to K2, he spent 8 years at Microsoft where he was a programming writer, beta lead, and support professional. While at Microsoft, he worked with product teams on supportability issues and wrote about InfoPath, SharePoint, and Excel. He currently resides in Colorado with his wife, daughter, and two sons. You can reach him at mtnswin@gmail.com

Dedication

This is dedicated to the fans of `DataPigTechnologies.com` ... all twelve of you.

—Michael Alexander

Author's Acknowledgments

My deepest thanks to Katie Mohr and Susan Cohen, for all the hours of work put into making this book as clear as it can be. Thanks also to the brilliant team of professionals who helped bring this book to fruition. Finally, a special thank you goes to my family for putting up with all the time spent away on this project.

—Michael Alexander

Acquisitions, Editorial, and Media Development

Project Editor: Susan B. Cohen

Acquisitions Editor: Katie Mohr

Copy Editor: Susan B. Cohen

Technical Editor: Mike Talley

Editorial Manager: Jodi Jensen

Editorial Assistant: Amanda Graham

Sr. Editorial Assistant: Cherie Case

Composition Services

Project Coordinator: Sheree Montgomery

Layout and Graphics: Carrie A. Cesavice

Proofreaders: John Greenough, Susan Hobbs, Lindsay Littrell

Indexer: BIM Indexing & Proofreading Services

Contents at a Glance

▶ Table of Contents

Part II: Excel Chart Basics

Part III: Going Beyond Tables and Charts

Part IV: Creating Advanced Dashboard Components

Part V: Automating Your Dashboards and Reports

Part VI: Working with the Outside World

INTRODUCTION

Business intelligence (BI) is what you get when you analyze raw data and turn that information into actionable knowledge. BI can help an organization identify cost-cutting opportunities, uncover new business opportunities, recognize changing business environments, identify data anomalies, and create widely accessible reports.

The BI concept is overtaking corporate executives who are eager to turn impossible amounts of data into useful knowledge. As a result of this trend, software vendors who focus on BI and build dashboards are coming out of the woodwork. Dashboards are ideal mechanisms for delivering this targeted information in a graphical, user-friendly form. New consulting firms touting their BI knowledge are popping up virtually every week. And even the traditional enterprise solution providers like Business Objects and SAP are offering new BI capabilities presented in a dashboard format.

So maybe *you've* been hit with dashboard fever? Or maybe you are holding this book because someone is asking you to create BI solutions (that is, create a dashboard) in Excel.

Although many IT managers would scoff at the thought of using Excel as a BI tool to create your dashboard, Excel is inherently part of the enterprise BI tool portfolio. Whether IT managers are keen to acknowledge it or not, most of the data analysis and reporting done in business today is done by using a spreadsheet program. We see several significant reasons to use Excel as the platform for your dashboards and reports. They are, as follows:

> **Familiarity with Excel:** If you work in corporate America, you are conversant in the "language" of Excel. You can send even the most seasoned senior vice president an Excel-based presentation and trust he will know what to do with it. With an Excel dashboard, your users spend less time figuring how to use the tool and more time viewing the data.

> **Built-in flexibility:** With most enterprise dashboards, the ability to analyze the data outside of the predefined views is either disabled or unavailable. In Excel, features such as pivot tables, drop-down lists, and other interactive controls (such as a check box) don't lock your audience into one view. And because an Excel workbook contains multiple worksheets, the users have space to add their own data analysis as needed.

> **Rapid development:** Using Excel to build your own dashboards can liberate you from assorted resource and time limitations from within an organization. With Excel, you can develop dashboards faster, and adapt more quickly to changing business requirements.

1

> **Powerful data connectivity and automation capabilities:** Excel is not the toy application some IT managers make it out to be. With its own native programming language and its robust object model, Excel can help to automate certain processes and even connect with various data sources. With a few advanced techniques, your dashboard can practically run on its own.

> **Little to no incremental costs:** Not all of us can work for multi-billion dollar companies that can afford enterprise-level reporting solutions. In most companies, funding for new computers and servers is limited, let alone funding for expensive dashboard software packages. For those companies, Excel is frankly the most cost-effective way to deliver key business reporting tools without compromising too deeply on usability and function.

Excel contains so many functions and features that it's difficult to know where to start. Enter your humble authors, spirited into your hands via this book. Here, we show you how you can turn Excel into your own personal BI tool. With a few fundamentals and some of the new BI functionality Microsoft has included in this latest version of Excel, you can go from reporting data with simple tables, to creating meaningful dashboards sure to wow everyone.

What You Need to Know

The goal of this book is to show you how to leverage Excel functionality to build and manage better presentations. Each chapter in this book provides a comprehensive review of Excel functions and features, and the analytical concepts that will help you create better reporting components — components that can be used for both dashboards and reports. As you move through this book, you will be able to create increasingly sophisticated components.

After reading this book, you will be able to:

> Analyze large amounts of data and report those results in a meaningful way

> Get better visibility into data from different perspectives

> Add interactive controls to show various views

> Automate repetitive tasks and processes

> Create eye-catching visualizations

> Create impressive dashboards and What-If analyses

> Access external data sources to expand your message

What You Need to Have

In order to get the most out of this book, it's best that you have certain skills before diving into the topics highlighted in this book. The ideal candidate for this book will have:

➤ Some experience working with data and familiarity with the basic concepts of data analysis such as working with tables, aggregating data, and performing calculations.

➤ Experience using Excel with a strong grasp of concepts such as table structures, filtering, sorting, and using formulas.

Conventions in This Book

Take a minute to skim this section and learn some of the typographic conventions used throughout this book.

Keyboard conventions

You need to use the keyboard to enter formulas. In addition, you can work with menus and dialog boxes directly from the keyboard — a method you may find easier if your hands are already positioned over the keys.

Formula listings

Formulas usually appear on a separate line in `monospace font`. For example, we may list the following formula:

```
=VLOOKUP(StockNumber,PriceList,2,False)
```

Excel supports a special type of formula known as an *array formula*. When you enter an array formula, press Ctrl+Shift+Enter (not just Enter). Excel encloses an array formula in brackets in order to remind you that it's an array formula. When we list an array formula, we include the brackets to make it clear that it is, in fact, an array formula. For example:

```
{=SUM(LEN(A1:A10))}
```

Note

Do not type the brackets for an array formula. Excel will put them in automatically.

VBA code listings

This book also contains examples of VBA code. Each listing appears in a `monospace font`; each line of code occupies a separate line. To make the code easier to read, we usually use one or more tabs to create indentations. Indentation is optional, but it does help to delineate statements that go together.

If a line of code doesn't fit on a single line in this book, we use the standard VBA line continuation sequence: a space followed by an underscore character. This indicates that the line of code extends to the next line. For example, the following two lines comprise a single VBA statement:

```
If Right(cell.Value, 1) = "!" Then cell.Value _
    = Left(cell.Value, Len(cell.Value) - 1)
```

You can enter this code either exactly as shown on two lines, or on a single line without the trailing underscore character.

Key names

Names of keys on the keyboard appear in normal type, for example Alt, Home, PgDn, and Ctrl. When you should press two keys simultaneously, the keys are connected with a plus sign: "Press Ctrl+G to display the Go To dialog box."

Functions, procedures, and named ranges

Excel's worksheet functions appear in all uppercase, like so: "Use the SUM function to add the values in column A."

Macro and procedure names appear in normal type: "Execute the InsertTotals procedure." we often use mixed upper- and lowercase to make these names easier to read. Named ranges appear in italic: "Select the *InputArea* range."

Unless you're dealing with text inside of quotation marks, Excel is not sensitive to case. In other words, both of the following formulas produce the same result:

```
=SUM(A1:A50)
=sum(a1:a50)
```

Excel, however, will convert the characters in the second formula to uppercase.

Mouse conventions

The mouse terminology in this book is all standard fare: "pointing," "clicking," "right-clicking," "dragging," and so on. You know the drill.

What the icons mean

Throughout the book, icons appear to call your attention to points that are particularly important.

New Feature

This icon indicates a feature new to Excel 2010.

Note

We use Note icons to tell you that something is important — perhaps a concept that may help you master the task at hand or something fundamental for understanding subsequent material.

Tip

Tip icons indicate a more efficient way of doing something or a technique that may not be obvious. These will often impress your officemates.

On the Web

These icons indicate that an example file is on the companion Web site:

www.wiley.com/go/exceldr

Caution

We use Caution icons when the operation that I'm describing can cause problems if you're not careful.

Cross-Ref

We use the Cross Reference icon to refer you to other chapters that have more to say on a particular topic.

How This Book Is Organized

The chapters in this book are organized into six parts. Each of these parts includes chapters that build on the previous chapters' instruction. The idea is that as you go through each part, you will be able to build dashboards of increasing complexity until you're an Excel dashboarding guru.

Part I: Moving from Spreadsheets to Dashboards

Part I is all about helping you think about your data in terms of creating effective dashboards and reports. Chapter 1 introduces you to the topics of dashboards and reports, defining some of the basic concepts and outlining key steps to take to prepare for a successful project. Chapter 2 shows you how to build an effective data model that provides the foundation upon which your dashboard or report is built. In this chapter, you will learn the impact of poorly organized data, and will discover how to set up the source data for the most positive outcome.

Part II: Excel Chart Basics

Part II provides a solid foundation in visualizing data using Excel Charts. Chapter 3 starts with the basics, introducing you to Excel's charting engine. In Chapter 4, we discuss the various chart types available in Excel and show which charts are best to use in different scenarios. Chapters 5 and 6 focus on formatting techniques that enable you to build customized charts that fit your distinct needs. By the end of this section, you will be able to effectively leverage Excel charts to synthesize your data into meaningful visualizations.

Part III: Going Beyond Tables and Charts

In Part III, we offer an in depth look at some of Excel's other key dashboard and report components that you can leverage to create a cutting edge dashboard presentation. In Chapter 7 we introduce you to pivot tables, and explore how this Excel feature can play an integral role in Excel-based presentations. Chapter 8 provides a primer on building pivot charts, giving you a solid understanding of how Excel pivot charts work with pivot tables. Chapter 9 introduces the new sparkline functionality found in Excel 2010. Finally, Chapter 10 rounds out this section with a look at the various techniques that you can use to visualize data without the use of charts or graphs.

Part IV: Creating Advanced Dashboard Components

Part IV takes you beyond basic chart-building with a look at some advanced business techniques that can help make your dashboards more meaningful. Starting with Chapter 11, we demonstrate how to represent trending across multiple series and distinct time periods. In Chapter 12, we explore how best to use charts to group data into meaningful views. And Chapter 13 demonstrates some of charting techniques that can help you display and measure performance against a target.

Part V: Automating Your Dashboards and Reports

Part V focuses on techniques that will help you automate your reporting processes, and give your users an interactive UI. Chapter 14 provides a clear understanding of how macros can be leveraged to automate your reporting systems. Chapter 15 illustrates how interactive controls can provide your clients with a simple interface, allowing them to easily navigate through and interact with your dashboard or report.

Part VI: Working with the Outside World

The theme in Part VI is importing and exporting information to and from Excel. Chapter 16 explores some of the ways to incorporate data that does not originate in Excel. In this chapter, you will learn how to import data from external sources, such as Microsoft Access, as well as create systems that allow for dynamic refreshing of external data sources. Chapter 17 wraps up this look at Excel dashboards and reports by showing you the various ways to distribute and present your work in a safe and effective way.

About the Companion Web Site

This book contains many examples, and the workbooks for those examples are available on the companion Web site that is arranged in directories that correspond to the chapters. You can download example files for this book at the Web site:

```
www.wiley.com/go/exceldr
```

The example workbook files on the Web site are not compressed (installation is not required). These files are all Excel 2007/2010 files.

About the Power Utility Pak Offer

Toward the back of the book, you'll find a coupon that you can redeem for a discounted copy of John Walkenbach's award-winning Power Utility Pak — a collection of useful Excel utilities, plus many new worksheet functions. John developed this package using VBA exclusively.

You can also use this coupon to purchase the complete VBA source code for a nominal fee. Studying the code is an excellent way to pick up some useful programming techniques.

You can download a 30-day trial version of the most recent version of the Power Utility Pak from John's Web site:

```
http://spreadsheetpage.com
```

If you find it useful, use the coupon to purchase a licensed copy at a discount.

Reach Out

We're always interested in getting feedback on our books. The best way to provide this feedback is via e-mail. Send your comments and suggestions to

```
mha105@yahoo.com
john@j-walk.com
```

Unfortunately, we're not able to reply to specific questions. Posting your question to one of the Excel newsgroups is, by far, the best way to get such assistance.

Also, when you're out surfing the Web, don't overlook John's Web site ("The Spreadsheet Page"). You'll find lots of useful Excel information, including tips and downloads. The URL is

```
http://spreadsheetpage.com
```

Now, without further ado, it's time to turn the page and expand your horizons.

Moving from Spreadsheets to Dashboards

Introducing Dashboards

In This Chapter

- Defining dashboards and reports
- Determining user requirements
- Establishing visualization and design principles
- Reviewing your dashboard prior to distribution

Creating a dashboard in Excel is not the same as creating a standard table-driven analysis. It's tempting to jump right in and start building away, but a dashboard requires far more preparation than a typical Excel report. It calls for closer communication with business leaders, stricter data modeling techniques, and the following of certain best practices. It's helpful to be familiar with fundamental dashboard concepts before venturing off into the mechanics of building your own. In this chapter, we discuss basic dashboard concepts and design principles, and what it takes to prepare for a dashboarding project.

On the Web

All workbook examples that we list in this book are available on the companion Web site for this book at www.wiley.com/go/exceldr.

What are Dashboards and Reports?

It isn't difficult to use the words *report* and *dashboard* interchangeably. In fact, the line between dashboards and reports frequently get muddied. We see countless reports that are referred to as dashboards just because they include a few charts. Likewise, we see many examples of what could be considered dashboards, but are called reports.

Now this may all seem like semantics to you, but it is helpful to clear the air a bit and understand the core attributes of both dashboards and reports.

Defining reports

Reports are probably the most common way to communicate business intelligence. A report can be described as a document that contains data used for viewing and analysis. It can be as simple as a data table (or a database) or as complex as a subtotaled view with interactive drilling.

The key attribute of a report is that it does not lead a reader to a predefined conclusion. Although a report can include analysis, aggregations, calculations, and even charts, reports often require the reader to apply his own judgment and analysis to the data.

To clarify this concept, Figure 1-1 shows an example of a report. This report shows National Park visitor stats by year. Although this data can be useful, this report does not steer the reader to any predefined conclusions or in any directions; it simply presents the aggregated data.

	A	Y	Z	AA	AB	AC
4	Park Name	2002	2003	2004	2005	2006
5	Great Smoky Mountains NP	20,475,367	20,634,460	20,413,816	20,439,247	20,971,356
6	Hot Springs NP	3,458,465	3,864,555	3,856,535	3,765,652	3,825,330
7	Grand Canyon NP	4,339,139	4,464,399	4,672,911	4,470,235	4,356,147
8	Olympic NP	4,489,227	4,126,221	4,010,058	3,961,358	3,495,470
9	Yosemite NP	3,468,175	3,475,317	3,376,333	3,384,484	3,359,386
10	Grand Teton NP	3,987,585	4,065,185	4,000,697	3,907,354	3,848,633
11	Acadia NP	2,811,148	2,465,562	2,242,347	2,098,584	2,130,688
12	Yellowstone NP	3,915,111	3,959,211	3,805,796	3,775,629	3,840,867
13	Rocky Mountain NP	3,138,067	3,249,445	2,950,646	2,981,039	2,927,920
14	Hawaii Volcanoes NP	2,399,361	2,178,430	2,605,297	2,699,002	3,342,112
15	Saguaro NP	3,437,831	3,478,078	3,601,775	3,629,550	3,140,395
16	Zion NP	2,614,445	2,480,692	2,699,242	2,608,565	2,589,250
17	Cuyahoga Valley NP	3,218,791	2,880,515	3,306,811	2,534,403	2,469,289
18	Mount Rainier NP	1,899,514	1,857,562	1,812,979	1,757,909	1,619,117
19	Mammoth Cave NP	1,983,560	1,961,390	1,980,520	1,970,259	740,552
20	Glacier NP	1,911,334	1,671,851	2,043,028	1,937,043	1,972,804

Figure 1-1: Reports present data for viewing, but do not lead readers to predefined conclusions.

Defining dashboards

A dashboard is a visual interface that provides at-a-glance views into key measures relevant to a particular objective or business process. A dashboard consists of three key attributes.

> ➤ Displays data graphically (such as in charts). Provides visualizations that help focus attention on key trends, comparisons, and exceptions.

> ➤ Displays only data that is relevant to the goal of the dashboard.

> ➤ Contains predefined conclusions relevant to the goal of the dashboard and relieves the reader from performing his own analysis.

Figure 1-2 illustrates a dashboard that uses the same data shown in Figure 1-1. This dashboard displays information about National Park attendance. As you can see, this presentation has all the key attributes that define a dashboard. First, it's a visual display that allows you to quickly recognize the overall trend of the attendance. Second, not all the details of the data are shown in this presentation; only the key pieces of information that support the goal of this dashboard. Finally, by virtue of its objective, this dashboard effectively presents you with analysis and conclusions about the trending of attendance.

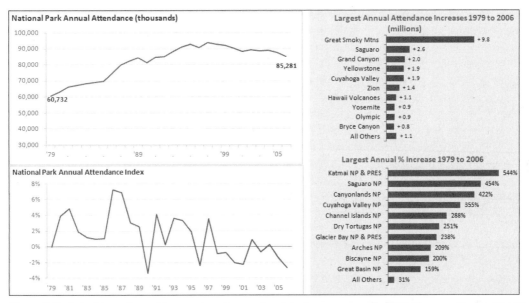

Figure 1-2: A dashboard provides an at-a-glance view into key measures relevant to a particular objective or business process.

As you take in this concept of reports versus dashboards, remember that Excel doesn't provide tools specifically designed for dashboards or reports. The beauty of Excel is that any of its tools can be used to perform virtually any task that you need. For example, you can use the chart, pivot tables, and macros features in a basic report or to play a key role in a dashboard presentation. In this book, we introduce you to the many ways that you can leverage everyday Excel tools to build your own dashboard components.

Establish the User Requirements

Imagine that your objective is to create a dashboard that provides information about monthly service subscriptions. Do you jump to action and slap together whatever comes to mind? Do you take a guess at what information would be useful in a dashboard like this? These questions sound ridiculous, but it happens more that you think. We are constantly called to action, but are rarely provided the time to gather the true requirements for the project. Between limited information and false deadlines, the end product often ends up not being used, or causing more work than value.

This brings me to one of the key steps in preparing to build a dashboard — collecting user requirements. These user requirements include defining your audience, data sources, performance measures, refresh schedules, and so on.

In the non-IT world of the Excel analyst, user requirements are practically useless because of the hard left and right turns we are asked to make every day. So the gathering of user requirements sometimes seems like a waste of valuable time in the ever-changing business environment.

But it's time to get into the dashboard state of mind. After all, would you rather spend your time up front gathering user requirements, or at the end painstakingly redesigning the dashboard you will surely come to hate?

Consider how many times you've been asked for an analysis, only to be told "No. I meant this." Or, "Now that I see it, I realize I need this." As frustrating as that can be for a single analysis, imagine running into this during the creation of a complex dashboard with several data integration processes.

The process of gathering user requirements doesn't have to be an overly complicated or formal one. Here are some simple things you can do to ensure that you have a solid idea of the purpose of the dashboard.

When collecting user requirements for your dashboard, focus on the types of data that you need, the dimensions of data that you require, the data sources that you will use, and so on. This is a good thing; without solid data processes, your dashboards won't be effective or maintainable.

Define the message(s)

When receiving requirements for a new dashboard project, don't be afraid to clarify the source of the initial request and talk to them about what they are really asking for. Discuss the purpose of the dashboard and the triggers that caused them to ask for a dashboard in the first place. You may find, after discussing the matter, a simple Excel report will meet their needs, foregoing the need for a full-on dashboard.

Establish the audience

If a dashboard is warranted, talk about who the end users will be. Take some time to meet with some of the end users and talk about how they plan to use the dashboard. For example, will the dashboard be used as a performance tool for regional managers, or perhaps to share data with external customers? Talking through these fundamentals with the right people will help align your thoughts and avoid missed requirements later.

Define the performance measures

Most dashboards are designed around a set of measures called Key Performance Indicators (KPIs). A KPI is an indicator of the level of performance of a task deemed to be essential to daily operations or processes. The idea around a KPI is that it will reveal performance that is outside the norm, signaling the need for attention and intervention. Although the measures you place into your dashboards may not officially be called KPIs, they undoubtedly serve the same purpose — to draw attention to problem areas.

Note

The topic of creating effective KPIs for your organization is a subject worthy of its own book and out of scope for this endeavor. For a detailed guide on KPI development strategies, pick up David Parmenter's "Key Performance Indicators: Developing, Implementing, and Using Winning KPIs," Wiley Publishing. This book provides an excellent step-by-step approach to developing and implementing KPIs.

The measures that you use on a dashboard should support the initial goal of that dashboard. For example, if you create a dashboard that focuses on supply chain processes, it may not make sense to have HR head count data included. It's generally good to avoid *nice-to-know* data in your dashboards simply to fill white space, or because the data is available. If the data does not support the core goal of the dashboard, leave it out.

Here's another tip. When gathering the measures required for the dashboard, we find that it often helps to write out a sentence to describe the measure needed. For example, instead of simply writing the word "Revenue" into our user requirements, we write what we call a "component question" such as, "What is the overall revenue trend for the last two years?" We call it a "component question" because we will ultimately task a single component, such as a chart or a table, to answer the question. For instance, if the component question is, "What is the overall revenue trend for the last two years?", you can imagine a chart component answering that question by showing the two year revenue trend.

We sometimes take this a step further and actually incorporate the "component questions" into a mock layout of the dashboard to get a high-level sense of what data the dashboard will require. Figure 1-3 illustrates an example.

Each box in this dashboard layout mockup represents a component on the dashboard and its approximate position. The questions within each box provide a sense of the types of data required to create the measures for the dashboard.

List the required data sources

After you have the list of measures that you need on the dashboard, it's important to take a tally of the available databases or other source systems to determine if the data required to produce those measures are available.

➤ Do you have access to the data sources necessary?

➤ How often are those data sources updated?

➤ Who owns and maintains those data sources?

➤ What are the processes to get the data from those resources?

➤ Does the data even exist?

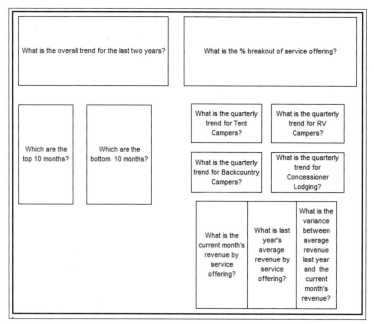

Figure 1-3: Each box in this dashboard layout mockup represents a component and the type of data required to create the measures.

You will need answers to these questions when negotiating development time, refresh intervals, and phasing.

Tip

Conventional wisdom says that the measures on your dashboard should not be governed by the availability of data. Instead, you should let dashboard KPIs and measures govern the data sources in your organization. Although we agree with the spirit of that statement, we've been involved in too many dashboard projects that have fallen apart because of lack of data. Real-world experience has taught us the difference between the ideal and the ordeal.

If your organizational strategy requires that you collect and measure data that is nonexistent or not available, press pause on the dashboard project, and turn your attention to creating a data collection mechanism that will help you to get the data you need.

Define the dimensions and filters

In the context of building a dashboard, a dimension is a data category that you use to organize business data. Examples of dimensions are region, market, branch, manager, or employee. When you define a dimension in the user requirements stage, you can determine how the measures should be grouped or distributed. For example, if your dashboard should report data by employee, you will need to ensure that your data collection processes include employee detail. As you can imagine, adding a new dimension after the dashboard is built can get complicated, especially when your processes require collecting data across multiple data sources. The bottom line is that locking down the dimensions for a dashboard early in the process will definitely save you headaches.

Along those same lines, you'll want to know the types of filters that you will need. Filters are mechanisms that allow you to narrow the scope of the data to a single dimension. For example, you can filter by year, employee, or region. Again, if you don't account for a particular filter while establishing your data collection process, you will likely be forced into an unpleasant redesign of both your processes and your dashboard.

Determine the need for drill down details

Many dashboards provide drill-down features that allow you to click through to the details of a specific measure. You'll want to get a clear understanding of the types of drill downs your users have in mind.

To most users, a drill-down feature means the ability to get a raw data table supporting the measures shown on the dashboard. Although this isn't always practical or possible, at minimum, you can set expectations and document the request for future dashboard versions. This allows you to plan for any macros, links, or other solutions that you may have to include with your dashboards.

Establish the update schedule

An update schedule refers to how often a dashboard is changed to reflect the latest information available. As the one who will build and maintain the dashboard, it's important that you have a say in these schedules. Your customer may not know what it will take to update the dashboard in question. While talking about this schedule, keep in mind the refresh rates of the different data sources you will need to get the measures. You won't be able to refresh your dashboard any faster than your data sources. Also, negotiate enough development time to build macros that will automate redundant and time consuming updating tasks.

A Quick Look at Dashboard Design Principles

Excel users live in a world of numbers and tables; not visualization and design. Your typical Excel analyst has no background in visual design, and is often left to rely on his own visual instincts to design his dashboards. As a result, most Excel-based dashboards have little thought given to effective visual design, often resulting in overly cluttered and ineffective UI.

The good news is that dashboards have been around for such a long time, so we have a vast knowledgebase of prescribed visualization and dashboard design principles. Although many of these principles seem like common sense, these are concepts that we Excel users don't find ourselves thinking about regularly. Let's break that trend and review a few dashboard design principles that will improve the design of your Excel dashboards.

Note

Many of the concepts in this section come from the work of Stephen Few, visualization expert and author of several books and articles on dashboard design principles. As this book is focused on the technical aspects of building dashboards in Excel, this section offers a high-level look at dashboard design. If you find that you are captivated by the subject, feel free to visit `www.perceptualedge.com` to see Stephen Few's Web site.

Rule number 1: Keep it Simple

Dashboard design expert, Stephen Few, has the mantra, "Simplify, Simplify, Simplify." A dashboard that is cluttered with too many measures and too much eye candy can dilute the significant information that you are trying to present. How many times has someone told you that your reports look "busy?" In essence they are saying that you have too much going on in the page or screen, making it hard to see the actual data.

Here are few actions you can take to ensure a simpler and more effective dashboard design.

Don't turn your dashboard into a Data Mart

Admit it. You include as much information in a report as possible, primarily to avoid being asked for additional information. We all do it. But in the dashboard state of mind, you'll have to fight the urge to force every piece of data available onto your dashboard.

Overwhelming users with too much data can cause them to lose sight of the primary goal of the dashboard, and focus on inconsequential data. The measures used on a dashboard should support the initial purpose of that dashboard. Avoid the urge to fill white space for the sake of symmetry and appearances. Don't include nice-to-know data just because the data is available. If the data does not support the core purpose of the dashboard, leave it out.

Forget about the fancy formatting

The key to communicating effectively with your dashboard is to present your data as simply as possible. There is no need to wrap it in eye candy to make it more interesting. It's okay to have a dashboard with little to no color or formatting. You'll find that the lack of fancy formatting only calls attention to the actual data. Focus on the data and not shiny happy graphics.

To help drive this point home, we've created the chart shown in Figure 1-4 (formatting and all). Excel makes it easy to achieve these types of effects with its layout and style features. The problem is that these effects subdue the very data we are trying to present. Furthermore, if we include this chart on a page with five to ten other charts with the same formatting, we get a dashboard that's difficult to look at — much less to read.

Figure 1-5 shows the same data without the fancy formatting. Not only is the chart easier to read, but you can process the data more effectively from this chart.

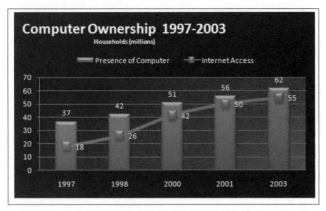

Figure 1-4: Fancy formatting can be overwhelming, subduing the very data you are trying to present.

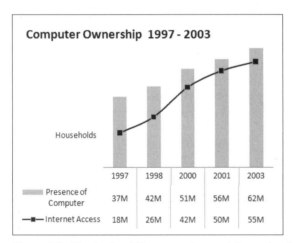

Figure 1-5: Charts should be present your data as simply as possible.

Here are some simple tips to keep from overdoing the fancy factor:

➤ Avoid using colors or background fills to organize your dashboards. Colors, in general, should be used sparingly, and reserved only for information about key data points. For example, assigning red, yellow, and green to measures traditionally indicates performance level. Coloring sections of your dashboard only distracts your audience from your message.

➤ De-emphasize borders, backgrounds, and other elements that define dashboard areas. Try to use the natural white space between your components to partition your dashboard. If borders are necessary, format them to lighter hues than your data. Light grays are typically ideal for borders. The idea is to indicate sections without distracting from the information displayed.

➤ Excel 2010 makes it easy to apply effects that make everything look shiny, glittery, and generally happy. Although these formatting features make for great marketing tools, they don't do you or your dashboard any favors. Avoid applying fancy effects such as gradients, pattern fills, shadows, glow, soft edges, and other formatting.

➤ Don't try to enhance your dashboard with clip art or pictures. Not only do they do nothing to further data presentation, they often just look tacky.

Skip the unnecessary chart junk

Data visualization pioneer Edward Tufte introduced the notion of data to ink ratio. Tufte's basic idea is that a large percentage of the ink on your chart (or on your dashboard) should be dedicated to data. Very little ink should represent what he calls chart junk: borders, gridlines, trend lines, labels, backgrounds, and so on.

Figure 1-6 illustrates the impact that chart junk can have on the ability to effectively communicate your data. Notice how convoluted and cramped the data looks in the top chart.

The bottom chart actually contains the same data. Yet, it more effectively presents the core message that driver registrations in Texas rose from approximately 10.5 million to almost 17 million. This message was diluted in the top chart by excess clutter. So you can see from this simple example how your chart dramatically improves by simply removing elements that don't directly contribute to the core message.

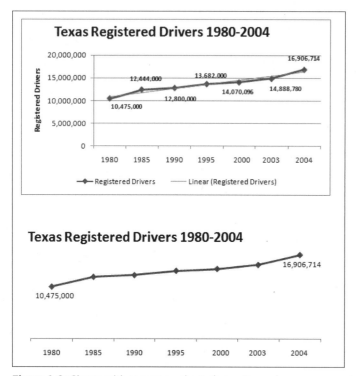

Figure 1-6: Charts with too many chart elements can become convoluted and hard to read. Removing the unnecessary elements clarifies the message.

Here are a few ways to avoid chart junk and ensure your charts clearly present your data.

➤ **Remove gridlines:** Gridlines (both vertical and horizontal) are almost always unnecessary. The implied reason for gridlines is that they help to visually gauge the value represented by each data point. The truth is, however, we typically gauge the value of a data point by comparing its position to the other data points in the chart. So gridlines become secondary reference points that simply take up ink.

➤ **Remove borders:** You'll find that eliminating borders and frames give your charts a cleaner look and helps you avoid the dizzying lines you get when placing multiple charts with borders on a single dashboard. Instead of borders, make use of the white space between the charts as implied borders.

➤ **Skip the trend lines:** Seldom does a trend line provide insight that can't be gained with the already plotted data or a simple label. In fact, trend lines often state the obvious and sometimes confuse readers into thinking they are another data series. Why place a trend line on a line chart when the line chart is in and of itself a trend line of sorts? Why place a trend line on a bar chart when it's just as easy to look at the tops of the bars? In lieu of trend lines, add a simple label that states what you are trying to say about the overall trend of the data.

➤ **Avoid unnecessary data labels:** Nothing states that you need to show the data label for every value on your chart. It's okay to plot a data point and not display its value. You'll find that your charts have more impact when you show only numbers that are relevant to your message.

➤ **Don't show a legend if you don't have to:** When you are plotting one data series, you do not need to display a space-taking chart legend. Allow your chart title to identify the data that your chart represents.

➤ **Remove any axis that doesn't add value:** The purpose of the X and Y axes are to help a user visually gauge and position the values represented by each data point. However, if the nature and utility of the chart doesn't require a particular axis, you should remove it. In Figure 1-6, there is no real need for Y axis because the two data points I'm trying to draw attention to are already labeled. Again, the goal here is not to hack away at your chart. The goal is to only include those chart elements that directly contribute to the core message of your chart.

Limit each dashboard to one viewable page or screen

A dashboard should provide an at-a-glance view into key measures relevant to a particular objective or business process. This implies that all of the data is immediately viewable at one time. Although this isn't always the easiest thing to do, it is best to see all the data on one page or screen. You can compare sections more easily, you can process cause and effect relationships more effectively, and you rely less on short-term memory. When a user has to scroll left, right, or down, these benefits are diminished. Furthermore, users tend to believe that when information is placed out of normal view (areas that require scrolling), it is somehow less important.

But what if you can't fit all the data in one viewable area (one page or one screen)? First, review the measures on your dashboard and determine if they really need to be there. Next, format your dashboard to use less space (format fonts, reduce white space, adjust column and row widths). Finally, try adding interactivity to your dashboard, allowing users to dynamically change views to show only those measures that are relevant to them.

We discuss how to add interactive features in Chapter 15.

Cross-Ref

Use layout and placement to draw focus

As discussed earlier in this chapter, only include measures that support your dashboard's goal. However, just because all measures on your dashboard are significant, they may not always have the same level of importance. In other words, you will frequently want one component of your dashboard to stand out from the others.

Instead of using bright colors or exaggerated sizing differences, you can leverage location and placement to draw focus to the most important components on your dashboard.

Various studies have shown that readers have a natural tendency to focus on particular regions of a document. For example, researchers at the Poynter Institute's Eyetracker III project have found that readers view various regions on a screen in a certain order, paying particular attention to specific regions on the screen. They use the diagram in Figure 1-7 to illustrate what they call "priority zones." Regions with the number 1 in the diagram seem to have high prominence, attracting the most attention for longer periods of time. Meanwhile number 3 regions seem to have low prominence.

1	1	2	3
1	1	2	2
2	2	2	3
3	3	3	3

Figure 1-7: Studies show that users pay particular attention to the upper left and middle left of a document.

You can leverage these priority zones to promote or demote certain components based on significance. If one of the charts on your dashboard warrant special focus, you can simply place that chart in a region of prominence.

Tip

Note that surrounding colors, borders, fonts, and other formatting can affect the viewing patterns of your readers, de-emphasizing a previously high prominence region.

Format numbers effectively

Undoubtedly, you will use lots of numbers in your dashboards. Some of them will be in charts, while others will be in tables. Remember that every piece of information on your dashboard should have a purpose. It's important that you format your numbers effectively so your users can understand the information they represent without confusion or hindrance.

Here are some guidelines to keep in mind when formatting the numbers in your dashboards and reports.

➤ Always use commas to make numbers easier to read. For example, instead of 2345 show 2,345.

➤ Only use decimal places if that level of precision is required. For instance, there is rarely benefit for showing the decimal places in a dollar amount such as $123.45. Likewise in percentages, use only the minimum number of decimals required to represent the data effectively. For example instead of 43.21%, you may be able to get away with 43%.

➤ Only use the dollar symbol when you need to clarify that you are referring to monetary values. If you have a chart or table that contains all revenue values, and there is a label clearly stating this, you can save rooms and pixels by leaving out the dollar symbol.

➤ Format very large numbers to thousands or millions place. For instance, instead of displaying 16,906,714, you can format the number to read 17M.

To help illustrate the benefit of formatting large numbers, take a look at Figure 1-8. The values here displayed are formatted so that they read 10M and 17M instead of the hard-to-read 10,475,000 and 16,906,714.

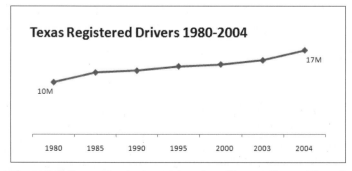

Figure 1-8: Formatting large numbers to millions or thousands makes a chart clearer.

You can easily format large numbers in Excel by using the Format Cells dialog box, shown in Figure 1-9. To specify a custom number format, select Custom in the Category list and indicate the desired number format code in the Type box. In Figure 1-9, the format code **0,,"M"**ensures that the numbers are formatted to millions with an M appendage.

Figure 1-9: Select Custom in the Category list and enter a number format code in the Type box.

Table 1-1 lists some common format codes and how they affect numbers.

Table 1-1: Common Number Format Codes

Number Format Code	How 16,906,714 Would be Displayed
0,	16907
0,0,	16,907
0.00,	16,906.71
0,"K"	16907K
0.00,"K"	16,906.71K
$0,0,"K"	$16,907K
0,,	17
0,,"M"	17M
0.0,,"M"	16.9M
0.00,,"M"	16.91M
$0.0,,"M"	$16.9M

Use titles and labels effectively

It's common sense, but we often fail to label items on our dashboard effectively. If your customer looks at your dashboard and asks you "What is this telling me?", you likely have labeling issues. Here are a few guidelines for effective labeling in your dashboards and reports.

> ➤ Always include a timestamp on your dashboard or report. This minimizes confusion when distributing the same dashboard or report in monthly or weekly installments.

> ➤ Always include some text indicating when the data for the measures was retrieved. In many cases, timing of the data is a critical piece of information for analyzing a measure.

> ➤ Use descriptive titles for each component. This allows users to clearly identify what they are looking at. Be sure to avoid cryptic titles with lots of acronyms and symbols.

> ➤ Although it may seem counterintuitive, it's generally good practice to de-emphasize labels by formatting them to lighter hues than your data. Lightly colored labels give your users the information they need without distracting them from the information that is displayed. Ideal colors to use for labels are colors that are commonly found in nature: soft grays, browns, blues, and greens.

Key Questions to Ask Before Distributing Your Dashboard

Before you send out your finished dashboard, it's worth your time to step back and measure it against some of the design principles we discuss in this chapter. Here are some key questions you can use as a checklist before distributing your dashboard.

Does my dashboard present the right information?

Look at the information you are presenting and determine if it meets the purpose of the dashboard identified during requirements gathering. Don't be timid about clarifying the purpose of the dashboard again with your core users. You want to avoid building the dashboard in a vacuum. Allow a few test users to see iterations as you develop it. This way, communication remains open, and you won't go too far in the wrong direction.

Does everything on my dashboard have a purpose?

Take an honest look at how much information on your dashboard doesn't support its main purpose. In order to keep your dashboard as valuable as possible, you don't want to dilute it with nice-to-know data that's interesting, but not actionable. Remember, if the data does not support the core purpose of the dashboard, leave it out. Nothing says you have to fill every bit of white space on the page.

Does my dashboard prominently display the key message?

Every dashboard has one or more key messages. You want to ensure that these messages are prominently displayed. To test if the key messages in a dashboard are prominent, stand back and squint your eyes while you look at the dashboard. Look away and then look at the dashboard several times. What jumps out at you first? If it's not the key components you want to display, then you'll have to change something. Here are a few actions you can take to ensure your key components have prominence.

➤ Place the key components of your dashboard in the upper left or middle left of the page. Studies show that these areas attract the most attention for longer periods of time.

➤ De-emphasize borders, backgrounds, and other elements that define dashboard areas. Try to use the natural white space between your components to partition your dashboard. If borders are necessary, format them to lighter hues than your data.

➤ Format labels and other text to lighter hues than your data. Lightly colored labels give your users the information they need without distracting them from the information displayed.

Can I maintain this dashboard?

There is a big difference between updating a dashboard and rebuilding a dashboard. Before you excitedly send out the sweet-looking dashboard you just built, take a moment to think about the maintenance of such a dashboard. You want to think about the frequency of updates, and what processes you need to go through each time you update the data. If it's a one-time reporting event, then set that expectation with your users. If you know it will become a recurring report, you'll want to really negotiate development time, refresh intervals, and phasing before agreeing to any time table.

Does my dashboard clearly display its scope and shelf life?

A dashboard should clearly specify its scope and shelf life. That is to say, anyone should be able to look at your dashboard and know the time period it's relevant to and the scope of the information on the dashboard. This comes down to a few simple things you can do to effectively label your dashboards and reports.

➤ Always include a timestamp on your dashboard. This minimizes confusion when distributing the same dashboard or report in monthly or weekly installments.

➤ Always include some text indicating when the data for the measures was retrieved. In many cases, timing of the data is a critical piece of information when analyzing a measure.

➤ Use descriptive titles for each component in your dashboard. Be sure to avoid cryptic titles with lots of acronyms and symbols.

Is my dashboard well documented?

It's important to document your dashboard and the data model behind it. Anyone who has ever inherited an Excel worksheet knows how difficult it can be to translate the various analytical gyrations that go into a report. If you're lucky, the data model will be small enough to piece together in a week or so. If you're not so lucky, you'll have to ditch the entire model and start from scratch. By the way, the Excel data model doesn't even have to be someone else's. I've actually gone back to a model that I built, and after 6 or so months I had forgotten what I had done. Without documentation, it took me a few days to remember and decipher my own work.

The documentation doesn't even have to be highfalutin fancy stuff. A few simple things can help in documenting your dashboard.

> **Add a Model Map tab to your data model.** The Model Map tab is a separate sheet you can use to summarize the key ranges in the data model, and how each range interacts with the reporting components in the final presentation layer.

> **Use comments and labels liberally.** It's amazing how a few explanatory comments and labels can help clarify your model even after you've been away from your data model for a long period of time.

> **Use colors to identify the ranges in your data model**. Using colors in your data model enables you to quickly look at a range of cells and get a basic indication of what that range does. Each color can represent a range type. For example, yellow could represent staging tables, gray could represent formulas, and purple could represent reference tables.

Cross-Ref
In Chapter 2, we introduce you to data models and building a data model map.

Is my dashboard user-friendly?

Before you distribute your dashboard, you want to ensure that it's user-friendly. It's not difficult to guess what user-friendly means.

> **Intuitive:** Your dashboard should be intuitive to someone who has never seen it before. Test it out on someone and ask them if it makes sense. If you have to start explaining what the dashboard says, something is wrong. Does the dashboard need more labels, less complicated charts, a better layout, more data, less data? It's a good idea to get feedback from several users.

> **Easy to navigate:** If your dashboard is dynamic, allowing for interactivity with macros or pivot tables, then you want to make sure that the navigation works well. Does the user have to click several places to get to their data? Is the number of drill-downs appropriate? Does it take too long to switch from one view to another? Again, you'll want to test your dashboard on several users. And be sure to test any interactive dashboard features on several computers other than yours.

➤ **Prints properly:** Nothing is more annoying than printing a dashboard only to find that the person who created the dashboard didn't take the time to ensure that it prints correctly. Be sure you set the print options on your Excel files so that your dashboards print properly.

Is my dashboard accurate?

Nothing kills a dashboard or report faster than the perception that the data in it is inaccurate. It's not within my capabilities to tell you how to determine if your data is accurate. I can, however, highlight three factors that establish the perception that a dashboard is accurate.

➤ **Consistency with authoritative sources:** It's obvious that if your data does not match other reporting sources, you'll have a data credibility issue — especially if those other sources are deemed to be the authoritative sources. Be sure you are aware of the data sources that are considered to be gospel in your organization. If your dashboard contains data associated with an authoritative source, compare your data with that source to ensure consistency.

➤ **Internal consistency:** It's never fun to explain why one part of your dashboard doesn't jive with other parts of the same dashboard. You want to ensure some level of internal consistency within your dashboard. Be sure comparable components in different areas of your dashboard are consistent with each other. If there is a reason for inconsistency, be sure to clearly notate those reasons. It's amazing how well a simple notation clears up questions about the data.

➤ **Personal experience:** Have you ever seen someone look at a report and say, "That doesn't look right?" They are using what some people call "gut feel" to evaluate the soundness of the data. None of us look at numbers in a vacuum. When we look at any analysis, we bring with us years of personal knowledge, interaction, and experience. We subconsciously use these experiences in our evaluation of information. When determining the accuracy of your dashboard, take into consideration organizational "anecdotal knowledge." If possible, show your dashboard to a few content experts in your company.

Developing Your Data Model

In This Chapter

- Setting up the data, analysis, and presentation layers
- Applying data model best practices
- Leveraging Excel functions to deliver data
- Using Excel tables that expand with data

A *data model* provides the foundation upon which your dashboard or report is built. When you collect and analyze data, you're essentially building a data model that feeds your presentation. In this chapter, we discuss how to build and manage an efficient data model. Although you'll discover how to build cool dashboard components in later chapters, they won't do you any good if you can't construct an effective data model. On that note, let's get started.

Building a Data Model

Building an effective data model isn't as complicated as you may think. The problem is that most people spend little time thinking about the data model that supports a final presentation. If they think about it at all, they usually start by imagining a mock-up of the finished dashboard and work backward from there.

So try thinking a bit about the end-to-end process. Where does the source data reside? How should that data be organized? What calculations do you need to perform? How will those results be fed to the dashboard? How will the dashboard be updated?

Obviously the answers to these questions are situation-specific. But here is a good place to start.

Separating the data, analysis, and presentation layers

One of the key concepts of a data model is the organization of data into three layers: data, analysis, and presentation. The basic idea is that you don't want your data to become too tied into any one particular way of presenting that data.

For example, think about a business invoice. The financial data on that invoice is not the true source of that data. It's merely a presentation of the actual data that's stored in some database. That data can then be organized and presented to you in many ways: in charts, in tables, on dashboards, or even on Web sites. This sounds obvious, but Excel users often fuse the data, analysis, and presentation layers together into one final project.

The best approach is to create three layers in your data model. You can think of these layers as three different worksheets in an Excel workbook. Sometimes this also is a good way to organize your data model. One sheet holds the raw data that feeds your report, one sheet serves as a staging area where the calculations are performed, and one serves as the final presentation. Figure 2-1 illustrates the three layers of an effective data model.

Tip

> **You don't necessarily have to place your data, analysis, and presentation layers on different worksheets. In small data models, you may find it easier to place your data in one area of a worksheet while building your staging tables in another area of the same worksheet.**

Why even bother with the three tiered data model? Imagine you have only the table in Figure 2-2. Hard-coded tables, such as this, are common. This table is an combination of data, calculations, and presentation. Not only does this table tie you to a specific analysis, but there's little to no transparency into the content of the analysis. Also, what happens when you need to report by quarters or when another dimension of analysis is needed? Do you import a table that consists of more columns and rows? How does that affect your data model?

Taking the easy route and avoiding the extra work of separating the data, analysis and presentation layers can lead to more problems later. Let's take a moment to define each layer and the role it plays in building out your dashboard model.

The data layer

As you can see in Figure 2-1, the data layer consists of the raw data that feeds your dashboard. The data in the data layer is typically used "as is" from whatever source you derived it from. That is to say, you perform no analysis in the data layer.

However, you'll find that not all data makes for effective data modeling. For example, the data shown in Figure 2-3 would make it impractical to apply any analysis outside what's already there. For instance, how would you calculate and present the average of all bike sales? How would you calculate a list of the top ten best performing markets?

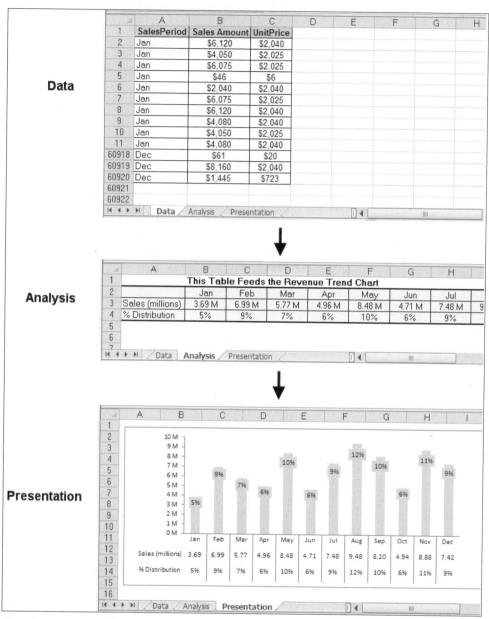

Figure 2-1: An effective data model separates data, analysis, and presentation layers.

A	B	C	D	E	F	G	H	I
		Jan	Feb	Mar	Apr	May	Jun	Jul
	Sales	3.69 M	6.99 M	5.77 M	4.96 M	8.48 M	4.71 M	7.48 M
	% Distribution	5%	9%	7%	6%	10%	6%	9%

Figure 2-2: Avoid using hard-coded tables that fuse data, analysis, and presentation.

	A	B	C	D	E	F	G
1							
2		Europe				North America	
3	France				Canada		
4	Segment	Sales Amount	Unit Price		Segment	Sales Amount	Unit Price
5	Accessories	$48,942	$7,045		Accessories	$119,303	$22,381
6	Bikes	$3,597,879	$991,098		Bikes	$11,714,700	$3,908,691
7	Clothing	$129,508	$23,912		Clothing	$383,022	$72,524
8	Components	$871,125	$293,854		Components	$2,246,255	$865,410
9							
10	Germany				Northeast		
11	Segment	Sales Amount	Unit Price		Segment	Sales Amount	Unit Price
12	Accessories	$35,681	$5,798		Accessories	$51,246	$9,666
13	Bikes	$1,602,487	$545,175		Bikes	$5,690,285	$1,992,517
14	Clothing	$75,593	$12,474		Clothing	$163,442	$30,969
15	Components	$337,787	$138,513		Components	$1,051,702	$442,598
16							
17	United Kingdom				Northwest		
18	Segment	Sales Amount	Unit Price		Segment	Sales Amount	Unit Price
19	Accessories	$43,180	$7,419		Accessories	$53,308	$11,417
20	Bikes	$3,435,134	$1,094,354		Bikes	$10,484,495	$3,182,041
21	Clothing	$120,225	$21,981		Clothing	$201,052	$40,055
22	Components	$712,588	$253,458		Components	$1,784,207	$695,876

Figure 2-3: Not all data can be a good source for your data layer.

With this setup, you're forced into very manual processes that are difficult to maintain month after month. Any analysis outside the high-level ones already in the report is basic at best — even with fancy formulas. Furthermore, what happens when you're required to show bike sales by month? When your data model requires analysis with data that isn't in the worksheet report, you're forced to search for other data.

Ideally, you will want your data layer to come in one of two forms:

> **Flat data tables:** Data repositories organized by row and column. Each row corresponds to a set of data elements, or a *record*. Each column is a *field*. A field corresponds to a unique data element in record. Figure 2-4 contains the same data as the data shown in Figure 2-3 but is in flat data table format. Flat tables lend themselves nicely to data modeling in Excel because they can be detailed enough to hold the data that you need and still be conducive to a wide array of simple formulas and calculations in your analysis layer — SUM, AVERAGE, VLOOKUP, and SUMIF, just to name a few. Later in this chapter, we discuss functions that come in handy in a data model.

> **Tabular data set:** Ideal for pivot table driven data models. Figure 2-5 illustrates a tabular data set. Note the primary difference between a tabular data set, as shown in Figure 2-5, and a flat data file is that the column labels don't double as actual data. For instance, in Figure 2-4, the month identifiers are integrated into the column labels. In Figure 2-5, the Sales Period column contains the month identifier. This subtle difference in structure is what makes tabular data sets optimal data sources for pivot tables. This structure ensures that key pivot table functions, such as sorting and grouping, work the way they should.

	A	B	C	D	E	F	
				Jan Sales	Feb Sales	Mar Sales	A
1	Region	Market	Business Segment	Amount	Amount	Amount	
2	Europe	France	Accessories	2,628	8,015	3,895	
3	Europe	France	Bikes	26,588	524,445	136,773	
4	Europe	France	Clothing	6,075	17,172	6,043	
5	Europe	France	Components	20,485	179,279	54,262	
6	Europe	Germany	Accessories	2,769	6,638	2,615	
7	Europe	Germany	Bikes	136,161	196,125	94,840	
8	Europe	Germany	Clothing	7,150	12,374	7,159	
9	Europe	Germany	Components	46,885	56,611	29,216	
10	Europe	United Kingdom	Accessories	4,205	2,579	5,745	
11	Europe	United Kingdom	Bikes	111,830	175,522	364,844	
12	Europe	United Kingdom	Clothing	7,888	6,763	12,884	
13	Europe	United Kingdom	Components	31,331	39,005	124,030	
14	North America	Canada	Accessories	3,500	12,350	9,768	
15	North America	Canada	Bikes	327,476	425,669	501,427	
16	North America	Canada	Clothing	11,387	26,165	26,514	

Figure 2-4: A flat data table.

	A	B	C	D	E	
1	Region	Market	Business Segment	Sales Period	Sales Amount	
2	Europe	France	Accessories	Jan	1,706	
3	Europe	France	Accessories	Feb	3,767	
4	Europe	France	Accessories	Mar	1,219	
5	Europe	France	Accessories	Apr	3,091	
6	Europe	France	Accessories	May	7,057	
7	Europe	France	Accessories	Jul	5,930	
8	Europe	France	Accessories	Aug	9,628	
9	Europe	France	Accessories	Sep	4,279	
10	Europe	France	Accessories	Oct	2,504	
11	Europe	France	Accessories	Nov	7,493	
12	Europe	France	Accessories	Dec	2,268	
13	Europe	France	Bikes	Jan	64,895	
14	Europe	France	Bikes	Feb	510,102	
15	Europe	France	Bikes	Mar	128,806	

Figure 2-5: A tabular data set.

The analysis layer

The analysis layer consists primarily of formulas that analyze and pull data from the data layer into formatted tables (commonly referred to as *staging tables*). These staging tables ultimately feed the reporting components in your presentation layer. In short, the sheet that contains the analysis layer becomes the staging area where data is summarized and shaped to feed the reporting components.

There are a couple of benefits to this setup:

1. You can easily update the entire data model by simply replacing the raw data with updated data. The formulas in the analysis tab then continue to work with the latest data.

2. You can create any added analyses easily by using different combinations of formulas on the analysis tab. If you need data that doesn't exist in the data layer, you can add a column to the end of the raw data without disturbing the analysis or presentation layers.

The presentation layer

The presentation layer is your store front. It contains all the charts, visualizations, and dashboard components that you want your audience to see. The presentation layer is the most flexible, as you can choose a plethora of tools, graphics, and charts to create the theme and style of your dashboard. And because the presentation layer feeds from the analysis layer, the data needed for each component is always consistent in content and format.

Data Model Best Practices

One of Excel's most attractive features is its flexibility. You can create an intricate system of calculations, linked cells, and formatted summaries that work together to create your final presentation. But creating a successful dashboard requires more than just slapping data onto a worksheet. A poorly designed data model can lead to hours of excess work maintaining and updating your presentation. On the other hand, an effective data model enables you to easily repeat monthly update processes without damaging your dashboards or your sanity.

In this section, we discuss some data modeling best practices that help you start your dashboard projects on the right foot.

Avoid storing excess data

In Chapter 1, you might have read that measures used on a dashboard should absolutely support the initial purpose of that dashboard. The same concept applies to the backend data model. You should only import data that's necessary to fulfill the purpose of your dashboard or report.

In an effort to have as much data at their fingertips, many Excel users bring into their worksheets every piece of data they can get their hands on. You can spot these people by the 40MB files they send through e-mail. You've seen these worksheets — two tabs that contain presentation and then six hidden tabs that contain thousands of lines of data (most of which isn't used). They essentially build a database in their worksheet.

What's wrong with utilizing as much data as possible? Well, here are a few issues:

> ➤ **Excess data increases the number of formulas.** If you're bringing in all raw data, you have to aggregate that data in Excel. This inevitably causes you to exponentially increase the number of formulas you have to employ and maintain. Remember your data model is a vehicle for presenting analyses, not processing raw data. The data that works best in the presentation layer is what's already been aggregated and summarized into useful views that can be navigated and fed to dashboard components. Importing data that's already been aggregated as much as possible is far better. For example, if you need to report on Revenue by Region and Month, there's no need to import sales transactions into your data model. Instead, use an aggregated table consisting of Region, Month, and Sum of Revenue.

➤ **Excess data degrades the performance of your presentation layer.** In other words, because your dashboard is fed by your data model, you need to maintain the model behind the scenes (likely in hidden tabs) when distributing the dashboard. Besides the fact that it causes the file size to be unwieldy, including too much data in your data model can actually degrade the performance of your dashboard. Why? When you open an Excel file, the entire file is loaded into memory (or *RAM*) to ensure quick data processing and access. The drawback to this behavior is that Excel requires a great deal of RAM to process even the smallest change in your worksheet. You may have noticed that when you try to perform an action on a large formula-intensive data, Excel is slow to respond, giving you a `Calculating` indicator in the status bar. The larger your data is, the less efficient the data crunching in Excel is.

➤ **Excess data limits the scalability of your data model.** Imagine that you're working in a small company and you're using monthly transactions in your data model. Each month holds 80,000 lines of data. As time goes on, you build a robust process complete with all the formulas, pivot tables, and macros you need to analyze the data that's stored in your neatly maintained tab. Now what happens after one year? Do you start a new tab? How do you analyze two data on two different tabs as one entity? Are your formulas still good? Do you have to write new macros?

You can avoid such issues by importing only aggregated and summarized data that's useful to the core purpose of your dashboard.

Use tabs to document and organize your data model

Wanting to keep your data model limited to one worksheet tab is natural. In our opinion, keeping track of one tab is much simpler than using different tabs. However, limiting your data model to one tab has its drawbacks, including the following:

➤ **Limits the quality of your analysis.** Because only so much text can fit on a tab, using one tab imposes real estate restrictions that can limit your analyses. Consider adding tabs to your data model to provide additional data and analysis that may not fit on just one tab.

➤ **Makes for a confusing data model.** When working with a large quantity of data, you need plenty of staging tables to aggregate and shape the raw data so that it can be fed to your dashboard components. If you use only one tab, you're forced to position these staging tables below or to the right of your data. Although this may provide all the elements needed to feed your presentation layer, a good deal of scrolling is necessary to view all the elements positioned in a wide range of areas. This makes the data model difficult to understand and maintain. Use separate tabs to hold your staging tables, particularly in data models that contain large quantities of data that take a lot of real estate.

➤ **Limits the amount of documentation you can include.** You'll find that your data models easily become a complex system of intertwining links among components, input ranges, output ranges, and formulas. Sure, it all makes sense while you're building your data model, but try coming back to it after a few months. You'll find that you've forgotten what each data range does and how each range interacts with the final presentation layer. To avoid this problem, consider adding a data model map tab to your data model. The map tab essentially summarizes the key ranges in the data model and allows you to document how each range interacts with the dashboard components in the final presentation layer. As you can see in Figure 2-6, the data model map is nothing fancy; just a table that lists some key information about each range in the model.

Tab	Range	Purpose	Linked Component/s
Analysis 1	A2:A11	Provides the data source for the trend graph component.	United States trend 1
Analysis 2	A3:A11	Data source for the List Box component.	List Box 1
Analysis 2	C1	Output range for the selected item in the List Box component.	Conditional trend icon
Analysis 2	D1:R1	Vlookup formulas that reference cell C1. This range also serves as the source data for the Combination Chart component.	Combination Chart 1
Data	C4:R48	Main data set for this data model.	

Figure 2-6: A data model map provides documentation that outlines how your data model works.

You can include any information you think appropriate in your data model map. The idea is to give yourself a handy reference that guides you through the elements in your data model.

 ## Speaking of documenting your data model . . .

Another way to document the logic in your data model is to use comments and labels liberally. It's amazing how a few explanatory comments and labels can help clarify your worksheets. The general idea here is that the logic in your model should be clear to you even after you've been away from your data model for a long period of time.

Also, consider using colors to identify the ranges in your data model. Using colors in your data model enables you to quickly look at a range of cells and get a basic indication of what that range does. The general concept behind this best practice is that each color represents a range type. For example, you could use yellow to represent staging tables used to feed the charts and the tables in your presentation layer. You could use gray to represent formulas that aren't to be altered or touched, or purple to represent reference tables used for lookups and drop-down lists.

You can use any color you want; it's up to you to give these colors meaning. The important thing is that you have a visual distinction between the various ranges being used in your data model.

Test your data model before building presentation components

This best practice is simple. Make sure that your data model does what it's supposed to do before building dashboard components on top of it. In that vein, here are a few things to watch for:

> ➤ **Test your formulas to be sure that they're working properly:** Make sure your formulas don't produce errors, and that each formula outputs expected results.

> ➤ **Double-check your main data to be sure that it's complete:** Check that your data table has not truncated when transferring to Excel. Also, be sure that each column of data you need is present with appropriate data labels.

> ➤ **Make sure all numeric formatting is appropriate:** Be sure that the formatting of your data is appropriate for the field. For example, check to see that dates are formatted as dates, currency values are formatted properly, and that the correct number of decimal places is displayed where needed.

The obvious goal here is to eliminate easily avoidable errors that may cause complications later.

Excel Functions for Your Data Model

As we discussed, the optimal data model for any dashboard separates data, analysis, and presentation into three distinct layers. Although all three layers are important, the analysis layer is where the real art comes into play. The fundamental task of the analysis layer is to extract information from the data layer for use in the staging tables that feed your charts, tables, and other dashboard components. To do this effectively, you need to use formulas that serve as data delivery mechanisms — formulas that deliver data to a destination range.

You see, the information you need lives in your data layer (typically a table containing aggregated data). *Data delivery formulas* are designed to get that data and deliver it to the analysis layer so it can be analyzed and shaped. The cool thing is that after you've set up your data delivery formulas, your analysis layer automatically updates each time your data layer is refreshed.

In this next section, we discuss a few Excel functions that work particularly well in data delivery formulas. As you go through the examples here, you'll start to see how these concepts come together.

The VLOOKUP function

The VLOOKUP function finds a specific value in the first column of a lookup table and returns the corresponding value in a specified table column. the lookup table is arranged vertically. In Figure 2-7, the table on the left shows sales by month and product number. The table on the right translates those product numbers to actual product names. The VLOOKUP function connects the appropriate product name to each respective product number.

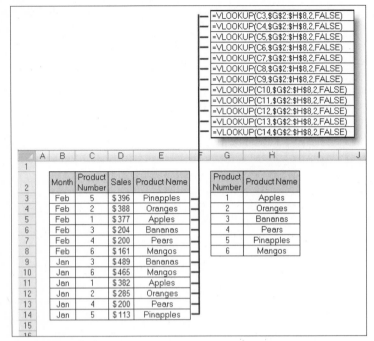

Figure 2-7: The VLOOKUP function finds the appropriate product name for each product number.

VLOOKUP basics

To see how the VLOOKUP function works, take a moment to review the basic syntax. A VLOOKUP function requires four arguments:

```
VLOOKUP(lookup_value,table_array,col_index_num,range_lookup)
```

> **lookup_value:** The value that you want to look up in the first column of the lookup table. In Figure 2-7, the lookup_value is the product number. Therefore, the first argument for all the formulas shown in Figure 2-7 references column C.

> **table_array:** The range that contains the lookup table. In Figure 2-7, that range is G2:H8. Please note that for the VLOOKUP function to work, the leftmost column of the table must be the matching value. For example, if you're matching product numbers, product numbers must be in the first column of the lookup table. Also, the reference that you use for this argument is an absolute reference. This means that the column and row references are prefixed with dollar ($) signs — as in $G$2:$H$8. This ensures that the references don't shift while you copy the formulas down or across.

> **col_index_num:** The column number from within the lookup table that contains the matching value. In Figure 2-7, the second (column H) contains the product name, so the formula uses the number 2. If the product name column was the fourth column in the lookup table, the number 4 would be used.

➤ **range_lookup:** Optional. You can specify whether you're looking for an exact match for your value or an approximate match. If an exact match is needed, type FALSE for this argument. If the closest match will do, type TRUE or leave the argument blank.

Adding VLOOKUP formulas to a data model

Using a few VLOOKUP formulas and a simple drop-down list, you can create a data model that not only delivers data to the appropriate staging table but allows you to dynamically change data views based on a selection you make. Figure 2-8 illustrates the setup.

On the Web

To see this effect in action, go to www.wiley.com/go/exceldr **to get the** Chapter 2 Sample File.xlsx **workbook. Open that workbook to see the VLOOKUP1 tab.**

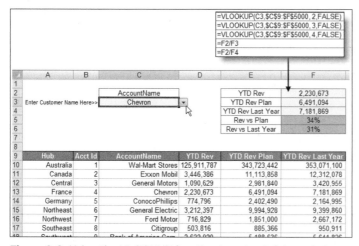

Figure 2-8: Using the VLOOKUP function to extract data and change data views.

The data layer in Figure 2-8 resides in the range A9:F209. The analysis layer displays in range E2:F6. The data layer consists of all the formulas that extract the appropriate data. As you can see, if you select Chevron in cell C3, the VLOOKUP formulas extracts the data for Chevron from the data layer.

Note

You may notice that the VLOOKUP formulas in Figure 2-8 specify a table_array argument of $C$9:$F$5000. So the lookup table that the formulas point to stretches from C9 to F5000. That may seem strange because the table ends at F209. Why would you force your VLOOKUP formulas to look at a range far past the end of the data table?

Remember that the idea behind separating the data layer and the analysis layer is that your analysis layer can automatically update when you update your data. So when you get new data next month, you can simply replace the data layer in the model without having to rework your analysis layer. Allowing for more rows than necessary in your VLOOKUP formulas ensures that if your data layer grows, records won't fall outside the lookup range of the formulas.

Later in this chapter, we show you how to automatically keep up with growing data tables by using the Excel table feature.

Using drop-down lists

In the example illustrated in Figure 2-8, the data model allows you to select customer names (that is, the AccountName field) from a drop-down list when you click cell C3. The customer name serves as the lookup value for the VLOOKUP formulas. Changing the customer name extracts a new set of data from the data layer. This allows you to quickly switch from one customer to another without having to remember and type the customer name.

Now, as cool as this seems, the reasons for this setup aren't all cosmetic. Practical reasons for adding drop-down lists to your data models.

Many of your models consist of multiple analysis layers. Although each analysis layer is different, they often need to revolve around a shared dimension, such as the same customer name, the market, or the region. For instance, when you have a data model that reports on Financials, Labor Statistics, and Operational Volumes, you want to ensure that when the model is reporting financials for the South region, the Labor statistics are for the South region as well.

An effective way to ensure this happens is to force your formulas to use the same dimension references. If cell C3 is where you switch customers, every analysis that is customer dependent should reference cell C3. Drop-down lists allow you to have a predefined list of valid variables located in a single cell. With a drop-down list, you can easily switch dimensions while building and testing multiple analysis layers.

Adding a drop-down list is a relatively easy thing to do with Excel's Data Validation functionality. To add a drop-down list:

1. Click the Data tab on the Ribbon.

2. Click the Data Validation button.

3. In the Data Validation dialog box, click the Settings tab (see Figure 2-9).

4. In the Allow drop-down list, select List.

5. In the Source box, specify the range of cells that contain your predefined selection list.

6. Click OK.

The HLOOKUP function

The HLOOKUP function is the less popular cousin of the VLOOKUP function. The H in HLOOKUP stands for horizontal. Because Excel data is typically vertically oriented, most situations require a vertical lookup (or VLOOKUP). However, some data structures are horizontally oriented, requiring a horizontal lookup; thus the HLOOKUP function comes in handy. The HLOOKUP searches a lookup table to find a single value from a row of data where the column label matches a given criterion.

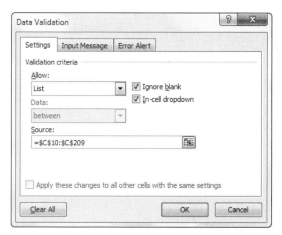

Figure 2-9: You can use data validation to create a predefined list of valid variables for your data model.

HLOOKUP basics

Figure 2-10 demonstrates a typical scenario where HLOOKUP formulas are used. The table in C3 requires quarter-end numbers (March and June) for 2010. The HLOOKUP formulas use the column labels to find the correct month columns and then locates the 2010 data by moving down the appropriate number of rows. In this case, 2010 data is in row 4, so the number 4 is used in the formulas.

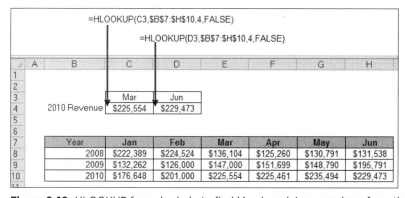

Figure 2-10: HLOOKUP formulas help to find March and June numbers from the lookup table.

To get your mind around how this works, take a look at the basic syntax of the HLOOKUP function.

```
HLOOKUP(lookup_value,table_array,row_index_num,range_lookup)
```

> ➤ **lookup_value:** The value that you want to look up. In most cases, these values are column names. In the example in Figure 2-10, the column labels are being referenced for the Lookup_value. This points the HLOOKUP function to the appropriate column in the lookup table.

➤ **table_array:** The range that contains the lookup table. In Figure 2-10, that range is B7:H10. Like the VLOOKUP examples earlier in this chapter, notice the references used for this argument are absolute. This means the column and row references are prefixed with dollar ($) signs — as in $B$7:$H$10. This ensures that the reference doesn't shift while you copy the formula down or across.

➤ **row_index_num:** The row number that contains the value that you're looking for. In the example in Figure 2-10, the 2010 data is located in row 4 of the lookup table. Therefore, the formulas use the number 4.

➤ **range_lookup:** You can specifies whether you're looking for an exact match or an approximate match. If an exact match is needed, enter FALSE for this argument. If the closest match will do, enter TRUE or leave the argument blank.

Applying HLOOKUP formulas to a data model

HLOOKUPs are especially handy for shaping data into structures appropriate for charting or other types of reporting. A simple example is demonstrated in Figure 2-11. With HLOOKUPs, the data shown in the raw data table at the bottom of the figure is reoriented in a staging table at the top. When the raw data is changed or refreshed, the staging table captures the changes.

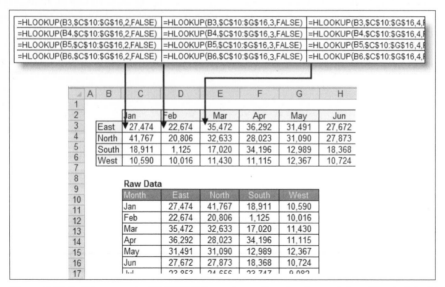

Figure 2-11: In this example, HLOOKUP formulas pull and reshape data without disturbing the raw data table.

The SUMPRODUCT function

The SUMPRODUCT function is actually listed under the math and trigonometry category of Excel functions. Because the primary purpose of SUMPRODUCT is to calculate the sum product, most people don't know you can actually use it to look up values. In fact, you can use this versatile function quite effectively in most data models.

SUMPRODUCT basics

The SUMPRODUCT function is designed to multiply values from two or more ranges of data and then add the results together to return the sum of the products. Take a look at Figure 2-12 to see a typical scenario where the SUMPRODUCT is useful.

In Figure 2-12, you see a common analysis where you need the total sales for the years 2009 and 2010. As you can see, to get the total sales for each year, you first have to multiply Price by the number of Units to get the total for each Region. Then you have to sum those results to get the total sales for each year.

	A	B	C	D	E	F	G
1							
2		Year	Region	Price	Units		
3		2010	North	$40	751	$30,040	=D3*E3
4		2010	South	$35	483	$16,905	=D4*E4
5		2010	East	$32	789	$25,248	=D5*E5
6		2010	West	$41	932	$38,212	=D6*E6
7		2009	North	$40	877	$35,080	=D7*E7
8		2009	South	$35	162	$5,670	=D8*E8
9		2009	East	$32	258	$8,256	=D9*E9
10		2009	West	$41	517	$21,197	=D10*E10
11							
12					2010 total	$110,405	=SUM(F3:F6)
13					2009 total	$70,203	=SUM(F7:F10)
14					Variance	$40,202	=F12-F13

Figure 2-12: Without the SUMPRODUCT, getting the total sales for each year involves a two step process: first multiply price and units and then sum the results.

With the SUMPRODUCT function, you can perform the two step analysis with just one formula. Figure 2-13 shows the same analysis with SUMPRODUCT formulas. Instead of using 11 formulas, you can accomplish the same analysis with just 3!

	A	B	C	D	E	F	G
1							
2		Year	Region	Price	Units		
3		2010	North	$40	751	$30,040	
4		2010	South	$35	483	$16,905	
5		2010	East	$32	789	$25,248	
6		2010	West	$41	932	$38,212	
7		2009	North	$40	877	$35,080	
8		2009	South	$35	162	$5,670	
9		2009	East	$32	258	$8,256	
10		2009	West	$41	517	$21,197	
11							
12					2010 total	$110,405	=SUMPRODUCT(D3:D6,E3:E6)
13					2009 total	$70,203	=SUMPRODUCT(D7:D10, E7:E10)
14					Variance	$40,202	=E12-E13

Figure 2-13: The SUMPRODUCT function allows you to perform the same analysis with just 3 formulas instead of 11.

The syntax of the SUMPRODUCT function is fairly simple:

```
SUMPRODUCT(array1,array2, ...)
```

The array argument represents a range of data. You can use anywhere from 2 to 255 arrays in a SUMPRODUCT formula. The arrays get multiplied together and then added. The only hard and fast rule you have to remember is that all the arrays must have the same number of values. That is to say, you can't use the SUMPRODUCT if range X has 10 values and Range Y has 11 values. Otherwise, you get the #VALUE! error.

A twist on the SUMPRODUCT function

The interesting thing about the SUMPRODUCT function is that it can be used to filter out values. Take a look at Figure 2-14 to see what I mean.

The formula in cell E12 is pulling the sum of total units for just the North region. Meanwhile, cell E13 is pulling the units logged for the North region in the year 2009.

	A	B	C	D	E	F
1						
2		Year	Region	Price	Units	
3		2010	North	$40	751	
4		2010	South	$35	483	
5		2010	East	$32	789	
6		2010	West	$41	932	
7		2009	North	$40	877	
8		2009	South	$35	162	
9		2009	East	$32	258	
10		2009	West	$41	517	
11						
12			North Units		$1,628	
13			2009 North Units		$877	
14						

```
=SUMPRODUCT((C3:C10="North")*(E3:E10))
=SUMPRODUCT((C3:C10="North")*(B3:B10=2009)*(E3:E10))
```

Figure 2-14: The SUMPRODUCT function can be used to filter data based on criteria.

To understand how this works, take a look at the formula in cell E12 shown in Figure 2-14. That formula reads SUMPRODUCT((C3:C10="North")*(E3:E10)).

In Excel, TRUE evaluates to 1 and FALSE evaluates to 0. Every value in Column C that equals "North" evaluates to TRUE or 1. Where the value is not "North", it evaluates to FALSE or 0.The part of the formula that reads (C3:C10="North") enumerates through each value in the range C3:C10, assigning a 1 or 0 to each value. Then internally, the SUMPRODUCT formula translates to

```
(1*E3)+(0*E4)+(0*E5)+(0*E6)+(1*E7)+(0*E8)+(0*E9)+(0*E10).
```

This gives you the answer of 1628 because this next formula equals 1628.

```
(1*751)+(0*483)+(0*789)+(0*932)+(1*877)+(0*162)+(0*258)+(0*517)
```

Applying SUMPRODUCT formulas to a data model

As always in Excel, you don't have to hard-code the criteria in your formulas. Instead of explicitly using "North" in the SUMPRODUCT formula, you could reference a cell that contains the filter value. You can imagine that cell A3 contains the word "North", in which case you can use (C3:C10=A3) instead of (C3:C10="North"). This way, you can dynamically change your filter criteria, and your formula keeps up.

Figure 2-15 demonstrates how you can use this concept to pull data into a staging table based on multiple criteria. Note that each of the SUMPRODUCT formulas shown here reference cells B3 and C3 to filter on Account and Product Line. Again, you can add data validation drop-down lists to cells B3 and C3, allowing you to easily change criteria.

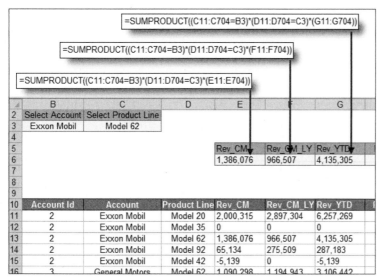

Figure 2-15: The SUMPRODUCT function can be used to pull summarized numbers from the data layer into staging tables.

The CHOOSE function

The CHOOSE function returns a value from a specified list of values based on a specified position number. For instance, if you'd enter the formulas CHOOSE(3,"Red", "Yellow", "Green", "Blue") into a cell, Excel would return Green because Green is the third item in the list of values. The formula CHOOSE(1,"Red", "Yellow", "Green", "Blue") would return Red. Although this may not look useful on the surface, the CHOOSE function can dramatically enhance your data models.

CHOOSE basics

Figure 2-16 illustrates how CHOOSE formulas can help pinpoint and extract numbers from a range cells. Note that instead of using hard-coded values, like Red, Green, and so on, you can use cell references to list the choices.

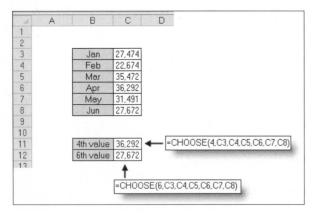

Figure 2-16: The CHOOSE function allows you to find values from a defined set of choices.

Take a moment to review the basic syntax of the CHOOSE function:

```
CHOOSE(index_num,value1,value2,...)
```

> **index_num:** Allows you to specifies the position number of the chosen value in the list of values. If the third value in the list is needed, the Index_num is 3. The Index_num argument must be an integer between one and the maximum number of values in the defined list of values. That is to say, if there are ten choices defined in the CHOOSE formula, the Index_num argument can't be more than ten.

> **value:** Represents a choice in the defined list of choices for that CHOOSE formula. The value arguments can be hard-coded values, cell references, defined names, formulas, or functions. Starting in Excel 2007, you can have up to 255 choices listed in your CHOOSE functions. In Excel 2003, you were limited to 29 value arguments.

Applying CHOOSE formulas to a data model

The CHOOSE function is especially valuable in data models where there are multiple layers of data that need to be brought together. Figure 2-17 illustrates an example where CHOOSE formulas help pull data together.

In this example, you have two data tables: one for Revenues and one for Net Income. Each contains numbers for separate regions. The idea is to create a staging table that pulls data from both tables so that the data corresponds to a selected region.

To understand what's going on, focus on the formula in cell F3 shown in Figure 2-17. The formula is CHOOSE($C$2,F7,F8,F9,F10). The index_num argument is actually a cell reference that looks at the value in cell C2, which happens to be the number 2. As you can see, cell C2 is actually a VLOOKUP formula that pulls the appropriate index number for the selected region. The list of defined choices in the CHOOSE formula is essentially the cell references that make up the revenue values for each region: F7, F8, F9, and F10. So the formula in cell F3 translates to CHOOSE(2, 27474, 41767, 18911, 10590). The answer is 41,767.

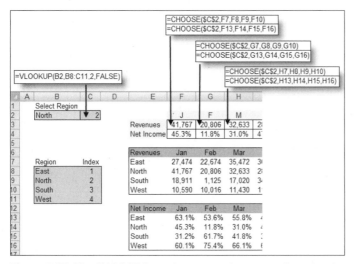

Figure 2-17: The CHOOSE formulas ensure the appropriate data is synchronously pulled from multiple data feeds.

Working with Excel Tables

One of the challenges you can encounter when building a data model is a data table that expands over time. That is to say, as you add new data, the number of records increase. Take a look at Figure 2-18. In this figure, you see a simple table that serves as the source for the bar chart. Notice that the table lists data for January through June.

Imagine that next month, this table expands to include July data. You'll have to manually update your chart to include July data. Now imagine you had this same issue across your data model, with multiple data tables that link to multiple staging tables and dashboard components. You can imagine it'd be an extremely painful task to keep up with changes each month.

To solve this issue, you can use Excel's table feature (you can tell they spent all night coming up with that name). The table feature allows you to convert a range of data into a defined table that's treated independently of other rows and columns on the worksheet. After a range is converted to a table, Excel views the individual cells in the table as a single object that has functionality that a normal data range doesn't have.

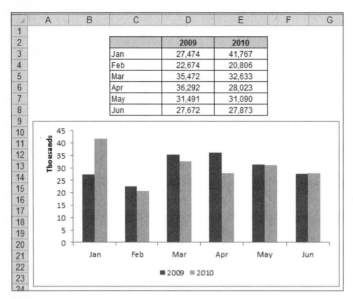

Figure 2-18: This table has the potential to grow every month.

For instance, Excel tables offer the following features:

➤ Drop-down lists in the Header row that allow you to filter and sort data in each column easily.

➤ A Total row feature with various aggregate functions.

➤ Ability to apply distinct formatting to the table independent of the rest of the worksheet.

➤ Automatically expand in dimensions to accommodate new data (key for data modeling purposes).

The table feature did exist in Excel 2003 under a different name. In Excel 2003, this feature was the List feature (found in Excel's Data menu). The benefit of this fact is that Excel tables are fully compatible with Excel 2003!

Tip

Converting a range to an Excel table

To convert a range of data to an Excel table, follow these steps:

1. Highlight the range of cells that contain the data you want to include in your Excel table.

2. On the Insert tab of the Ribbon, click the Table button.

   The Create Table dialog box opens, as shown in Figure 2-19.

3. In the Create Table dialog box, verify the range for the table and specify whether the first row of the selected range is a Header row.

4. Click OK.

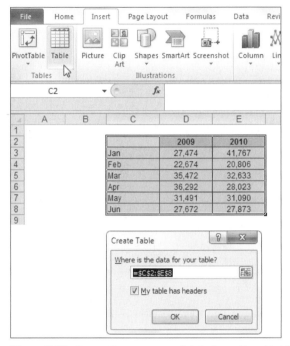

Figure 2-19: Converting a range of data to an Excel table.

After the conversion takes place, notice a few small changes. Excel put drop-down lists in each Header row, the rows in your table now have alternate shading, and any header that didn't have a value has been named by Excel.

You can use Excel tables as the source for charts, pivot tables, list boxes, or anything else for which you'd normally use a data range. In Figure 2-20, a bar chart has been linked to the Excel table.

Here's the impressive bit. When data is added to the table, Excel automatically expands the range of the table and incorporates the new range into any linked object. That's just a fancy way of saying that any chart or pivot table tied to an Excel table automatically captures new data without manual intervention.

For example, if I added July and August data to the end of the Excel table, the chart automatically updates to capture the new data. In Figure 2-21, I added July with no data and August with data to show you that the chart captures any new records and automatically plots the data given.

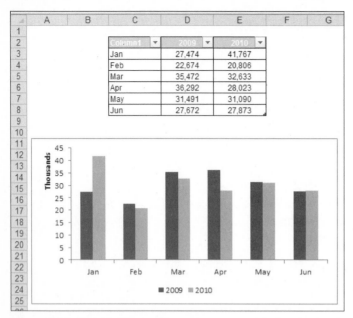

Figure 2-20: Excel tables can be used as source data for charts, pivot tables, named ranges, and so on.

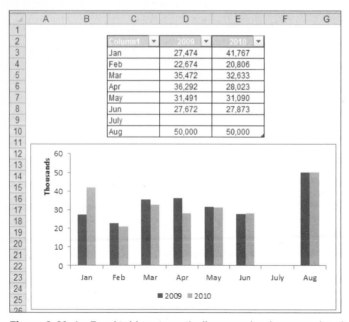

Figure 2-21: An Excel table automatically expands when new data is added.

Take a moment to think about what Excel tables mean to a data model. Pivot tables never have to be reconfigured, charts automatically capture new data, and ranges automatically keep up with changes.

Converting an Excel table back to a range

If you want to convert an Excel table back to a normal range, you can follow these steps:

1. Place your cursor in any cell inside the Excel table and select the Table Tools Design sub tab in the Ribbon.

2. Choose the Convert to Range command, as shown in Figure 2-22.

3. When asked if you're sure (via a message box), click Yes.

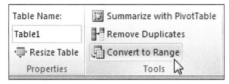

Figure 2-22: To remove Excel table functionality, convert the table back to a range.

Excel Chart Basics

Introducing Excel Charts

In This Chapter

- What is a chart?
- How Excel handles charts
- Embedded charts versus chart sheets
- The parts of a chart
- The basic steps for creating a chart
- Working with charts

No other tool is more synonymous with dashboards and reports than the chart. Charts offer a visual representation of numeric values, at-a-glance views that allow you to specify relationships between data values, point out differences, and observe business trends. Few mechanisms allow you to absorb data faster than a chart, which can be a key component in your dashboard.

While most people think of a spreadsheet product such as Excel, they think of crunching rows and columns of numbers. But, Excel is no slouch when it comes to presenting data visually, in the form of a chart. In this chapter we present an overview of Excel's charting ability, and show you how to create and customize your own charts using Excel.

What Is a Chart?

Let's start with the basics. A *chart* is a visual representation of numeric values. Charts (also known as graphs) have been an integral part of spreadsheets since the early days of Lotus 1-2-3. Charts generated by early spreadsheet products were extremely crude by today's standards. But, over the years, quality and flexibility have improved significantly. You'll find that Excel provides you with the tools to create a wide variety of highly customizable charts that can help you effectively communicate your message.

Displaying data in a well-conceived chart can make your numbers more understandable. Because a chart presents a picture, charts are particularly useful for summarizing a series of numbers and their interrelationships. Making a chart can often help you spot trends and patterns that might otherwise go unnoticed.

Figure 3-1 shows a worksheet that contains a simple column chart that depicts a company's sales volume by month. Viewing the chart makes it very apparent that sales were off in the summer months (June through August), but they increased steadily during the final four months of the year. You could, of course, arrive at this same conclusion simply by studying the numbers. But viewing the chart makes the point much more quickly.

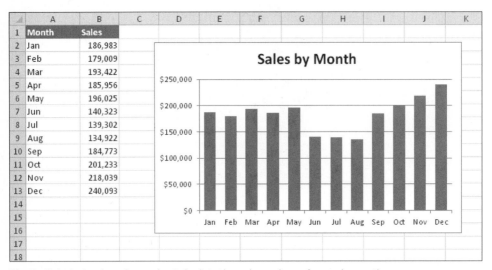

Figure 3-1: A simple column chart depicts the sales volume for each month.

A column chart is just one of many different types of charts that you can create with Excel. By the way, creating this chart is simple: Select the data in A1:B13, and press Alt+F1.

On the Web

All the charts pictured in this chapter are available at www.wiley.com/go/exceldr **in a workbook file named** introductory examples.xlsx.

How Excel Handles Charts

Before you can create a chart, you must have some numbers — sometimes known as data. The data, of course, is stored in the cells in a worksheet. Normally, the data that is used by a chart resides in a single worksheet, but that's not a strict requirement. A chart can use data that's stored in any number of worksheets, and the worksheets can even be in different workbooks. The decision to use data from one sheet or multiple sheets really depends on your data model, the nature of your data sources, and the interactivity you want to give your dashboard.

A chart is essentially an "object" that Excel creates upon request. This object consists of one or more *data series,* displayed graphically. The appearance of the data series depends on the selected *chart type.* For example, if you create a line chart that uses two data series, the chart contains two lines, and each line represents one data series. The data for each series is stored in a separate row or column. Each point on the line is determined by the value in a single cell, and is represented by a marker. You can distinguish the lines by their thickness, line style, color, or data markers.

Figure 3-2 shows a line chart that plots two data series across a 9-year period. The series are identified by using different data markers (squares versus circles), shown in the *legend* at the bottom of the chart. The lines also use different colors, which is not apparent in the grayscale figure.

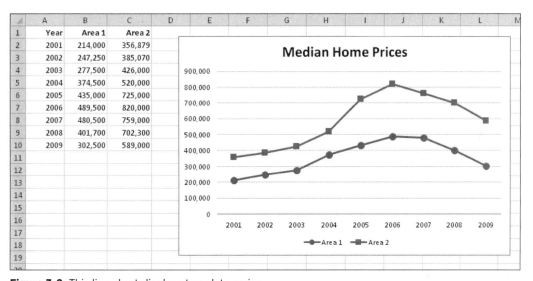

Figure 3-2: This line chart displays two data series.

A key point to keep in mind is that charts are dynamic. In other words, a chart series is linked to the data in your worksheet. If the data changes, the chart is updated automatically to reflect those changes so your dashboard can show the most current information.

After you've created a chart, you can always change its type, change the formatting, add new data series to it, or change an existing data series so that it uses data in a different range.

Charts can reside in either of two locations in a workbook:

> ➤ On a worksheet (an embedded chart)
> ➤ On a separate chart sheet

Embedded charts

An *embedded chart* basically floats on top of a worksheet, on the worksheet's drawing layer. The charts shown previously in this chapter are both embedded charts.

As with other drawing objects (such as a text box or a shape), you can move an embedded chart, resize it, change its proportions, adjust its borders, and add effects such as a shadow. Using embedded charts enables you to view the chart next to the data that it uses. Or, you can place several embedded charts together so that they print on a single page.

As discussed in Chapter 2, you would ideally place your charts in the presentation layer, presenting the relevant charts in a single viewable area that would fit on one page or a single screen.

When you create a chart, it always starts off as an embedded chart. The exception to this rule is when you select a range of data and press F11 to create a default chart. Such a chart is created on a chart sheet.

To make any changes to the actual chart in an embedded chart object, you must click it to *activate* the chart. When a chart is activated, Excel displays the three Chart Tools context tabs shown in Figure 3-3: Chart Tools ➜ Design, Chart Tools ➜ Layout, and Chart Tools ➜ Format.

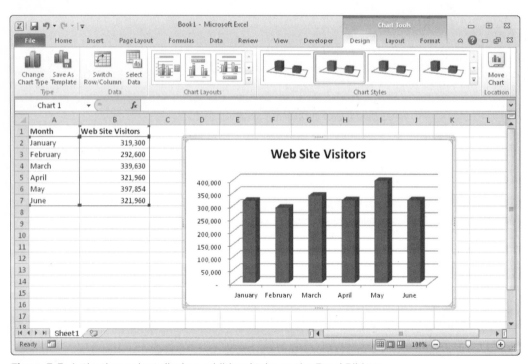

Figure 3-3: Activating a chart displays additional tabs on the Excel Ribbon.

Chart sheets

You can move an embedded chart to its own chart sheet, so you can view it by clicking a sheet tab. When you move a chart to a chart sheet, the chart occupies the entire sheet. If you plan to print a chart on a page by itself, using a chart sheet is often your better choice. If you have many charts to create, you may want to put each one on a separate chart sheet to avoid cluttering your worksheet. This technique also makes locating a particular chart easier because you can change the names of the chart sheets' tabs to provide a description of the chart that it contains. Although chart sheets are not typically used in traditional dashboards, they can come in handy when producing reports that will be viewed in a multi-tab workbook.

Figure 3-4 shows a chart on a chart sheet. When a chart sheet is activated, Excel displays the Chart Tools context tabs, as described in the previous section.

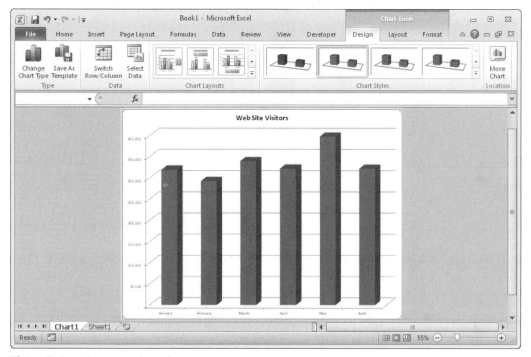

Figure 3-4: A chart on a chart sheet.

Parts of a Chart

A chart is made up of many different elements, and all of these elements are optional. Yes, you can create a chart that contains no chart elements — an empty chart. It's not very useful, but Excel allows it.

Refer to the chart in Figure 3-5 as you read the following description of the chart's elements.

This particular chart is a combination chart that displays both columns and a line. The chart has two *data series:* Income and Profit Margin. Income is plotted as vertical columns, and the Profit Margin is plotted as a line with square markers. Each bar (or marker on the line) represents a single *data point* (the value in a cell).

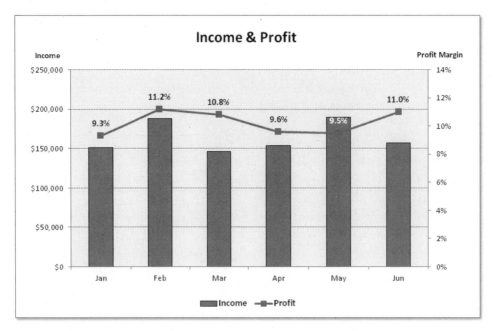

Figure 3-5: Parts of a chart.

The chart has a horizontal axis, known as the *category axis.* This axis represents the category for each data point (January, February, and so on). This axis doesn't have a label because the category units are obvious.

Notice that this chart has two vertical axes. These are known as *value axes,* and each one has a different scale. The axis on the left is for the column series (Income), and the axis on the right is for the line series (Profit Margin).

The value axes also display scale values. The axis on the left displays scale values from 0 to 250,000, in major unit increments of 50,000. The value axis on the right uses a different scale: 0 percent to 14 percent, in increments of 2 percent. For a value axis, you can control the minimum and maximum values, as well as the increment value.

A chart with two value axes is appropriate because the two data series vary dramatically in scale. If the Profit Margin data was plotted using the left axis, the line would not even be visible.

If a chart has more than one data series, you'll usually need a way to identify the data series or data points. A *legend,* for example, is often used to identify the various series in a chart. In this example, the legend appears at the bottom of the chart. Some charts also display *data labels* to identify specific data points. The example chart displays data labels for the Profit Margin series, but not for the Income series. In addition, most charts (including the example chart) contain a *chart title* and additional labels to identify the axes or categories.

The example chart also contains horizontal *gridlines* (which correspond to the values on the left axis). Gridlines are basically extensions of the value axis scale, which makes it easier for the viewer to determine the magnitude of the data points.

In addition, all charts have a *chart area* (the entire background area of the chart) and a *plot area* (the part that shows the actual chart, including the plotted data, the axes, and the axis labels).

Charts can have additional parts or fewer parts, depending on the chart type. For example, a pie chart (see Figure 3-6) has "slices" and no axes. A 3-D chart may have *walls* and a *floor* (see Figure 3-7).

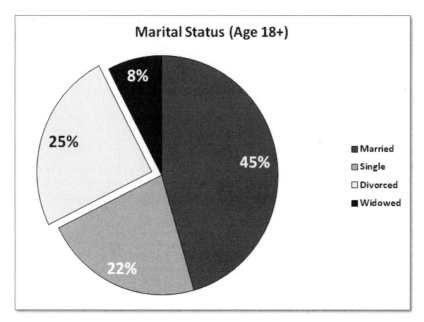

Figure 3-6: A pie chart.

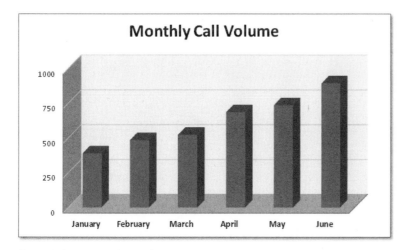

Figure 3-7: A 3-D column chart.

▶ Chart limitations

The following table lists the limitations of Excel charts.

Item	Limitation
Charts in a worksheet	Limited by available memory
Worksheets referred to by a chart	255
Data series in a chart	255
Data points in a data series	32,000
Data points in a data series (3-D charts)	4,000
Total data points in a chart	256,000

Most users never find these limitations to be a problem. However, one item that frequently *does* cause problems is the limit on the length of the SERIES formula. Each argument is limited to 255 characters, and in some situations, that's simply not enough characters. Refer to Chapter 5 for more information about SERIES formulas.

Several other types of items can be added to a chart. For example, you can add a *trend line* or display *error bars.*

Basic Steps for Creating a Chart

Creating a chart is relatively easy. The following sections describe how to create and then customize a basic chart in Excel 2007 and Excel 2010 to best communicate your business goals.

Creating the chart

Follow these general steps to create a chart using the data in Figure 3-8:

1. Select the data that you want to use in the chart.

    Make sure that you select the column headers, if the data has them. Another option is to select a single cell within a range of data. Excel then uses the entire data range for the chart.

◢	A	B	C	D
1		**Projected**	**Actual**	
2	Jan	2,000	1,895	
3	Feb	2,500	2,643	
4	Mar	3,500	3,648	
5				
6				
7				

Figure 3-8: This data would make a good chart.

2. Click the Insert tab, and then click a Chart icon in the Charts group.

   The icon expands into a gallery list that shows subtypes (see Figure 3-9).

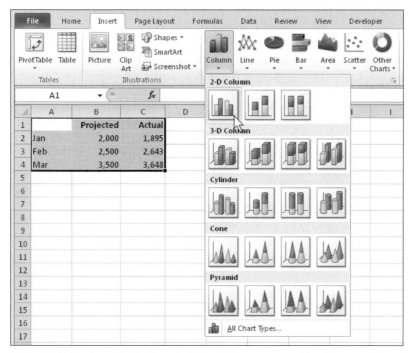

Figure 3-9: The icons in the Insert ➜ Charts group expand to show a gallery of chart subtypes.

3. Click a Chart subtype, and Excel then creates the chart of the specified type.

   Figure 3-10 shows a column chart created from the data.

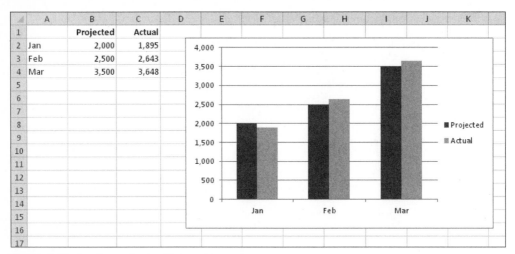

Figure 3-10: A column chart with two data series.

Tip

To quickly create a default chart, select the data and press Alt+F1 to create an embedded chart, or press F11 to create a chart on a chart sheet.

Switching the row and column orientation

When Excel creates a chart, it uses an algorithm to determine whether the data is arranged in columns or in rows. Most of the time Excel guesses correctly, but if it creates the chart using the wrong orientation, you can quickly change it by selecting the chart and choosing Chart Tools ➔ Design ➔ Data ➔ Switch Row/Column. This command is a toggle, so if changing the data orientation doesn't improve the chart, just choose the command again (or click the Undo button found on the Quick Access toolbar).

The orientation of the data has a drastic effect on the look (and, perhaps, understandability) of your chart. Figure 3-11 shows the column chart in Figure 3-10 after changing the orientation. Notice that the chart now has three data series, one for each month. If the goal of your dashboard is to compare actual with projected values for each month, this version of the chart is much more difficult to interpret because the relevant columns are not adjacent.

Cross-Ref

To learn more about effectively communicating your message with charts, see Chapter 4.

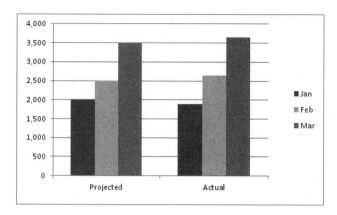

Figure 3-11: The column chart, after swapping the row/column orientation.

Changing the chart type

After you've created a chart, you can easily change the chart type. Although a column chart may work well for a particular data set, there's no harm in checking out some other chart types. You can choose Chart Tools → Design → Type → Change Chart Type to display the Change Chart Type dialog box and experiment with other chart types. Figure 3-12 shows the Change Chart Type dialog box.

Note

If your chart uses more than one data series, make sure that a chart element other than a data series is selected when you choose the Chart Tools → Design → Type → Change Chart Type command. If you select a series, the command changes the chart type of the selected series only. Selecting a single series before you issue the Change Chart Type command is the basis of creating combination charts (see Chapter 4 for more information about chart types and creating combination charts).

In the Change Chart Type dialog box, the main categories are listed on the left, and the subtypes are shown as icons. Select an icon and click OK, and Excel displays the chart using the new chart type. If you don't like the result, click the Undo button.

Tip

If the chart is an embedded chart, you can also change a chart's type by using the icons in the Insert → Charts group. In fact, this method is more efficient because it doesn't involve a dialog box.

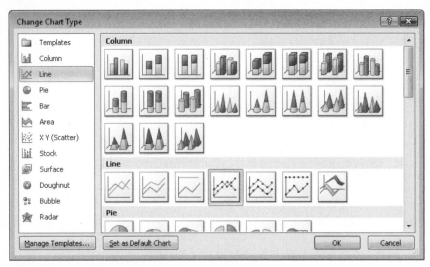

Figure 3-12: The Change Chart Type dialog box.

Applying a chart layout

Each chart type has a number of prebuilt layouts that you can apply with a single mouse click. A layout contains additional chart elements, such as a title, data labels, axes, and so on. This step is optional, but one of the prebuilt designs might be just what you're looking for. Even if the layout isn't exactly what you want, it may be close enough that you need to make only a few adjustments.

To apply a layout, select the chart and use the Chart Tools ➜ Design ➜ Chart Layouts gallery. Figure 3-13 shows how a column chart would look using various layouts.

Applying a chart style

The Chart Tools ➜ Design ➜ Chart Styles gallery contains quite a few styles that you can apply to your chart. The styles consist of various color choices and some special effects. Again, this step is optional.

Tip

The styles displayed in the gallery depend on the workbook's theme. When you choose Page Layout ➜ Themes to apply a different theme, you'll see a new selection of chart styles designed for the selected theme.

Adding and deleting chart elements

In some cases, applying a chart layout (as described previously) gives you a chart with all the elements you need. Most of the time, however, you'll need to add or remove some chart elements and fine-tune the layout. You do this using the controls on the Chart Tools ➜ Layout tab.

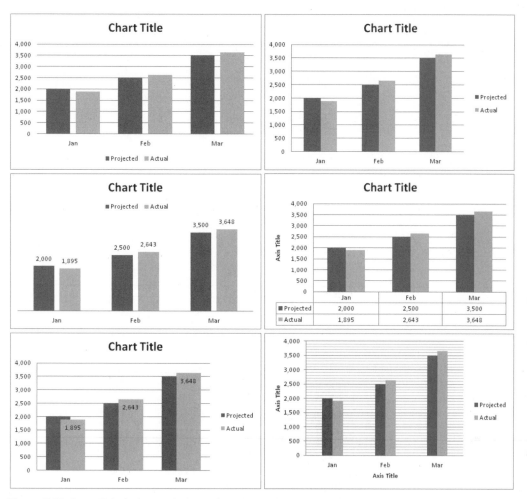

Figure 3-13: One-click design variations of a column chart.

For example, to give a chart a title, choose Chart Tools ➜ Layout ➜ Labels ➜ Chart Title. The control displays some options that determine where the title is placed. Excel inserts a title with the text "Chart Title." Click the text and replace it with your actual chart title.

Formatting chart elements

Every element in a chart can be formatted and customized in many ways. Many users are content with charts that are created using the steps described earlier in this chapter. But because you're reading this book, you probably want to find out how to customize charts for maximum impact.

Cross-Ref

For more detailed information about formatting and customizing your chart, see Chapter 6.

Excel provides two ways to format and customize individual chart elements. Both of the following methods require that you select the chart element first:

➤ Use the Ribbon controls on the Chart Tools ➡ Format tab.

➤ Press Ctrl+1 to display the Format dialog box that's specific to the selected chart element.

If you use Excel 2010, you can also double-click a chart element to display the Format dialog box for the element.

Note

The Ribbon controls contain only a subset of the formatting options. For maximum control, use the Format dialog box.

For example, assume that you'd like to change the color of the columns for one of the series in the chart. Click any column in the series (which selects the entire series). Then, choose Chart Tools ➡ Format ➡ Shape Styles ➡ Shape Fill and choose a color from the displayed list. To change the properties of the outline around the columns, use the Chart Tools ➡ Format ➡ Shape Styles ➡ Shape Outline control. To change the effects used in the columns (for example, add a shadow), use the Chart Tools ➡ Format ➡ Shape Styles ➡ Shape Effects control.

Alternatively, you can select a series in the chart, press Ctrl+1, and use the Format Data Series dialog box shown in Figure 3-14. Note that this is a tabbed dialog box. Click a tab along the left side to view additional controls. It's also a stay-on-top dialog box, so you can click another element in the chart. In other words, you don't have to close the dialog box to see the changes you specify.

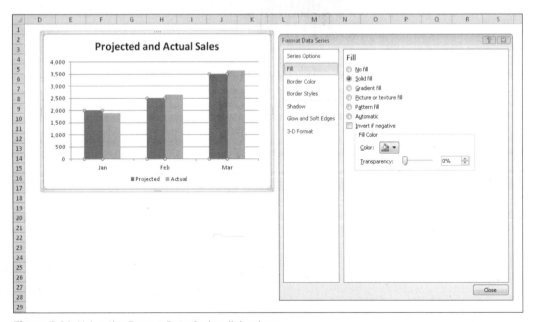

Figure 3-14: Using the Format Data Series dialog box.

Working with Charts

The following sections cover these common chart modifications:

- ➤ Moving and resizing charts
- ➤ Converting an embedded chart to a chart on a chart sheet
- ➤ Copying a chart
- ➤ Deleting a chart
- ➤ Adding chart elements
- ➤ Moving and deleting chart elements
- ➤ Formatting chart elements
- ➤ Copying a chart's formatting
- ➤ Renaming a chart
- ➤ Printing charts

Note

Before you can modify a chart, you must activate it. To activate an embedded chart, click it. Doing so activates the chart and also selects the element that you click. To activate a chart on a chart sheet, just click its sheet tab.

Moving and resizing a chart

If your chart is an embedded chart, you can freely move and resize it with your mouse. Click the chart's border and then drag the border to move the chart. Drag any of the eight "handles" to resize the chart. The handles consists of three dots that appear on the chart's corners and edges when you click the chart's border. When the mouse pointer turns into a double arrow, click and drag to resize the chart.

When a chart is selected, you can use the Chart Tools ➜ Format ➜ Size controls to adjust the height and width of the chart. Use the spinners, or type the dimensions directly into the Height and Width controls. Oddly, Excel does not provide similar controls to specify the top and left positions of the chart.

To move an embedded chart, just click its border at any location except one of the eight resizing handles. Then drag the chart to its new location. You also can use standard cut-and-paste techniques to move an embedded chart. Select the chart and choose Home ➜ Clipboard ➜ Cut (or press Ctrl+X). Then activate a cell near the desired location and choose Home ➜ Clipboard ➜ Paste (or press Ctrl+V). The new location can be in a different worksheet or even in a different workbook. If you paste the chart to a different workbook, it will be linked to the data in the original workbook. Another way to move a chart to a different location is to choose Chart Tools ➜ Design ➜ Location ➜ Move Chart. This command displays the Move Chart dialog box, which lets you specify a new sheet for the chart (either a chart sheet or a worksheet).

Converting an embedded chart to a chart sheet

When you create a chart using the icons in the Insert ➜ Charts group, the result is always an embedded chart. If you'd prefer that your chart be located on a chart sheet, you can easily move it.

To convert an embedded chart to a chart on a chart sheet, select the chart and choose Chart ➜ Tools ➜ Design ➜ Location ➜ Move Chart to display the Move Chart dialog box shown in Figure 3-15. Select the New Sheet option and (optionally) provide a different name for the chart sheet.

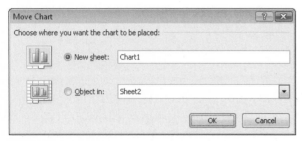

Figure 3-15: Use the Move Chart dialog box to move an embedded chart to a chart sheet (or vice versa).

To convert a chart on a chart sheet to an embedded chart, activate the chart sheet and then choose Chart ➜ Tools ➜ Design ➜ Location ➜ Move Chart to display the Move Chart dialog box. Select the Object In option and specify the sheet by using the drop-down control.

Copying a chart

To make an exact copy of an embedded chart, select the chart and choose Home ➜ Clipboard ➜ Copy (or press Ctrl+C). Then activate a cell near the desired location and choose Home ➜ Clipboard ➜ Paste (or press Ctrl+V). The new location can be in a different worksheet or even in a different workbook. If you paste the chart to a different workbook, it will be linked to the data in the original workbook.

To copy a chart on a chart sheet, press Ctrl while you drag the sheet tab to a new location in the tab list.

Deleting a chart

To delete an embedded chart, press Ctrl and click the chart (this selects the chart as an object). Then press Delete. When the Ctrl key is pressed, you can select multiple charts and then delete them all with a single press of the Delete key.

To delete a chart sheet, right-click its sheet tab and choose Delete from the shortcut menu. To delete multiple chart sheets, select them by pressing Ctrl while you click the sheet tabs.

Adding chart elements

To add new elements to a chart (such as a title, legend, data labels, or gridlines), use the controls in the Chart Tools ➜ Layout group. These controls are arranged into logical groups, and they all display a drop-down list of options.

Moving and deleting chart elements

Some of the elements within a chart can be moved. The movable chart elements include the plot area, titles, the legend, and data labels. To move a chart element, click it to select it. Then drag its border. The easiest way to delete a chart element is to select it and then press Delete. You can also use the controls in the Chart Tools ➜ Layout group to turn off the display of a particular chart element. For example, to delete data labels, choose Chart Tools ➜ Layout ➜ Labels ➜ Data Labels ➜ None.

Note that deleting a chart element by using the controls in the Chart Tools ➜ Layout group deletes the element (it doesn't just hide it). For example, assume that you add a chart title and apply formatting to it. Then you use the Chart Tools ➜ Layout ➜ Labels ➜ Chart Title ➜ None command to hide the title. If you later decide that you want the title, the previously formatted title is gone and you need to re-apply the formatting.

A few chart elements consist of multiple objects. For example, the data labels element consists of one label for each data point. To move or delete one data label, click once to select the entire element and then click a second time to select the specific data label. You can then move or delete the single data label.

Formatting chart elements

Many users are content to stick with the predefined chart layouts and chart styles. For more precise customizations, Excel allows you to work with individual chart elements and apply additional formatting. You can use the Ribbon commands for some modifications, but the easiest way to format chart elements is to right-click the element and choose Format from the shortcut menu. The exact command depends on the element you select. For example, if you right-click the chart's title, the shortcut menu command is Format Chart Title. Alternatively, you can press Ctrl+1 to display the Format dialog box for the selected element.

The Format command displays a stay-on-top tabbed dialog box, with options for the selected element.

Tip

If you've applied formatting to a chart element and decide that it wasn't such a good idea, you can revert to the original formatting for the particular chart style. Right-click the chart element and choose Reset to Match Style from the shortcut menu. To reset the entire chart, select the chart area when you issue the command.

Copying a chart's formatting

If you create a nicely formatted chart, and realize that you need to create several more charts that have the same formatting, you have these three choices:

➤ Make a copy of the original chart, and then change the data used in the copied chart. One way to change the data used in a chart is to choose the Chart Tools ➜ Design ➜ Data ➜ Select Data command and make the changes in the Select Data Source dialog box.

➤ Create the other charts, but don't apply any formatting. Then, activate the original chart and press Ctrl+C. Select one of the other charts, and choose Home ➜ Clipboard ➜ Paste ➜ Paste Special. In the Paste Special dialog box, click the Formats option and then click the OK button. Repeat for each additional chart.

➤ Create a chart template, and then use the template as the basis for the new charts. Or, you can apply the new template to existing charts. See Chapter 4 for more information about chart templates.

Renaming a chart

When you activate an embedded chart, its name appears in the Name box (located to the left of the Formula bar). It seems logical that you can use the Name box to change the name of a chart — but you can't.

To change the name of an embedded chart, use the Chart Tools ➜ Layout ➜ Properties ➜ Chart Name box. Just type the new name and press Enter.

Why rename a chart? If a worksheet has many charts, you may prefer to activate a particular chart by name. Just type the chart's name in the Name box and press Enter. It's much easier to remember a chart named Monthly Sales as opposed to a chart named Chart 9.

Note

> When you rename a chart, Excel allows you to use a name that already exists for another chart. Normally, it doesn't matter if multiple charts have the same name, but it can cause problems if you use VBA macros that select a chart by name.

Printing charts

Printing embedded charts is nothing special; you print them the same way that you print a worksheet. As long as you include the embedded chart in the range that you want to print, Excel prints the chart as it appears on-screen. When printing a sheet that contains embedded charts, it's a good idea to preview first (or use Page Layout View) to ensure that your charts do not span multiple pages. If you created the chart on a chart sheet, Excel always prints the chart on a page by itself.

Tip   **If you select an embedded chart and choose File → Print, Excel prints the chart on a page by itself (as if it were a chart sheet) and does *not* print the worksheet.**

If you don't want a particular embedded chart to appear on your printout, select the background area of the chart(the chart area), right-click and choose Format. In the Format Chart Area dialog box, click the Properties tab and deselect the Print Object check box (see Figure 3-16).

Figure 3-16: Specifying that a chart should not be printed with the worksheet.

Understanding Chart Types

In This Chapter

- Types of charts Excel can generate

- Examples of each chart type

- Creating and using chart templates

If you are an experienced professional, you've probably been exposed to many types of charts: bar charts, line charts, pie charts, and so on. Excel supports all these common chart types and even some esoteric chart types, such as radar charts and doughnut charts.

This chapter explores each of these chart types, along with information that may help you determine which type of chart can best display your data.

Conveying a Message with a Chart

People who create charts usually do so to make a point or to communicate a specific message. Often, the message is explicitly stated in the chart's title or in a text box within the chart. The chart itself provides visual support for the message.

Choosing the correct chart type is often a key factor in making the message compelling. Therefore, it's often well worth your time to experiment with various chart types to determine which one is most effective.

In almost every case, the underlying message in a chart is some type of *comparison.* Examples of some general types of comparisons include the following:

> ➤ **Compare items:** A chart may compare sales volume in each of a company's sales regions.

> ➤ **Compare data over time:** A chart may display sales amounts by month, to indicate a trend over time.

➤ **Make relative comparisons:** A common pie chart can depict relative values in terms of pie slices.

➤ **Compare data relationships:** A scatter chart is ideal for this. You may create a chart to show the relationship between monthly marketing expenditures and sales.

➤ **Compare frequency:** A common histogram, for example, can display the number (or percentage) of students who had a test score within several ranges of scores.

➤ **Identify "outliers" or unusual situations:** If you have thousands of data points, creating a chart may help identify data that is not representative.

Choosing a Chart Type

A common question among Excel users is, "How do I know which chart type to use for my data?" Unfortunately, there is no cut-and-dried answer to this question. Perhaps the best answer is a vague one: *Use the chart type that gets your message across in the simplest way.*

Figure 4-1 shows the same set of data plotted using six different chart types. Although all six charts represent the same information (monthly visitors to a Web site), they look quite different from one another.

On the Web

To get this workbook, go to www.wiley.com/go/exceldr **and download the file named** six chart types.xlsx.

The column chart (upper left) is probably the best choice for this particular set of data because it clearly shows the information for each month in discrete units. The bar chart (upper right) is similar to a column chart, but the axes are swapped. Most people are more accustomed to seeing time-based information extend from left to right rather than from top to bottom.

The line chart (middle left) may not be the best choice because it seems to imply that the data is continuous — that points exist in between the 12 actual data points. This same argument could be made against using an area chart (middle right).

The pie chart (lower left) is simply too confusing and does nothing to convey the time-based nature of the data. Pie charts are most appropriate for a data series in which you want to emphasize proportions among a relatively small number of data points. If you have too many data points, a pie chart can be impossible to interpret. For some reason, pie charts are wildly popular — even though they are often not the best choice.

The radar chart (lower right) is clearly inappropriate for this data. People are not accustomed to viewing time-based information in a circular direction!

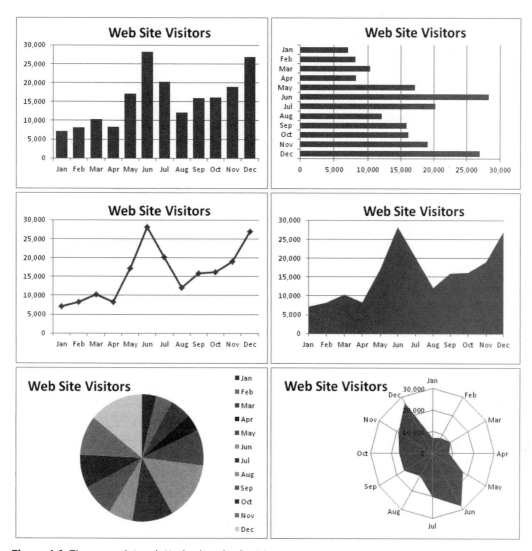

Figure 4-1: The same data, plotted using six chart types.

Fortunately, changing a chart's type is very easy, so you can experiment with various chart types until you find the one that represents your data accurately and clearly — and as simply as possible. To change a chart's type, select the chart and choose Chart Tools ➜ Design ➜ Change Chart Type. Then select the chart type from the Change Chart Type dialog box. Or, you can select a chart and use the chart options in the Insert ➜ Charts group.

Note If your chart has more than one data series, make sure that something other than a chart series is selected when you issue the Chart Tools ➜ Design ➜ Change Chart Type command. If a series is selected, only the type for that series will be changed. In other words, you'll end up with a combination chart — a chart that incorporates two or more different chart types. I describe combination charts later in this chapter.

The remainder of this chapter contains lots of information about Excel's various chart types. The examples and discussion may give you a better handle on determining the most appropriate chart type for your data.

Excel's Chart Types

To create a chart, first select the cells that contain the data for the chart. Then, click an icon in the Insert ➜ Charts group for the chart type. The icon then expands so that you can select the sub-type. For example, if you choose Insert ➜ Charts ➜ Pie, the control expands to display the six pie chart subtypes, as shown in Figure 4-2. When you hover your mouse over a chart subtype, Excel displays a brief description.

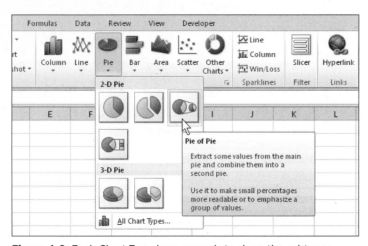

Figure 4-2: Each Chart Type icon expands to show the subtypes.

If you click the All Chart Types link, you get a dialog box that lists all charts and their subtypes.

Note that you create the less frequently used chart types by choosing the Insert ➜ Charts ➜ Other Charts command. The charts available from this control are stock charts, surface charts, doughnut charts, bubble charts, and radar charts.

Column charts

Column charts are one of the most common chart types. A column chart displays each data point as a vertical column, the height of which corresponds to the value. The value scale is displayed on the vertical axis, which is usually on the left side of the chart. You can specify any number of data series, and the corresponding data points from each series can be stacked on top of each other. Typically, each data series is depicted in a different color or pattern.

Column charts are often used to compare discrete items, and they can depict the differences between items in a series or items across multiple series.

Table 4-1 lists and describes Excel's 19 column chart subtypes.

Table 4-1: Column Chart Subtypes

Chart Type	Description
Clustered column	Standard column chart.
Stacked column	Column chart with data series stacked.
100% stacked column	Column chart with data series stacked and expressed as percentages.
3-D clustered column	Column chart with a perspective look.
Stacked column in 3-D	Column chart with a perspective look. Data series are stacked.
100% stacked column in 3-D	Column chart with a perspective look. Data series are stacked and expressed as percentages.
3-D column	Column chart with multiple series arranged along a third axis.
Clustered cylinder	Like a 3-D clustered column chart, but the columns are cylindrical.
Stacked cylinder	Like a stacked column in 3-D chart, but the columns are cylindrical.
100% stacked cylinder	Like a 100% stacked column in 3-D chart, but the columns are cylindrical.
3-D cylinder	Like a 3-D column chart, but the columns are cylindrical.
Clustered cone	Like a 3-D clustered column chart, but the columns are conical.
Stacked cone	Like a stacked column in 3-D chart, but the columns are conical.
100% stacked cone	Like a 100% stacked column in 3-D chart, but the columns are conical.
3-D cone	Like a 3-D column chart, but the columns are conical.
Clustered pyramid	Like a 3-D clustered column chart, but the columns are pyramidal.
Stacked pyramid	Like a stacked column in 3-D chart, but the columns are pyramidal.
100% stacked pyramid	Like a 100% stacked column in 3-D chart, but the columns are pyramidal.
3-D pyramid	Like a 3-D column chart, but the columns are pyramidal.

Figure 4-3 shows an example of a clustered column chart that depicts annual sales for two products. From this chart, it is clear that Sprocket sales have always exceeded Widget sales. In addition, Widget sales have been declining over the years, whereas Sprocket sales are increasing.

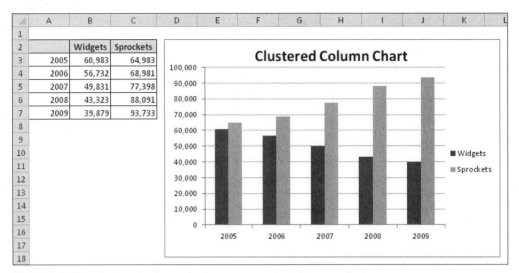

Figure 4-3: This clustered column chart compares sales of two products.

On the Web

To get the chart examples in this section, go to www.wiley.com/go/exceldr **and download the workbook named** column charts.xlsx.

The same data, in the form of a stacked column chart, is shown in Figure 4-4. This chart has the added advantage of depicting the combined sales over time (note the scale of the vertical axis). It shows that total sales have remained relatively steady over the years, but the relative proportions of the two products have changed.

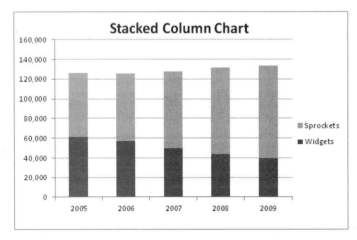

Figure 4-4: This stacked column chart displays sales by product and depicts the total sales.

Figure 4-5 shows the same sales data plotted as a 100% stacked column chart. This chart type shows the relative contribution of each product by year. Notice that the value axis displays percentage values, not sales amounts. This chart provides no information about the actual sales numbers. This type of chart is often a good alternative to using several pie charts. Instead of using a round pie to show the relative sales volume in each year, the chart uses a rectangular column for each year.

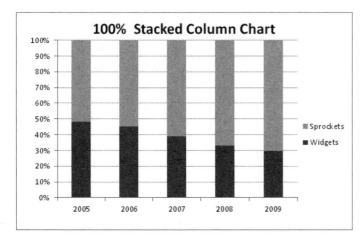

Figure 4-5: This 100% stacked column chart displays annual sales as a percentage.

The data is plotted using a 3-D column chart in Figure 4-6. Many people use this type of chart because it has more visual pizzazz. Although it may be more appealing visually, this type of chart often makes it difficult to make precise comparisons because of the distorted perspective view. If you must use a 3-D column chart, save it for situations in which you want to show general trends rather than allow precise comparisons.

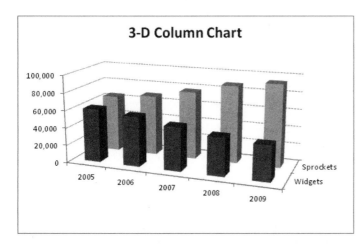

Figure 4-6: A 3-D column chart.

3-D or not 3-D? That is the question

Some of Excel's charts are referred to as *3-D charts.* This terminology can be somewhat confusing, because some of these so-called 3-D charts aren't technically 3-D charts. Rather, they are 2-D charts with a perspective look to them; that is, they appear to have some depth. The accompanying figure shows two "3-D" charts.

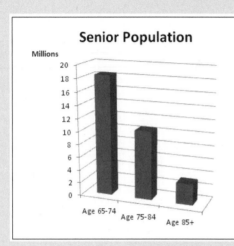
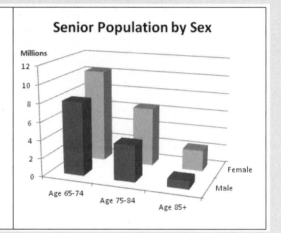

The chart on the left is a 3-D clustered column chart. However, it's not a true 3-D chart. It's just a 2-D chart that uses perspective to add depth to the columns. The chart on the right (a 3-D column chart) is a true 3-D chart because the data series extend into the third (depth) dimension.

A true 3-D chart has three axes: a value axis (the height dimension), a category axis (the width dimension), and a series axis (the depth dimension). The series axis is always a category axis — it cannot depict scaled numerical values.

When a 3-D chart is active (whether it's a true 3-D chart or not), you can change the chart's perspective and viewpoint by using the Chart Tools ➜ Layout ➜ Background ➜ 3-D Rotation command. This command displays the 3-D Rotation tab of the Format Chart Area dialog box. You'll find that you have a great deal of control. You can distort the chart so much that it becomes virtually useless.

The final column chart variation is shown in Figure 4-7. This is a stacked cone chart. This chart subtype (as well as the cylinder and pyramid variations) is usually more difficult to interpret, compared to a standard column chart. This particular chart can be a bit misleading because the Sprockets series may be viewed as being less important because of the reduced volume at the top of the cones. In addition, note the perspective distortion. Although the combined sales for the products exceeds 120,000 for all years, that fact is not apparent in this 3-D chart.

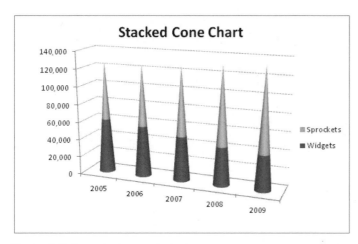

Figure 4-7: A stacked cone chart.

Bar charts

A *bar chart* is essentially a column chart that has been rotated 90 degrees clockwise. One distinct advantage to using a bar chart is that the category labels may be easier to read. Figure 4-8 shows a bar chart that displays a value for each of ten survey items. The category labels are lengthy, and it would be difficult to display them legibly using a column chart.

On the Web

To get the chart examples in this section, go to `www.wiley.com/go/exceldr` **and download the workbook file named** `line charts.xlsx`.

Table 4-2 lists Excel's 15 bar chart subtypes.

Table 4-2: Bar Chart Subtypes

Chart Type	Description
Clustered bar	Standard bar chart.
Stacked bar	Bar chart with data series stacked.
100% stacked bar	Bar chart with data series stacked and expressed as percentages.
Clustered bar in 3-D	Standard bar chart with a perspective look.
Stacked bar in 3-D	Bar chart with a perspective look. Excel stacks data series.
100% stacked bar in 3-D	Bar chart with a perspective look. Excel stacks data series and expresses them as percentages.
Clustered horizontal cylinder	Like a clustered bar chart, but the bars are cylindrical.
Stacked horizontal cylinder	Like a stacked bar chart, but the bars are cylindrical.
100% stacked horizontal cylinder	Like a 100% stacked bar chart, but the bars are cylindrical.
Clustered horizontal cone	Like a clustered bar chart, but the bars are conical.

continued

Table 4-2: Bar Chart Subtypes *(continued)*

Chart Type	Description
Stacked horizontal cone	Like a stacked bar chart, but the bars are conical.
100% stacked horizontal cone	Like a 100% stacked bar chart, but the bars are conical.
Clustered horizontal pyramid	Like a clustered bar chart, but the bars are pyramidal.
Stacked horizontal pyramid	Like a stacked bar chart, but the bars are pyramidal.
100% stacked horizontal pyramid	Like a 100% stacked bar chart, but the bars are pyramidal.

Note

Unlike a column chart, there is no subtype that displays multiple series along a third axis (that is, there is no 3-D Bar Chart subtype).

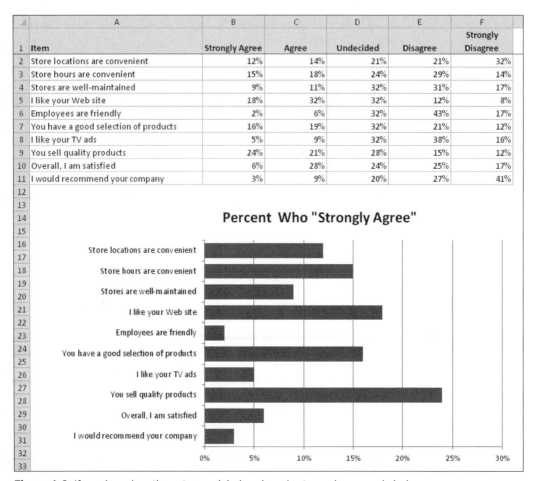

Figure 4-8: If you have lengthy category labels, a bar chart may be a good choice.

As with a column chart, you can include any number of data series in a bar chart. In addition, the bars can be "stacked" from left to right. Figure 4-9 shows a 100% stacked bar chart. This chart summarizes the percentage of survey respondents who replied to each option.

Cross-Ref

In some situations, you may prefer to use Excel's data bar conditional formatting in lieu of a bar chart. Using conditional formatting offers some advantages if you need to create many different bar charts. See Chapter 10 for details.

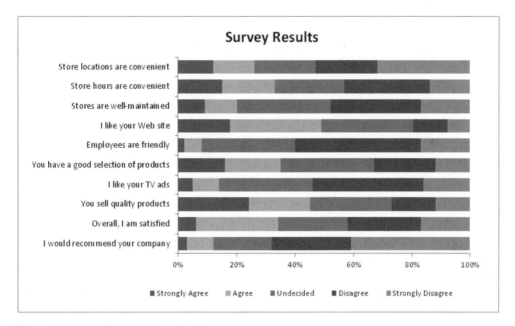

Figure 4-9: A 100% stacked bar chart.

Line charts

Line charts are often used to plot continuous data and are useful for identifying trends over time. For example, plotting daily sales as a line chart may help you to identify sales fluctuations over time. Normally, the category axis for a line chart displays equal intervals.

Table 4-3 lists Excel's seven line chart subtypes.

Table 4-3: Line Chart Subtypes

Chart Type	Description
Line	Standard line chart.
Stacked line	Line chart with stacked data series.
100% stacked line	Line chart with stacked data series expressed as percentages.
Line with markers	Line chart with data markers.
Stacked line with markers	Line chart with stacked data series and data markers.
100% stacked line with markers	Line chart with stacked data series and line markers, expressed as percentages.
3-D line	Chart that displays "ribbon-like" lines, using a third axis.

See Figure 4-10 for an example of a line chart that depicts daily sales (200 data points). Although the data varies quite a bit on a daily basis, the chart clearly depicts a general upward trend.

Figure 4-10: A line chart can often help you spot trends and patterns in your data.

A line chart can use any number of data series, and you distinguish the lines by using different colors, line styles, or markers. Figure 4-11 shows a line chart that uses three series, each with 55 data points. Each line is displayed in a different color and with a different marker, so the lines can be identified even if the chart is reproduced in grayscale.

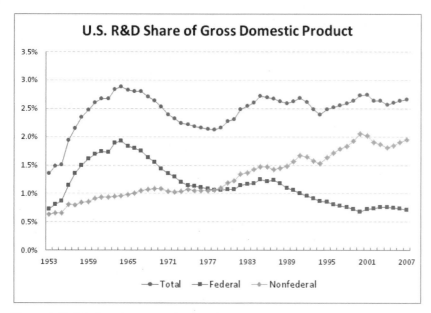

Figure 4-11: This line chart uses three series.

Figure 4-12 shows a 3-D line chart that depicts population growth for three states. Most would agree that a 3-D line chart is definitely *not* a good chart type for this data. For example, the 3-D perspective makes it virtually impossible to determine the relative growths of Washington and Oregon. In fact, the chart may present an optical illusion that makes it impossible to discern the order of the line series across the depth axis. Using a standard line chart, as in Figure 4-13, is a better choice.

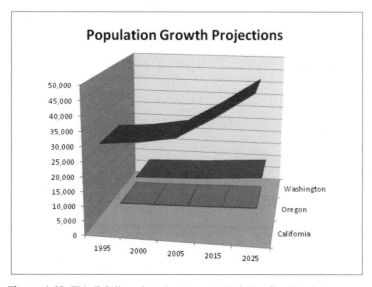

Figure 4-12: This 3-D line chart is not a good choice for this data.

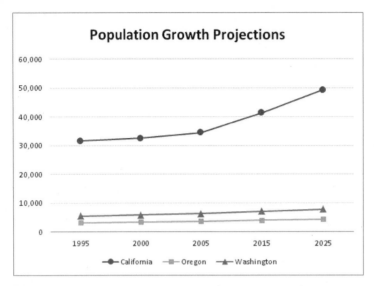

Figure 4-13: Using a standard line chart is a better choice for this data.

Pie charts

A *pie chart* is useful when you want to show relative proportions or contributions to a whole. A pie chart displays only one data series. Pie charts are most effective with a small number of data points. Generally, a pie chart should use no more than five or six data points (or slices). A pie chart with too many data points can be very difficult to interpret.

Note

The values used in a pie chart must all be positive numbers. If you create a pie chart that uses one or more negative values, those values will be converted to positive values — which is probably not what you intended!

You can "explode" one or more slices of a pie chart for emphasis (see Figure 4-14). Activate the chart and click any pie slice to select the entire pie. Then click the slice that you want to explode and drag it away from the center.

On the Web

The chart examples in this section are available at `www.wiley.com/go/exceldr` **in the workbook file named** `pie charts.xlsx`.

Table 4-4 lists Excel's six pie chart subtypes.

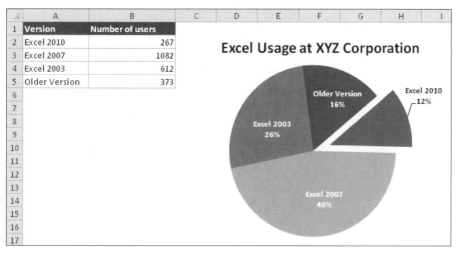

Figure 4-14: A pie chart with one slice exploded.

Table 4-4: Pie Chart Subtypes

Chart Type	Description
Pie	Standard pie chart.
Pie in 3-D	Pie chart with perspective look.
Pie of pie	Pie chart with one slice broken into another pie.
Exploded pie	Pie chart with one or more slices exploded.
Exploded pie in 3-D	Pie chart with perspective look, with one or more slices exploded.
Bar of pie	Pie chart with one slice broken into a column.

Figure 4-15 shows an example of a pie in 3-D chart. You have complete control over how the chart is rotated and how much the slices are separated. Keep in mind that 3-D pie charts are particularly prone to perspective distortion. In other words, this chart type can be very difficult to interpret.

The pie of pie and bar of pie chart types enable you to display a secondary chart that provides more detail for one of the pie slices. Refer to Figure 4-16 for an example. The pie chart shows the breakdown of four expense categories: Rent, Supplies, Utilities, and Salary. The secondary bar chart provides an additional regional breakdown of the Salary category. You control which values are used in the secondary chart by using the Series Options tab in the Format Data Series dialog box.

The `pie chart.xlsx` file in the companion files for this book includes an alternate presentation of this data, using a stack column chart.

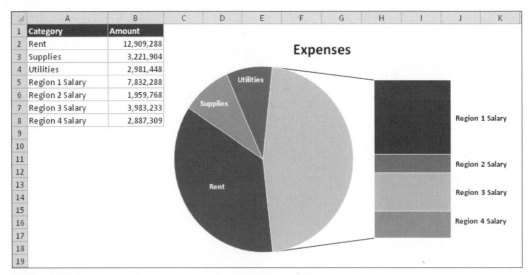

Figure 4-16: A bar of pie chart that shows detail for one of the pie slices.

Scatter charts

Another common chart type is a *scatter chart* (also known as an XY chart). A scatter chart differs from most other chart types in that both axes display values. (A scatter chart has no category axis.)

This type of chart often is used to show the relationship between two variables. Figure 4-17 shows an example of a scatter chart that plots the relationship between sales calls made during a month (horizontal axis) and actual sales for the month (vertical axis). The chart shows that these two variables are positively related: Months in which more calls were made typically had higher sales volumes.

On the Web

The chart examples in this section are available at www.wiley.com/go/exceldr **in the workbook file named** scatter charts.xlsx.

Note

Although these data points correspond to time, it's important to understand that the chart does not convey any time-related information. In other words, the data points are plotted based only on their two values. The Year and Month columns are not used.

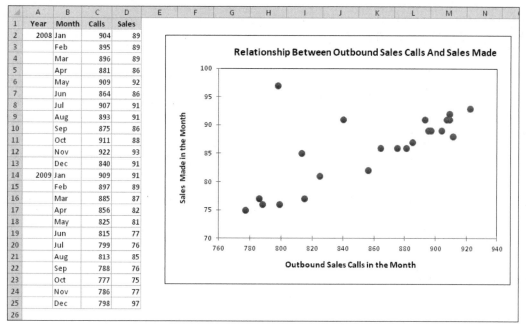

Figure 4-17: A scatter chart shows the relationship between two variables.

Table 4-5 lists Excel's five scatter chart subtypes.

Table 4-5: Scatter Chart Subtypes

Chart Type	Description
Scatter with only markers	A scatter chart with data markers and no lines.
Scatter with smooth lines and markers	A scatter chart with data markers and smoothed lines.
Scatter with smooth lines	A scatter chart with smoothed lines and no data markers.
Scatter with straight lines and markers	A scatter chart with lines and data markers.
Scatter with straight lines	A scatter chart with lines and no data markers.

Another scatter chart example is shown in Figure 4-18. This chart displays 200 x-y data points, using a smoothed line and no markers. This is also an example of a minimalist chart. All the chart elements (except the data series) are removed.

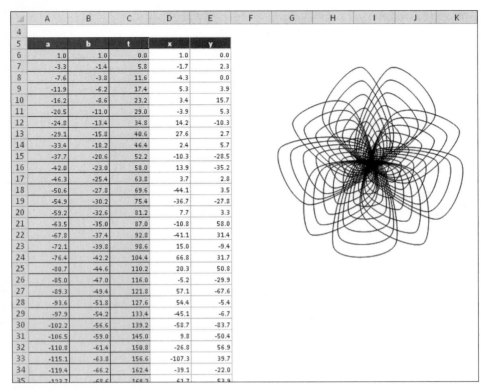

◢	A	B	C	D	E	F	G	H	I	J	K
4											
5	**a**	**b**	**t**	**x**	**y**						
6	1.0	1.0	0.0	1.0	0.0						
7	-3.3	-1.4	5.8	-1.7	2.3						
8	-7.6	-3.8	11.6	-4.3	0.0						
9	-11.9	-6.2	17.4	5.3	3.9						
10	-16.2	-8.6	23.2	3.4	15.7						
11	-20.5	-11.0	29.0	-3.9	5.3						
12	-24.8	-13.4	34.8	14.2	-10.3						
13	-29.1	-15.8	40.6	27.6	2.7						
14	-33.4	-18.2	46.4	2.4	5.7						
15	-37.7	-20.6	52.2	-10.3	-28.5						
16	-42.0	-23.0	58.0	13.9	-35.2						
17	-46.3	-25.4	63.8	3.7	2.8						
18	-50.6	-27.8	69.6	-44.1	3.5						
19	-54.9	-30.2	75.4	-36.7	-27.8						
20	-59.2	-32.6	81.2	7.7	3.3						
21	-63.5	-35.0	87.0	-10.8	58.0						
22	-67.8	-37.4	92.8	-41.1	31.4						
23	-72.1	-39.8	98.6	15.0	-9.4						
24	-76.4	-42.2	104.4	66.8	31.7						
25	-80.7	-44.6	110.2	20.3	50.8						
26	-85.0	-47.0	116.0	-5.2	-29.9						
27	-89.3	-49.4	121.8	57.1	-67.6						
28	-93.6	-51.8	127.6	54.4	-5.4						
29	-97.9	-54.2	133.4	-45.1	-6.7						
30	-102.2	-56.6	139.2	-58.7	-83.7						
31	-106.5	-59.0	145.0	9.8	-50.4						
32	-110.8	-61.4	150.8	-26.8	56.9						
33	-115.1	-63.8	156.6	-107.3	39.7						
34	-119.4	-66.2	162.4	-39.1	-22.0						
35	-123.7	-68.6	168.2	61.7	53.9						

Figure 4-18: 200 data points displayed in a scatter chart.

Area charts

Think of an *area chart* as a line chart in which the area below the line has been colored in. Table 4-6 lists Excel's six area chart subtypes.

Table 4-6: Area Chart Subtypes

Chart Type	Description
Area	Standard area chart.
Stacked area	Area chart; data series stacked.
100% stacked area	Area chart; data series stacked and expressed as percentages.
3-D area	A true 3-D area chart with a third axis.
Stacked area in 3-D	Area chart with a perspective look; data series stacked.
100% stacked area in 3-D	Area chart with a perspective look; data series stacked and expressed as percentages.

Figure 4-19 shows an example of a stacked area chart. Stacking the data series enables you to see clearly the total sales for each quarter, plus the contribution by each series.

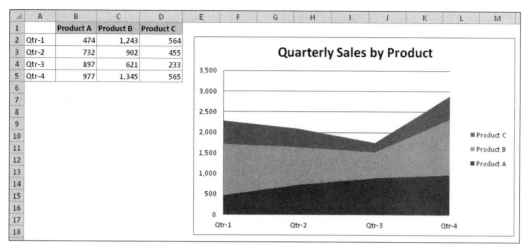

	Product A	Product B	Product C
Qtr-1	474	1,243	564
Qtr-2	732	902	455
Qtr-3	897	621	233
Qtr-4	977	1,345	565

Figure 4-19: A stacked area chart.

On the Web

The chart examples in this section are available at www.wiley.com/go/exceldr in the workbook file named area charts.xlsx.

Figure 4-20 shows the same data, plotted as a 3-D area chart. Although this chart has lots of visual appeal, it has a serious weakness: The data toward the back is often obscured. In this example, the first three quarters for Product C are not even visible.

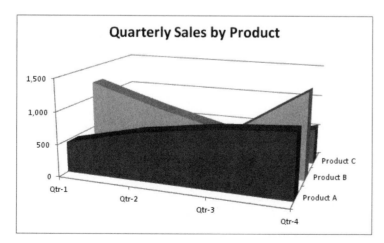

Figure 4-20: The first three quarters for Product C are not visible in this 3-D area chart.

Cross-Ref
Problems with data visibility in 3-D area charts can sometimes be solved by rotating or changing the elevation of the 3-D chart to provide a different view. In some cases, plotting the series in reverse order reveals the obscured data. For the most control, you can manually change the plot order of the series. These procedures are described in Chapter 6.

Doughnut charts

A *doughnut chart* is similar to a pie chart, with two exceptions: It has a hole in the middle, and it can display more than one series of data. Figure 4-21 shows an example of a doughnut chart with two series (1st Half Sales and 2nd Half Sales). The legend identifies the data points. The arrows and series descriptions were added manually. Oddly, a doughnut chart does not provide a direct way to identify the series.

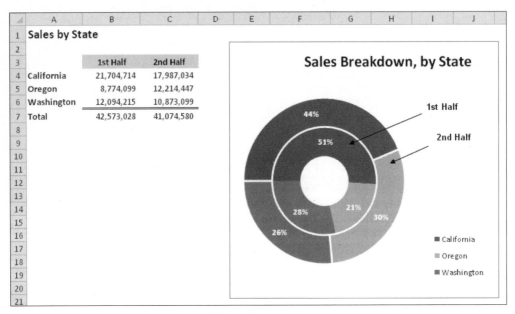

Figure 4-21: A doughnut chart with two data series

On the Web
The chart examples in this section are available at www.wiley.com/go/exceldr in the workbook file named doughnut charts.xlsx.

Notice that Excel displays the data series as concentric rings. As you can see, a doughnut chart with more than one series can be very difficult to interpret. For example, the relatively larger sizes of the slices toward the outer part of the doughnut can be deceiving. Consequently, doughnut charts should be used sparingly. In many cases, a stacked or clustered column chart for such comparisons expresses your meaning better than does a doughnut chart. Figure 4-22 shows the same data, displayed in a stacked column chart.

Perhaps the best use for a doughnut chart is to plot a single series as a visual alternative to a pie chart. Figure 4-23 shows a single-series doughnut chart, with one slice exploded.

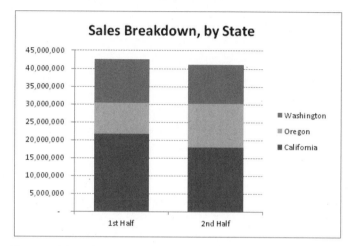

Figure 4-22: Using a stacked column chart as a doughnut chart replacement.

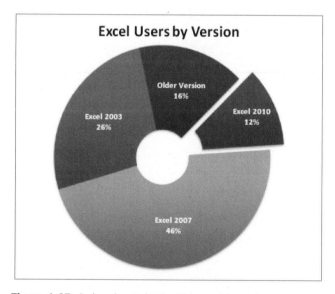

Figure 4-23: A doughnut chart with one data series.

Table 4-7 lists Excel's two doughnut chart subtypes.

Table 4-7: Doughnut Chart Subtypes

Chart Type	Subtype
Doughnut	Standard doughnut chart.
Exploded doughnut	Doughnut chart with all slices exploded.

Radar charts

You may not be familiar with radar charts. A *radar chart* has a separate axis for each category, and the axes extend outward from the center of the chart. The value of each data point is plotted on the corresponding axis.

Figure 4-24 shows an example of a radar chart. This chart plots two data series across 12 categories (months) and shows the seasonal demand for snow skis versus water skis.

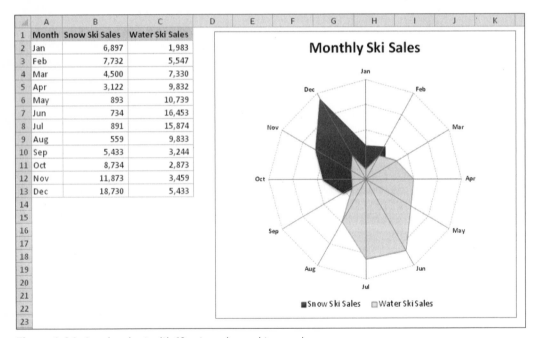

	A	B	C
1	Month	Snow Ski Sales	Water Ski Sales
2	Jan	6,897	1,983
3	Feb	7,732	5,547
4	Mar	4,500	7,330
5	Apr	3,122	9,832
6	May	893	10,739
7	Jun	734	16,453
8	Jul	891	15,874
9	Aug	559	9,833
10	Sep	5,433	3,244
11	Oct	8,734	2,873
12	Nov	11,873	3,459
13	Dec	18,730	5,433

Figure 4-24: A radar chart with 12 categories and two series.

On the Web

The chart examples in this section are available at `www.wiley.com/go/exceldr` in the workbook file named `radar charts.xlsx`.

It's probably a safe bet that the vast majority of people would have no idea how to interpret the ski sale chart. Figure 4-25 shows a much better way to present the data: a stacked column chart.

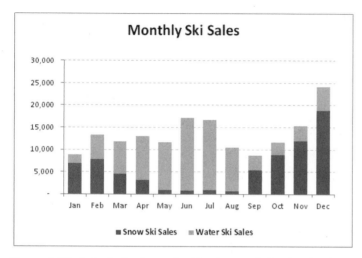

Figure 4-25: A stacked column chart is a better choice for the ski sale data.

Figure 4-26 shows another radar chart, with three categories. This chart depicts the red, green, and blue components for a color using the RGB color system. In the RGB color system, each color is represented by a value (between 0 and 255) for red, green, and blue.

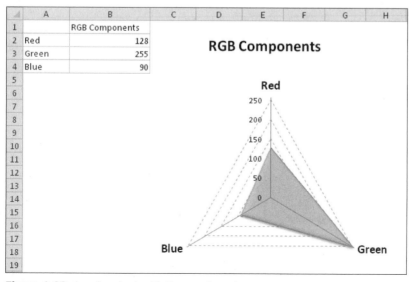

Figure 4-26: A radar chart with three categories.

Table 4-8 lists Excel's three radar chart subtypes.

Table 4-8: Radar Chart Subtypes

Chart Type	Subtype
Radar	Standard radar chart (lines only).
Radar with markers	Radar chart with lines and data markers.
Filled radar	Radar chart with lines colored in.

Surface charts

A *surface chart* displays two or more data series as a three-dimensional surface. As Figure 4-27 shows, these charts can be quite interesting.

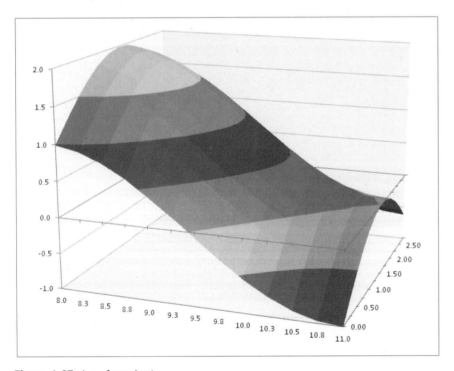

Figure 4-27: A surface chart.

Unlike other charts, Excel uses color to distinguish values, not to distinguish the data series. The number of colors used is determined by the major unit scale setting for the value axis. Each color corresponds to one major unit.

The chart examples in this section are available at www.wiley.com/go/exceldr **in the workbook file named** surface charts.xlsx.

Table 4-9 lists Excel's four 3-D surface chart subtypes.

Table 4-9: Surface Chart Subtypes

Chart Type	Description
3-D surface	Standard 3-D surface chart
Wireframe 3-D surface	3-D surface chart with no colors
Contour	3-D surface chart as viewed from above
Wireframe contour	3-D surface chart as viewed from above; no color

Note

You should understand that a surface chart does not plot 3-D data points. The series axis for a surface chart, as with all other 3-D charts, is a category axis — not a value axis. In other words, if you have data that is represented by x, y, and z coordinates, it cannot be plotted accurately on a surface chart unless the x and y values are equally spaced.

Bubble charts

Think of a *bubble chart* as a scatter chart that can display an additional data series, which is represented by the size of the bubbles. As with a scatter chart, both axes are value axes (there is no category axis).

Figure 4-28 shows an example of a bubble chart that depicts the results of a weight-loss program. The horizontal value axis represents the original weight, the vertical value axis shows the length of time in the program, and the size of the bubbles represents the amount of weight lost.

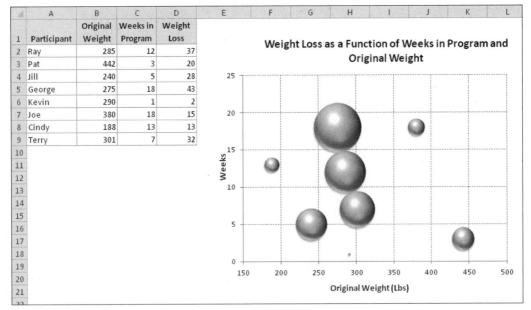

◢	A	B	C	D
1	Participant	Original Weight	Weeks in Program	Weight Loss
2	Ray	285	12	37
3	Pat	442	3	20
4	Jill	240	5	28
5	George	275	18	43
6	Kevin	290	1	2
7	Joe	380	18	15
8	Cindy	188	13	13
9	Terry	301	7	32

Figure 4-28: A bubble chart.

Note

Displaying quantitative information as bubble size can be confusing because most people cannot accurately judge the relative areas of the bubbles. Excel provides a bubble size option in the Series Options tab of the Format Data Series dialog box. You can choose to have values correspond to the area of the bubbles (default) or to the width of the bubbles.

On the Web

The chart examples in this section are available at www.wiley.com/go/exceldr in the workbook file named bubble charts.xlsx.

Table 4-10 lists Excel's two bubble chart subtypes.

Table 4-10: Bubble Chart Subtypes

Chart Type	Subtype
Bubble chart	Standard bubble chart.
Bubble with a 3-D effect	Bubble chart with 3-D bubbles.

Figure 4-29 shows another bubble chart, carefully crafted to resemble a cartoon mouse.

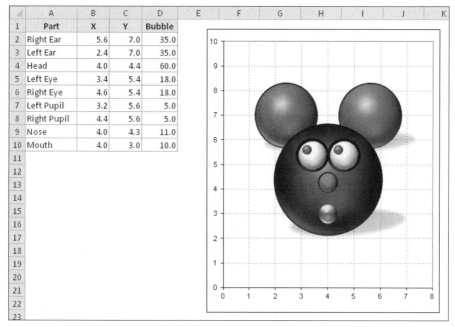

Figure 4-29: A less-serious bubble chart.

Stock charts

Stock charts are most useful for displaying stock market information, but they can be used to display other types of data. These charts require three to five data series, depending on the subtype.

Table 4-11 lists Excel's four stock chart subtypes.

Table 4-11: Stock Chart Subtypes

Chart Type	Subtype
High-low-close	Displays the stock's high, low, and closing prices. Requires three data series.
Open-high-low-close	Displays the stock's opening, high, low, and closing prices. Requires four data series.
Volume-high-low-close	Displays the stock's volume and high, low, and closing prices. Requires four data series.
Volume-open-high-low-close	Displays the stock's volume and open, high, low, and closing prices. Requires five data series.

Figure 4-30 shows an example of each of the four stock chart types. The two charts on the bottom display the trade volume and use two value axes. The daily volume, represented by columns, uses the axis on the left. The "up bars," sometimes referred to as candlesticks, depict the difference between the opening and closing price. A black up bar indicates that the closing price was lower than the opening price. These charts can be difficult to interpret because Excel does not display symbols in the legend for all series.

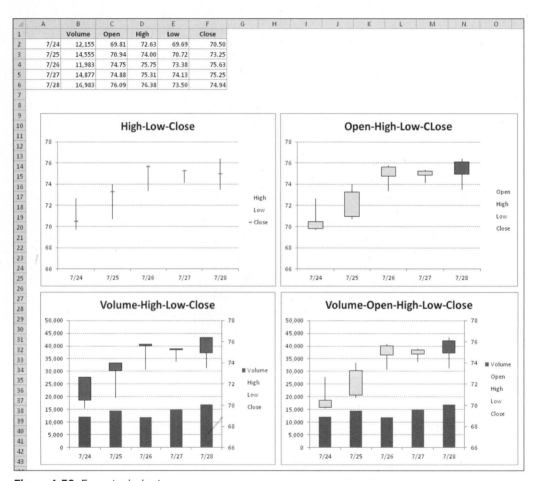

Figure 4-30: Four stock charts.

On the Web
The chart examples in this section are available at www.wiley.com/go/exceldr **in the workbook file named** stock charts.xlsx.

A stock market chart can display any number of data points. Figure 4-31, for example, shows three years of data for a company. This chart plots all four variables: volume, high, low, and close. With this many data points, individual days are not discernible, but trends are easy to identify.

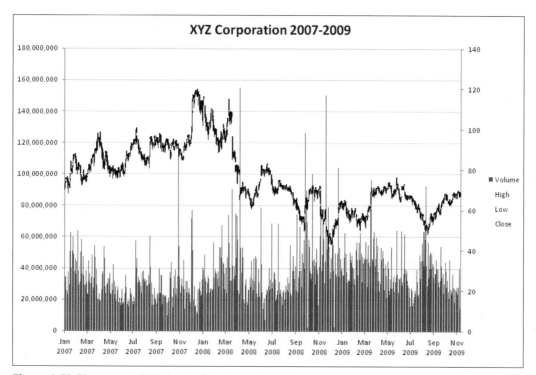

Figure 4-31: Three years (747 days) of stock market data.

Stock charts are not limited to financial data, and this chart type can be used for a variety of other purposes. Figure 4-32 shows an example of daily temperature data displayed in a stock chart. For each day, the chart shows the high temperature, the low temperature, and the average temperature.

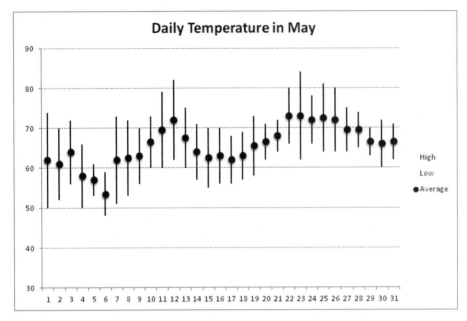

Figure 4-32: Stock charts aren't just for financial information.

Creating Combination Charts

A *combination chart* combines two different chart types, such as a column chart and a line chart. In such a case, each series is assigned its own chart type.

Excel doesn't provide a direct way to create a combination chart. In other words, you won't find "Combination Chart" in any of the drop-down controls in the Insert ➜ Charts group. However, creating a combination chart is easy. Just follow these steps:

1. Create a standard chart (for example, a column chart) that uses at least two data series.

2. Click one of the series to select it.

3. Choose Chart Tools ➜ Design ➜ Type ➜ Change Chart Type to display the Change Chart Type dialog box.

4. Select a chart type for the selected series, and click the OK button.

The chart of the selected series is changed to the type you specified.

Keep in mind that the Change Chart Type dialog box behaves differently, depending on the type of chart element that's selected when you issue the command. If a series is selected, the new chart type applies only to that series. If anything other than a series is selected, the chart type applies to all series in the chart.

Figure 4-33 shows a combination chart that contains two series. One series (Sales) is depicted as columns; the other series (Goal) is depicted as a line. This chart makes it very easy to see sales performance relative to each monthly goal.

Figure 4-33: A combination chart.

 The chart examples in this section are available at www.wiley.com/go/exceldr **in the workbook file named** combination charts.xlsx.

On the Web

In some cases, you might want to use a different vertical axis for the different chart series. Figure 4-34 shows a combination chart that displays a line chart for the average monthly temperature values and an area chart for the monthly precipitation. Because these two data series vary so widely in scale, the second vertical axis (for the precipitation) is necessary. If both series were plotted on the same axes, the precipitation series would not even be visible.

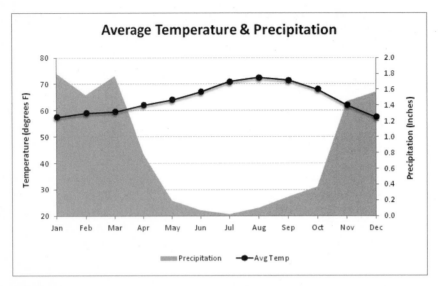

Figure 4-34: A combination chart that uses two vertical axes.

When you start experimenting with combination charts, you'll quickly discover that all 3-D charts are off limits for combination charts. In addition, you can't use stock charts or bubble charts as part of a combination chart. You'll also find that some combinations are of limited value. For example, it's unlikely that anyone would need to create a chart that combines a radar chart and a line chart.

Note

A combination chart uses a single plot area. Therefore, you can't create, say, a combination chart that displays three pie charts.

Creating and Using Chart Templates

If you find that you frequently make the same types of modifications to your charts, you might be able to save some time and energy by creating a chart template. Or, if you create lots of combination charts, you can create a combination chart template and avoid making the manual adjustments required for a combination chart.

To create a chart template, follow these steps:

1. Create a chart to serve as the basis for your template.

    The data you use for this chart is not critical, but for best results, it should be typical of the data that you'll eventually be plotting with your custom chart type.

2. Apply any formatting and customizations that you like.

   This step determines the appearance of the charts created from the template.

3. Activate the chart and choose Chart Tools ➜ Design ➜ Type ➜ Save as Template.

   Excel displays its Save Chart Template dialog box.

4. Provide a name for the template, and click the Save button.

Follow these steps to create a chart based on a template you've created and saved:

1. Select the data to be used in the chart.

2. Choose Insert ➜ Charts ➜ Other Charts ➜ All Chart Types.

   Excel displays its Insert Chart dialog box.

3. On the left side of the Insert Chart dialog box, select Templates.

   Excel displays an icon for each custom template that has been created.

4. Select the icon that represents the template you want to use, and click OK.

   Excel creates the chart based on the template you selected.

You can also apply a template to an existing chart. Select the chart and choose Chart Tools ➜ Design ➜ Change Chart Type.

5

Working with Chart Series

In This Chapter

- Adding and removing series from a chart
- Finding various ways to change the data used in a chart
- Using noncontiguous ranges for a chart
- Charting data from different worksheets or workbooks
- Dealing with missing data
- Controlling a data series by hiding data
- Unlinking a chart from its data
- Using secondary axes

Every chart consists of at least one series, and the data used in that series is (normally) stored in a worksheet. This chapter provides an in-depth discussion of data series for charts and presents lots of tips to help you select and modify the data used in your charts.

Specifying the Data for Your Chart

When you create a chart, you almost always start by selecting the worksheet data to be plotted. Normally, you select the numeric data as well as the category labels and series names, if they exist.

When creating a chart, a key consideration is the orientation of your data: by rows or by columns. In other words, is the data for each series in a single row or in a single column?

Excel attempts to guess the data orientation by applying a simple rule: If the data rows outnumber the data columns, each series is assumed to occupy a column. If the number of data columns is greater than or equal to the number of data rows, each series is assumed to occupy a row. In other words, Excel always defaults to a chart that has more category labels than series.

After you create the chart, it's a simple matter to override Excel's orientation guess. Just activate the chart and choose Chart Tools ➜ Design ➜ Data ➜ Switch Row/Column.

Your choice of orientation determines how many series the chart has, and it affects the appearance and (possibly) the legibility of your chart. Figure 5-1 shows two charts that use the same data. The chart on the left displays three series, arranged in columns. The chart on the right shows four series, arranged in rows.

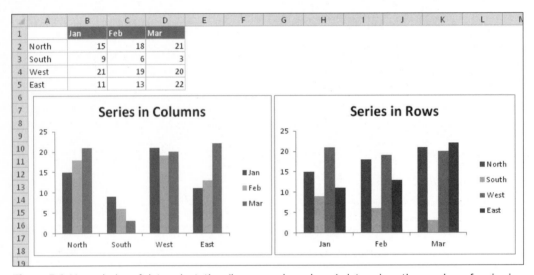

Figure 5-1: Your choice of data orientation (by row or by column) determines the number of series in the chart.

In many situations, you may find it necessary to modify the ranges used by a chart. Specifically, you may want to do the following:

➤ Add a new series to the chart.

➤ Delete a series from the chart.

➤ Extend the range used by a series (show more data).

➤ Contract the range used by a series (show less data).

➤ Add or modify the series names.

All these topics are covered in the following sections.

Dealing with numeric category labels

It's not uncommon to have category labels that consist of numbers. For example, you may create a chart that shows sales by year, and the years are numeric values. If your category labels include a heading, Excel will (incorrectly) interpret the category labels as a data series, and use generic category labels that consist of integers (1, 2, 3, and so on). The following figure shows an example.

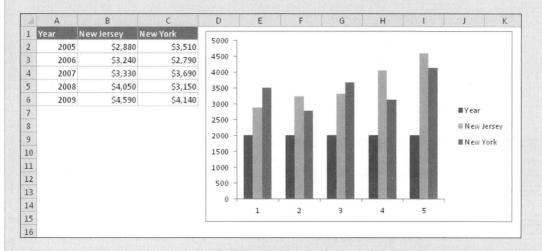

You can, of course, choose Chart Tools ➜ Design ➜ Data ➜ Select Data and use the Select Data Source dialog box to fix the chart. But a more efficient solution is to make a simple change before you create the chart: Remove the header text above the category labels! The following figure shows the chart that was created when the heading was removed from the category label column.

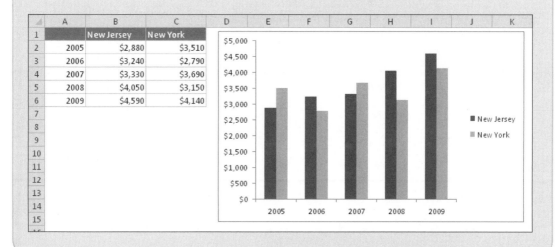

Note

Chart types vary in the number of series that they can use. All charts are limited to a maximum of 255 series. Other charts require a minimum number of series. For example, a high-low-close stock chart requires three series. A pie chart can use only one series.

Adding a New Series to a Chart

Excel provides four ways to add a new series to an existing chart:

> Copy the range, and then paste the data into the chart.

> Use the Select Data Source dialog box.

> Select the chart and extend the blue highlighting rectangle to include the new series.

> Activate the chart, click in the Formula bar, and type a SERIES formula manually.

These techniques are described in the sections that follow.

Note

Attempting to add a new series to a pie chart has no apparent effect, because a pie chart can have only one series. The series, however, is added to the chart but is not displayed. If you select a different chart type for the chart, the added series is then visible.

Adding a new series by copying a range

One way to add a new series to a chart is to perform a standard copy/paste operation. Follow these steps:

1. Select the range that contains the data to be added (including the series name).

2. Choose Home ➜ Clipboard ➜ Copy (or press Ctrl+C).

3. Click the chart to activate it.

4. Choose Home ➜ Clipboard ➜ Paste (or press Ctrl+V).

For more control when adding data to a chart, choose Home ➜ Clipboard ➜ Paste ➜ Paste Special in Step 4. This command displays the Paste Special dialog box. Figure 5-2 shows a new series (using data in row 5) being added to a line chart.

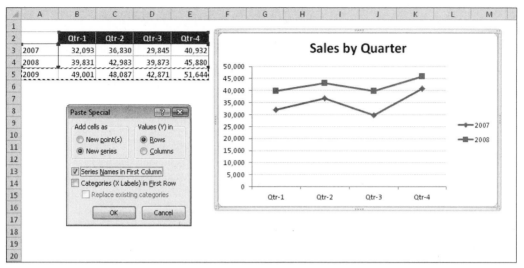

Figure 5-2: Using the Paste Special dialog box to add a series to a chart.

Following are some pointers to keep in mind when you add a new series using the Paste Special dialog box:

> ➤ Make sure that the New Series option is selected.

> ➤ Excel will guess at the data orientation, but you should verify that the Rows or Columns option is guessed correctly.

> ➤ If the range you copied included a cell with the series name, ensure that the Series Names in First Row/Column option is selected.

> ➤ If the first column of your range selection included category labels, make sure that the Categories (X Labels) in First Column/Row check box is selected.

> ➤ If you want to replace the existing category labels, select the Replace Existing Categories check box.

Adding a new series by extending the range highlight

When you select a series in a chart, Excel displays an outline around the data used by that series. When you select something other than a series in a chart, Excel displays an outline around the entire data range used by the chart — but only if the data is in a contiguous range of cells.

If you need to add a new series to a chart (and the new series is contiguous with the existing chart's data), you can just drag the blue range highlight to add the new series. Start by selecting any chart element *except* a series. Excel highlights the range with a blue outline. Drag a corner of the blue outline to include the new data, and Excel creates a new series in the chart.

Adding a new series using the Select Data Source dialog box

The Select Data Source dialog box provides another way to add a new series to a chart, as follows:

1. Click the chart to activate it.

2. Choose Chart Tools → Design → Data → Select Data to display the Select Data Source dialog box.

3. Click the Add button to display the Edit Series dialog box.

4. Use the range selector controls to specify the cell for the Series Name (optional) and Series Values (see Figure 5-3).

5. Click the OK button to close the Edit Series dialog box and return to the Select Data Source dialog box.

6. Click the OK button to close the Select Data Source dialog box, or click the Add button to add another series to the chart.

Note

The configuration of the Edit Series dialog box varies, depending on the chart type. For example, if the chart is a scatter chart, the Edit Series dialog box displays range selectors for the Series Name, the Series X Values, and the Series Y Values. If the chart is a bubble chart, the dialog box displays an additional range selector for the Series Bubble Size.

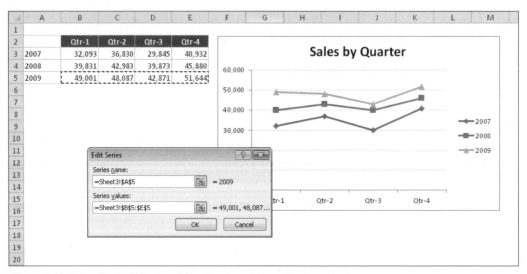

Figure 5-3: Using the Edit Series dialog box to add a series to a chart.

Adding a new series by typing a new SERIES formula

Excel provides yet another way to add a new series: Type a new SERIES formula. Follow these steps:

1. Click the chart to activate it.

2. Click the Formula bar.

3. Type the new SERIES formula and press Enter.

This method is certainly not the most efficient way to add a new series to a chart. It requires that you understand how the SERIES formula works, and (as you might expect) it can be rather error-prone. Note, however, that you don't need to type the SERIES formula from scratch. You can copy an existing SERIES formula, paste it into the Formula bar, and then edit the SERIES formula to create a new series.

Cross-Ref

For more information about the SERIES formula, see the "SERIES formula syntax" sidebar, later in this chapter.

Deleting a Chart Series

The easiest way to delete a series from a chart is to select the series and press Delete.

Note

Deleting the only series in a chart does not delete the chart. Rather, it gives you an empty chart. If you'd like to delete this empty chart, just press Delete a second time.

You can also use the Select Data Source dialog box to delete a series. Choose Chart Tools ➜ Design ➜ Data ➜ Select Data to display this dialog box. Then select the series from the list and click the Remove button.

Modifying the Data Range for a Chart Series

After you've created a chart, you may want to modify the data ranges used by the chart. For example, you may need to expand the range to include new data. Or, you might need to substitute an entirely different range. Excel offers a number of ways to perform these operations:

➤ Drag the range highlights

➤ Use the Select Data Source dialog box

➤ Edit the SERIES formula

Each of these techniques is described in the sections that follow.

Tip

If you create your chart from data in a table (created by using Insert ➔ Tables ➔ Table) the chart will adjust automatically if you add new data to the table.

Using range highlighting to change series data

When you select a series in a chart, Excel highlights the worksheet ranges used in that series. This range highlighting consists of a colored outline around each range used by the series. Figure 5-4 shows an example in which the chart series (Region 1) is selected. Excel highlights the following ranges:

> ➤ C2 (the series name)

> ➤ B3:B8 (the category labels)

> ➤ C3:C8 (the values)

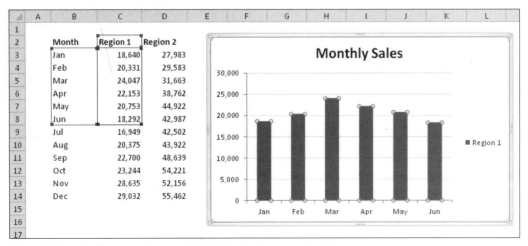

Figure 5-4: Selecting a chart series highlights the data used by the series.

Each of the highlighted ranges contains a small "handle" at each corner. You can perform two operations with the highlighted data:

> ➤ **Expand or contract the data range:** Click one of the handles and drag it to expand the outlined range (specify more data) or contract the data range (specify less data). When you move your cursor over a handle, the mouse pointer changes to a double arrow.

> ➤ **Specify an entirely different data range:** Click one of the borders of the highlight and then drag it to highlight a different range. When you move the cursor over a border, the mouse pointer changes to a 4-way arrow.

Figure 5-5 shows the chart after the data range has been changed. In this case, the highlight around cell C2 was dragged to cell D2, and the highlight around C3:C8 was dragged to D3:D8 and then expanded to include D3:D14. Notice that the range for the category labels (B3:B8) has not been modified — and the missing labels are not shown in the chart. To finish the job, that range needs to be expanded to B3:B14.

Modifying chart source data by using the range highlights is probably the simplest method. Note, however, that this technique works only with embedded charts (not with chart sheets). In addition, it does not work when the chart's data is in a worksheet other than the sheet that contains the embedded chart.

Note

A surface chart is a special case. You cannot select an individual series in a surface chart. But when you select the plot area of a surface chart, Excel highlights all the data used in the chart. You can then use the range highlighting to change the ranges used in the chart.

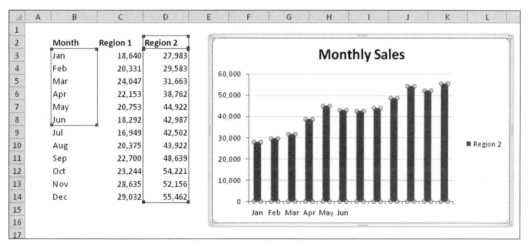

Figure 5-5: The chart's data range has been modified.

Using the Select Data Source dialog box to change series data

Another method of modifying a series data range is to use the Select Data Source dialog box. Select your chart and then choose Chart Tools ➜ Design ➜ Data ➜ Select Data. Figure 5-6 shows the Select Data Source dialog box.

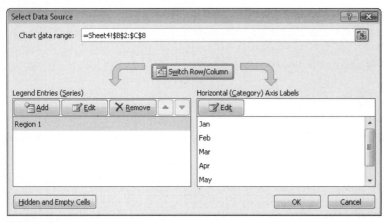

Figure 5-6: The Select Data Source dialog box.

Notice that the Select Data Source dialog box has three parts:

> ➤ The top part of the dialog box shows the entire data range used by the chart. You can change this range by selecting new data.

> ➤ The lower-left part displays a list of each series. Select a series and click the Edit button to display the Edit Series dialog box to change the data used by a single series.

> ➤ The lower-right part displays the category axis labels. Click the Edit button to display the Axis Labels dialog box to change the range used as the axis labels.

Note

The Edit Series dialog box can vary somewhat, depending on the chart type. The Edit Series dialog box for a bubble chart, for example, has four range selector controls: Series Name, Series X Values, Series Y Values, and Series Bubble Size.

Editing the SERIES formula to change series data

Every chart series has its own SERIES formula. When you select a data series in a chart, its SERIES formula appears in the Formula bar. In Figure 5-7, for example, you can see one of two SERIES formulas in the Formula bar for a chart that displays two data series.

Although a SERIES formula is displayed in the Formula bar, it is not a "real" formula. In other words, you can't put this formula into a cell, and you can't use worksheet functions within the SERIES formula. You can, however, edit the arguments in the SERIES formula to change the ranges used by the series. To edit the SERIES formula, just click in the Formula bar and use standard editing techniques. Refer to the sidebar, "SERIES formula syntax," to find out about the various arguments for a SERIES formula.

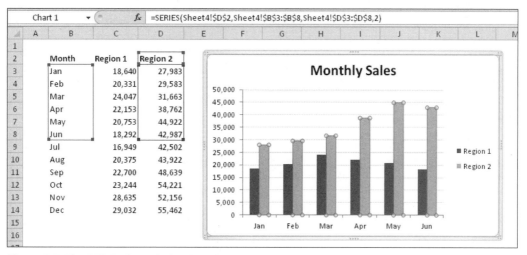

Figure 5-7: The SERIES formula for the selected data series appears in the Formula bar.

Note When you modify a series data range using either of the techniques discussed previously in this section, the SERIES formula is also modified. In fact, those techniques are simply easy ways of editing the SERIES formula.

Following is an example of a SERIES formula:

```
=SERIES(Sheet4!$D$2,Sheet4!$B$3:$B$8,Sheet4!$D$3:$D$8,2)
```

This SERIES formula does the following:

> Specifies that cell D2 (on Sheet4) contains the series name

> Specifies that the category labels are in B3:B8 on Sheet4

> Specifies that the data values are in D3:D8, also on Sheet4

> Specifies that the series will be plotted second on the chart (the final argument is 2)

Notice that range references in a SERIES formula always include the worksheet name, and the range references are always absolute references. An absolute reference, as you may know, uses a dollar sign before the row and column part of the reference. If you edit a SERIES formula and remove the sheet name or make the cell references relative, Excel will override these changes.

SERIES formula syntax

A SERIES formula has the following syntax:

```
=SERIES(series_name, category_labels, values, order, sizes)
```

The arguments you can use in the SERIES formula include the following:

- *series_name*: (Optional) A reference to the cell that contains the series name used in the legend. If the chart has only one series, the name argument is used as the title. This argument can also consist of text, in quotation marks. If omitted, Excel creates a default series name (for example, Series 1).
- *category_labels*: (Optional) A reference to the range that contains the labels for the category axis. If omitted, Excel uses consecutive integers beginning with 1. For scatter charts, this argument specifies the *x* values. A noncontiguous range reference is also valid. (The ranges' addresses are separated by a comma and enclosed in parentheses.) The argument may also consist of an array of comma-separated values (or text in quotation marks) enclosed in braces.
- *values*: (Required) A reference to the range that contains the values for the series. For scatter charts, this argument specifies the *y* values. A noncontiguous range reference is also valid. (The ranges' addresses are separated by a comma and enclosed in parentheses.) The argument may also consist of an array of comma-separated values enclosed in braces.
- *order*: (Required) An integer that specifies the plotting order of the series. This argument is relevant only if the chart has more than one series. Using a reference to a cell is not allowed.
- *sizes*: (Only for bubble charts) A reference to the range that contains the values for the size of the bubbles in a bubble chart. A noncontiguous range reference is also valid. (The ranges' addresses are separated by a comma and enclosed in parentheses.) The argument may also consist of an array of values enclosed in braces.

Understanding Series Names

Every chart series has a name, which is displayed in the chart's legend. If you don't explicitly provide a name for a series, it will have a default name, such as Series1, Series2, and so on.

The easiest way to name a series is to do so when you create the chart. Typically, a series name is contained in a cell adjacent to the series data. For example, if your data is arranged in columns, the column headers usually contain the series names. If you select the series names along with the chart data, those names will be applied automatically.

Figure 5-8 shows a chart with three series. The series names, which are stored in B3:D3, are Main, N. County, and Westside. The SERIES formula for the first data series is as follows:

```
=SERIES(Sheet1!$B$3,Sheet1!$A$4:$A$9,Sheet1!$B$4:$B$9,1)
```

Note that the first argument for this SERIES formula is a reference to the cell that contains the series name.

Changing a series name

The series name is the text that appears in a chart's legend. In some cases, you may prefer the chart to display a name other than the text that's in the worksheet. To change the name of a series, follow these steps:

1. Activate the chart.

2. Choose Chart Tools ➔ Design ➔ Data ➔ Select Data to display the Select Data Source dialog box.

3. In the Select Data Source dialog box, select the series that you want to modify, and click the Edit button to display the Edit Series dialog box.

4. Type the new name in the Series Name box.

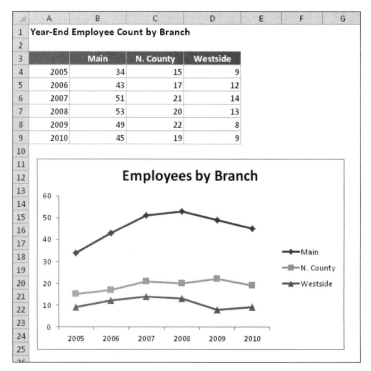

Figure 5-8: The series names are picked up from the worksheet.

Normally, the Series Name box contains a cell reference. But you can override this and enter any text.

Note

If you go back to a series that you've already renamed, you'll find that Excel has converted your text into a formula — an equal sign, followed by the text you entered (the new series name), in quotation marks.

Figure 5-9 shows the previous chart, after changing the series names. The first argument in each of the SERIES formulas no longer displays a cell reference. It now contains the literal text. For example, the SERIES formula for the first series is as follows:

```
=SERIES("Branch 1",Sheet1!$A$4:$A$9,Sheet1!$B$4:$B$9,1)
```

You can also change the name of a series by editing the SERIES formula directly. Select the series, click the Formula bar, and replace the first argument with your text (make sure that the text is enclosed in quotation marks).

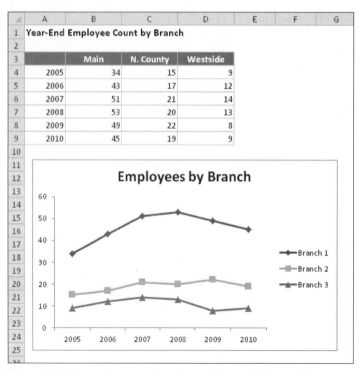

Figure 5-9: The series names have been changed; the new names are shown in the legend.

Deleting a series name

To delete a series name, use the Edit Series dialog box as described previously. Highlight the range reference (or text) in the Series Name box and press Delete.

Alternatively, you can edit the SERIES formula and remove the first argument. Here's an example of a SERIES formula for a series with no specified name (it will use the default name):

```
=SERIES(,Sheet2!$A$2:$A$6,Sheet2!$B$2:$B$6,1)
```

Note

> When you remove the first argument in a SERIES formula, make sure that you do not delete the comma that follows the first argument. The comma is required as a place-holder to indicate the missing argument.

To create a series with no name, use a set of empty quotation marks for the first argument in the SERIES formula. A series with no name still appears in the chart's legend, but no text is displayed.

Adjusting the Series Plot Order

Every chart series has a plot order parameter. A chart's legend usually displays the series names in the order in which they are plotted. I say usually, because you do find exceptions. For example, consider a combination chart that displays a column series and a line series. Changing the series order does not change the order in which the series are listed in the legend.

To change the plot order of a chart's data series, use the Select Data Source dialog box. In the lower-left list, the series are listed in the order in which they are plotted. Select a series, and then use the up- or down-arrow buttons to adjust its position in the list — which also changes the plot order of the series.

Alternatively, you can edit the SERIES formulas — specifically, the fourth parameter in the SERIES formulas. See the "SERIES formula syntax" sidebar, earlier in this chapter, for more information about SERIES formulas.

For some charts, the plot order is not important. For others, however, you may want to change the order in which the series are plotted. Figure 5-10 shows a stacked column chart generated from the data in A2:E6. Notice that the columns are stacked, beginning with the first data series (Region 1) on the bottom. You might prefer to stack the columns in the order in which the data appears. To do so, you need to change the plot order.

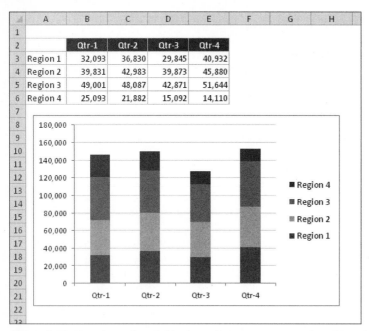

Figure 5-10: The plot order of this chart does not correspond to the order of the data.

After changing the plot order of the series, the chart now appears as in Figure 5-11.

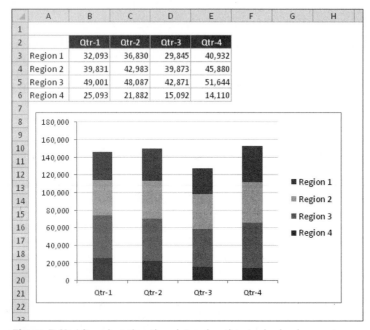

Figure 5-11: After changing the plot order, the stacked columns correspond to the order of the data.

Figure 5-12 shows another example. This chart displays three data series in a 3-D column chart. The columns for the Laptops and PDAs series are obscured by the columns for the Desktops series. The best solution is to uses a different chart type, but if you must use this type of chart, you can edit the plot order parameter of the SERIES formulas, as described previously. But in this case, you can use a more direct solution. Follow these steps:

1. Select the depth axis (which contains the series names), and press Ctrl+1 to display the Format Axis dialog box.

2. Click the Axis Options tab in the Format Axis dialog box.

3. Select the Series in Reverse Order check box.

The result, shown in Figure 5-13, is a much more legible chart. Note that the option to plot the series in reverse order does not actually change the plot order for the SERIES formulas. The SERIES formulas remain the same, but Excel displays them in reverse order on the series axis. Consequently, if the chart has a legend, the order of the entries in the legend remains the same.

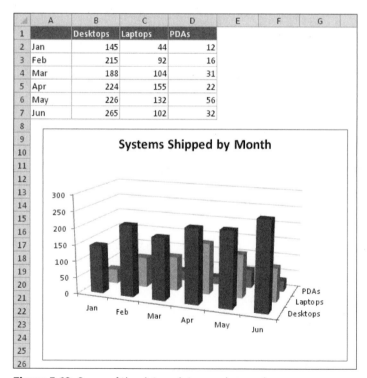

	A	B	C	D	E	F	G
1		Desktops	Laptops	PDAs			
2	Jan	145	44	12			
3	Feb	215	92	16			
4	Mar	188	104	31			
5	Apr	224	155	22			
6	May	226	132	56			
7	Jun	265	102	32			

Systems Shipped by Month

Figure 5-12: Some of the data points are obscured.

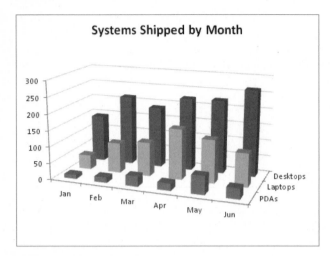

Figure 5-13: After reversing the series axis, the chart is more legible.

Charting a Noncontiguous Range

Most of the time, a chart series consists of a contiguous range of cells. But Excel does allow you to plot data that is not in a contiguous range. Figure 5-14 shows an example of a noncontiguous series. This chart displays monthly data for the first and fourth quarter. The data in this single series is contained in rows 2:4 and 11:13. Notice that the category labels display Jan, Feb, Mar, Oct, Nov, and Dec.

The SERIES formula for this series is as follows:

```
=SERIES(,(Sheet1!$A$2:$A$4,Sheet1!$A$11:$A$13),(Sheet1!$B$2:$B$4,Sheet1!$B$11
   :$B$13),1)
```

The first argument is omitted, so Excel uses the default series name. The second argument specifies six cells in column A as the category labels. The third argument specifies six corresponding cells in column B as the data values. Note that the range arguments for the noncontiguous ranges are displayed in parentheses, and each subrange is separated by a comma.

Note

When a series uses a noncontiguous range of cells, Excel does not display the range highlights when the series is selected. Therefore, the only way to modify the series is to use the Select Data Source dialog box or to edit the SERIES formula manually.

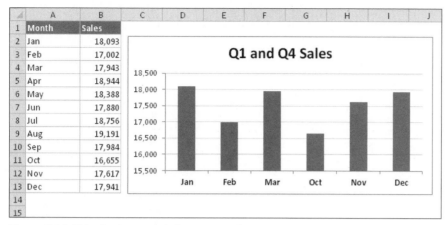

Figure 5-14: This chart uses data in a noncontiguous range.

Using Series on Different Sheets

Typically, data to be used on a chart resides on a single sheet. Excel, however, does allow a chart to use data from any number of worksheets, and the worksheets need not even be in the same workbook.

Normally, you select all the data for a chart before you create the chart. But if your chart uses data from different worksheets, you need to create an empty chart and then add the series. (see the section "Adding a New Series to a Chart," earlier in this chapter).

Figure 5-15 shows a chart that uses data from two other worksheets. Each of the three worksheets is shown in a separate window.

The SERIES formulas for this chart are as follows:

```
=SERIES(Region1!$B$1,Region1!$A$2:$A$7,Region1!$B$2:$B$7,1)
=SERIES(Region2!$B$1,Region1!$A$2:$A$7,Region2!$B$2:$B$7,2)
```

Tip

Another way to handle data in different worksheets is to create a summary range in a single worksheet. This summary range consists of simple formulas that refer to the data in other sheets. Then, you can create a chart from the summary range.

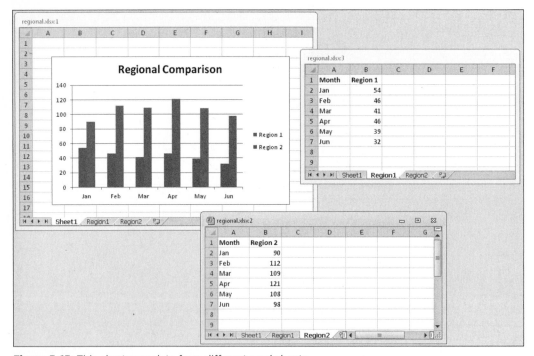

Figure 5-15: This chart uses data from different worksheets.

Handling Missing Data

Sometimes, data that you use in a chart may lack one or more data points. Excel offers the following ways to handle the missing data:

➤ Ignore the missing data. Plotted data series will have a gap.

➤ Treat the missing data as zero values.

➤ Interpolate the missing data (for line and scatter charts only).

For some reason, Excel makes these options rather difficult to locate. The Ribbon doesn't contain these options, and you don't specify these options in the Format Data Series dialog box. Rather, you must follow these steps:

1. Select your chart.

2. Choose Chart Tools ➔ Design ➔ Data ➔ Select Data to display the Select Data Source dialog box.

3. In the Select Data Source dialog box, click the Hidden and Empty Cells button. Excel displays the dialog box shown in Figure 5-16.

4. Choose the appropriate option, and click the OK button.

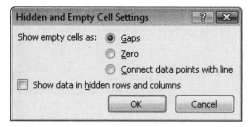

Figure 5-16: Use the Hidden and Empty Cell Settings dialog box to specify how to handle missing data.

The setting that you choose applies only to the active chart and applies to all series in the chart. In other words, you can't specify a different missing data option for different series in the same chart. In addition, not all chart types support all missing data options.

Figure 5-17 shows three charts that depict the three missing data options. The chart shows temperature readings at one-hour intervals, and four data points are missing. The "correct" missing data option depends on the message that you want to convey. In the top chart, the missing data is obvious because of the gaps in the line. In the middle chart, the missing data is shown as zero — which is clearly misleading. In the bottom chart, the missing data is interpolated. Because of the time-based and relatively "smooth" nature of the data, interpolating the missing data may be an appropriate choice.

Tip

For line charts, you can force Excel to interpolate missing values by placing =NA() in the empty cells. Those cell values will be interpolated, regardless of the missing data option that is in effect for the chart. For other charts, =NA() is interpreted as zero.

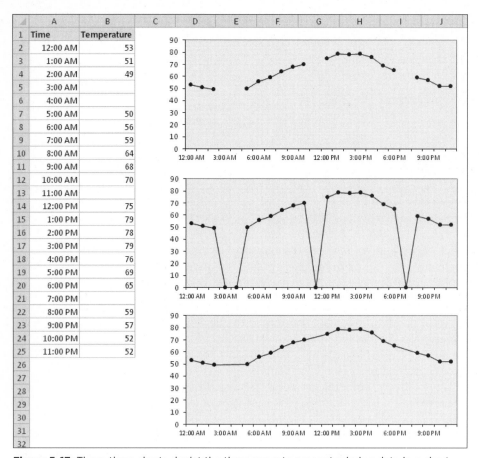

Figure 5-17: These three charts depict the three ways to present missing data in a chart.

Controlling a Data Series by Hiding Data

By default, Excel doesn't plot data that is in a hidden row or column. You can sometimes use this to your advantage, because it's an easy way to control what data appears in the chart.

Figure 5-18 shows a line chart that plots 365 days of data stored in a table (created by choosing Insert ➜ Tables ➜ Table). Figure 5-19 shows the same chart after I applied a filter to the table. The filter hides all rows except those in which the month is September.

Figure 5-18: A line chart that uses data in a table.

In some cases, when you're working with outlines or filtered tables (both of which use hidden rows), you may not like the idea that hidden data is removed from your chart. To override this, activate the chart and choose Chart Tools ➔ Design ➔ Data ➔ Select Data to display the Select Data Source dialog box. Click the Hidden and Empty Cells button, and select the Show Data in Hidden Rows and Columns check box.

Note

The Show Data in Hidden Rows and Columns setting applies only to the active chart. It is not a global setting that would be applied to all charts.

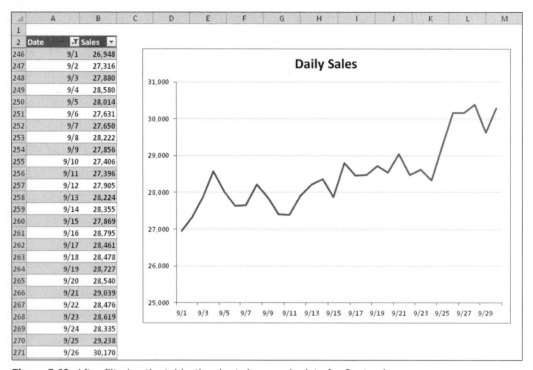

Figure 5-19: After filtering the table, the chart shows only data for September.

Unlinking a Chart Series from Its Data Range

Typically, an Excel chart uses data stored in a range. Change the data in the range, and the chart updates automatically. In some cases, you may want to "unlink" the chart from its data ranges and produce a *static chart* — a chart that never changes. For example, if you plot data generated by various what-if scenarios, you may want to save a chart that represents some baseline so that you can compare it with other scenarios. You can create such a chart in the following ways:

➤ Convert the chart to a picture

➤ Convert the range references to arrays

Converting a chart to a picture

To convert a chart to a static picture, follow these steps:

1. Create the chart as usual and make any necessary modifications.

2. Click the chart to activate it.

3. Choose Home ➜ Clipboard ➜ Copy (or press Ctrl+C).

4. Click any cell to deselect the chart.

5. Choose Home ➜ Clipboard ➜ Paste ➜ Picture.

The result is a picture of the original chart. This picture can be edited as a picture, but not as a chart. In other words, you can no longer modify properties such as chart type, data labels, and so on.

Although a chart converted to a picture cannot be edited as a chart, it can be edited as a picture. When you select such a picture, you see Excel's Picture Tools ➜ Format tab. Figure 5-20 shows a few examples of built-in formatting options applied to a picture of a chart.

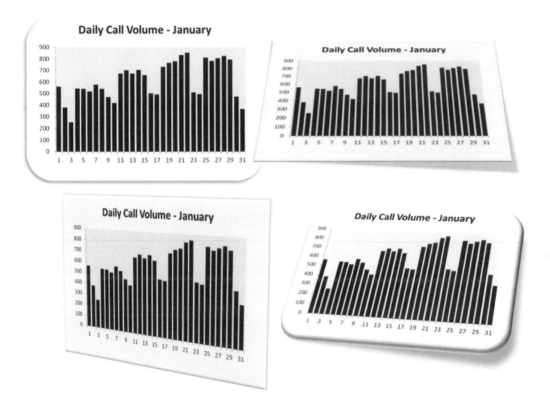

Figure 5-20: After converting a chart to a picture, you can apply various types of formatting to the picture.

Converting a range reference to arrays

The other way to unlink a chart from its data is to convert the SERIES formula range references to arrays. Figure 5-21 shows an example of a pie chart that does not use data stored in a worksheet. Rather, the chart's data is stored directly in the SERIES formula, which is as follows:

```
=SERIES(,{"Work","Sleep","Drive","Eat","Other"},{9,7,2.5,3,2.5},1)
```

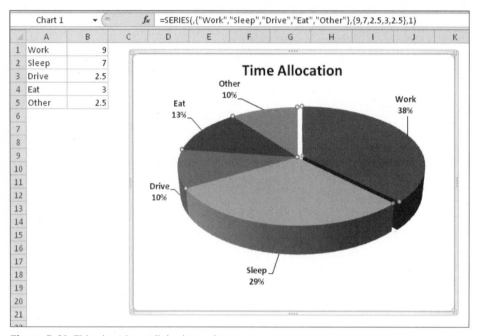

Figure 5-21: This chart is not linked to a data range.

The first argument, the series name, is omitted. The second argument consists of an array of five text strings. Notice that each array element appears in quotation marks and is separated by a comma. The array is enclosed in braces. The chart's data is stored as another array (the third argument).

This chart was originally created by using data stored in a range. Then, the SERIES formula was "delinked" from the range and the original data was deleted. The result is a chart that does not rely on data stored in a range.

Follow these steps to convert the range references in a SERIES formula to arrays:

1. Create the chart as usual.

2. Click the chart series.

   The SERIES formula appears in the Formula bar.

3. Click the Formula bar.

4. Press F9.

5. Press Enter, and the range references are converted to arrays.

Repeat this procedure for each series in the chart. This method of unlinking a chart series (as opposed to creating a picture) enables you to continue to edit the chart and apply formatting. Note that you can also convert just a single argument to an array. Highlight the argument in the SERIES formula and press F9.

Note

Excel imposes a 1,024-character limit to the length of a SERIES formula, so this technique does not work if a chart series contains a large number of values or category labels.

Working with Multiple Axes

An axis is a chart element that contains category or value information for a series. A chart can use zero, two, three, or four axes, and any or all of them can be hidden if desired.

Pie charts and doughnut charts have no axes. Common chart types, such as a standard column or line chart, use a single category axis and a single value axis. If your chart has at least two series — and it's not a 3-D chart — you can create a secondary value axis. Each series is associated with either the primary or the secondary value axis. Why use two value axes? Two value axes are most often used when the data being plotted in a series varies drastically in scale from the data in another series.

Creating a secondary value axis

Figure 5-22 shows a line chart with two data series: Income and Profit Margin. Compared to the Income values, the Profit Margin numbers (represented by squares) are so small that they barely show up on the chart. This is a good candidate for a secondary value axis.

To add a secondary value axis, follow these steps:

1. Select the Profit Margin series on the chart.

2. Press Ctrl+1 to display the Format Data Series dialog box.

3. In the Format Data Series dialog box, click the Series Options tab.

4. Choose the Secondary Axis option.

A new value axis is added to the right side of the chart, and the Profit Margin series uses that value axis. Figure 5-23 shows the dual-axis chart. I added axis titles (by choosing Chart Tools ➜ Layout ➜ Labels ➜ Axis Titles) so that the reader can identify the axis that applies to each data series.

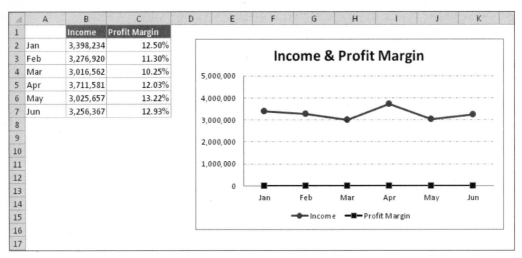

Figure 5-22: The values in the Profit Margin series are so small that they aren't visible in the chart.

Creating a chart with four axes

Very few situations warrant a chart with four axes. The problem, of course, is that using four axes almost always causes the chart to be difficult to understand. An exception is scatter charts. Figure 5-24 shows a scatter chart that has two series, and the series vary quite a bit in magnitude on both dimensions. If the objective is to compare the shape of the lines, this chart does not do a very good job because most of the chart consists of white space. Using four axes might solve the problem.

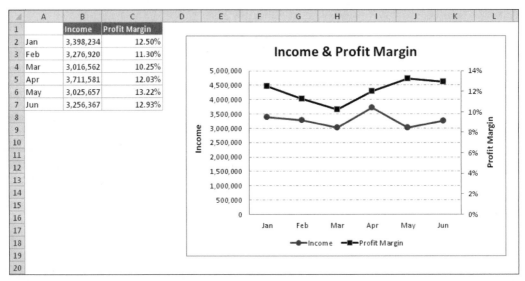

Figure 5-23: Using a secondary value axis for the Profit Margin series.

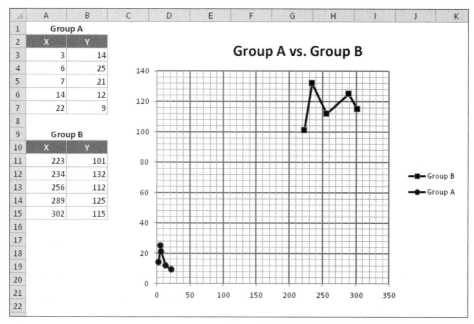

Figure 5-24: The two series vary in magnitude.

Follow these steps to add two new value axes for this scatter chart:

1. Select the Group B series.

2. Press Ctrl+1 to display the Format Data Series dialog box.

3. In the Format Data Series dialog box, click the Series Options tab.

4. Choose the Secondary Axis option.

   At this point, each of the series has its own *y*-value axis (one on the left, one on the right), but they share a common *x*-value axis.

5. Choose Chart Tools → Layout → Axes → Secondary Horizontal Axis → Show Default Axis.

   Note that this Ribbon command is available only if you've assigned a series to the secondary axis.

Figure 5-25 shows the result. The Group B series uses the left and bottom axes, and the Group A series uses the right and top axes. The chart also has four axis titles to clarify the axes for each group. If necessary, the scales for each axis can be adjusted separately.

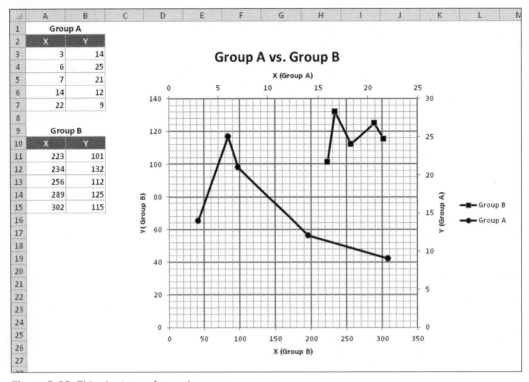

Figure 5-25: This chart uses four value axes.

Formatting and Customizing Charts

6

In This Chapter

- Getting an overview of chart formatting
- Formatting fill and borders
- Formatting chart background elements
- Working with chart titles
- Working with legends, data labels, gridlines, and data tables
- Understanding chart axes
- Formatting 3-D charts

If you create a chart for your own use, spending a lot of time on formatting and customizing the chart may not be worth the effort. But if you want to create the most effective chart possible, or if you need to create a chart for presentation purposes, you will want to take advantage of the additional customization techniques available in Excel.

This chapter discusses the ins and outs of formatting and customizing your charts. It's easy to become overwhelmed with all the chart customization options. However, the more you work with charts, the easier it becomes. Even advanced users tend to experiment a great deal with chart customization, and they rely heavily on trial and error — a technique that's highly recommend.

Chart Formatting Overview

Customizing a chart involves changing the appearance of its elements, as well as possibly adding new elements to it or removing elements from it. These changes can be purely cosmetic (such as changing colors or modifying line widths) or quite substantial (such as changing the axis scales).

Before you can customize a chart, you must activate it. To activate an embedded chart, click anywhere within the chart. To deactivate an embedded chart, just click anywhere in the worksheet, or press Esc (once or twice, depending on which chart element is currently selected). To activate a chart on a chart sheet, click its sheet tab.

Tip

If you press Ctrl while you activate an embedded chart, the chart is selected as an object. In fact, you can select multiple charts using this technique. When a group of charts is selected, you can move and resize them all at once. In addition, the tools in the Drawing Tools → Format → Arrange group are available. For example, you can align the selected charts vertically or horizontally.

Selecting chart elements

Modifying a chart is similar to everything else you do in Excel: First you make a selection (in this case, select a chart element); then you issue a command to do something with the selection.

You can select only one chart element at a time. For example, if you want to change the font for two axis labels, you must work on each label separately. The exceptions to the single-selection rule are elements that consist of multiple parts, such as gridlines. Selecting one gridline selects them all.

Excel provides three ways to select a particular chart element:

> Use the mouse

> Use the keyboard

> Use the Chart Elements control

These selection methods are described in the following sections.

Selecting with the mouse

To select a chart element with your mouse, just click the element.

Tip

To ensure that you've selected the chart element that you intended to select, check the name that's displayed in the Chart Elements control. The Chart Elements control is available in two Ribbon groups: Chart Tools → Layout → Current Selection, and Chart Tools → Format → Current Selection. The Chart Elements control displays the name of the selected chart element, and you can also use this control to select a particular element. See the "Selecting with the Chart Elements control" section later in this chapter.

When you move the cursor over a selected chart, a small "chart tip" displays the name of the chart element under the mouse pointer. When the mouse pointer is over a data point, the chart tip also displays the series, category, and value of the data point. If you find these chart tips annoying, you can turn them off in the Advanced tab in the Excel Options dialog box. In the

Chart section, you'll find two check boxes: Show Chart Element Names on Hover, and Show Data Point Values on Hover.

Some chart elements (such as a chart series, a legend, and data labels) consist of multiple items. For example, a chart series is made up of individual data points. To select a single data point, you need to click twice: First click the series to select it; then click the specific element within the series (for example, a column or a line chart marker). Selecting an individual element enables you to apply formatting only to a particular data point in a series. This might be useful if you'd like one marker in a line chart to stand out from the others.

Note

If you find that some chart elements are difficult to select with the mouse, you're not alone. If you rely on the mouse for selecting a chart element, it may take several clicks before the desired element is actually selected. And in some cases, selecting a particular element with the mouse is almost impossible. Fortunately, Excel provides other ways to select a chart element, and it's worth your while to be familiar with them.

Selecting with the keyboard

When a chart is active, you can use the up- and down-arrow keys on your keyboard to cycle among the chart's elements. Again, keep your eye on the Chart Elements control to verify which element is selected.

When a chart series is selected, use the left- and right-arrow keys to select an individual data point within the series. Similarly, when a set of data labels is selected, you can select a specific data label by using the left- or right-arrow key. And when a legend is selected, you can select individual elements within the legend by using the left- or right-arrow keys.

Selecting with the Chart Elements control

As noted earlier, the Chart Elements control displays the name of the selected chart element. This control contains a drop-down list of all chart elements (excluding shapes and text boxes), so you can also use it to select a particular chart element.

Tip

Although the Chart Elements control is available in two Ribbon groups (Chart Tools ➜ Layout ➜ Current Selection, and Chart Tools ➜ Format ➜ Current Selection), you may find that you also need to use it when the Chart Tools ➜ Design tab is displayed. You may prefer to put this control on your Quick Access toolbar so that it's always visible. Just right-click the drop-down arrow on the right side of the Chart Elements control and choose Add to Quick Access Toolbar from the shortcut menu.

The Chart Elements control is a drop-down list that lets you select a particular chart element from the active chart (see Figure 6-1). This control lists only the top-level elements in the chart. To select an individual data point within a series, for example, you need to select the series and then use one of the other techniques to select the desired data point.

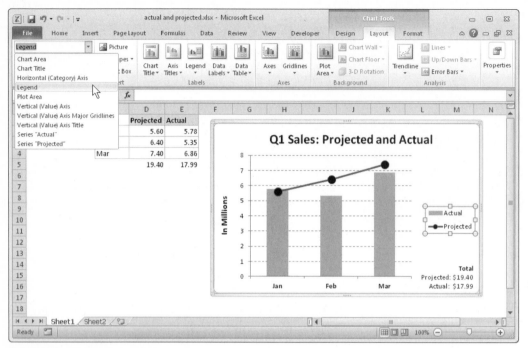

Figure 6-1: Use the Chart Elements control to select an element on a chart.

Note   When a single data point is selected, the Chart Elements control *will* display the name of the selected element, even though it's not actually available for selection in the drop-down list.

Common chart elements

Table 6-1 contains a list of the various chart elements that you may encounter. Note that the actual chart elements that are present in a particular chart depend on the chart type and on the customizations that you've performed on the chart.

Table 6-1: Chart Elements

Part	Description
Category Axis	The axis that represents the chart's categories.
Category Axis Title	The title for the category axis.
Chart Area	The chart's background.
Chart Title	The chart's title.
Data Label	A data label for a point in a series. The name is preceded by the series and the point. Example: Series 1 Point 1 Data Label.

Part	Description
Data Labels	Data labels for a series. The name is preceded by the series. Example: Series 1 Data Labels.
Data Table	The chart's data table.
Display Units Label	The units label for an axis.
Up/Down Bars	Vertical bars in a line chart or stock market chart.
Drop Lines	Lines that extend from each data point downward to the axis (line and area charts only).
Error Bars	Error bars for a series. The name is preceded by the series. Example: Series 1 Error Bars.
Floor	The floor of a 3-D chart.
Gridlines	A chart can have major and minor gridlines for each axis. The element is named using the axis and the type of gridlines. Example: Primary Vertical Axis Major Gridlines.
High-Low Lines	Vertical lines in a line chart or stock market chart.
Legend	The chart's legend.
Legend Entry	One of the text entries inside a legend.
Plot Area	The chart's plot area — the actual chart, without the legend.
Point	A point in a data series. The name is preceded by the series name. Example: Series 1 Point 2.
Secondary Category Axis	The second axis that represents the chart's categories.
Secondary Category Axis Title	The title for the secondary category axis.
Secondary Value Axis	The second axis that represents the chart's values.
Secondary Value Axis Title	The title for the secondary value axis.
Series	A data series.
Series Axis	The axis that represents the chart's series (3-D charts only).
Series Lines	A line that connects a series in a stacked column or stacked bar chart.
Trendline	A trend line for a data series.
Trendline Equation	The equation for a trend line.
Value Axis	The axis that represents the chart's values. There also may be a Secondary Value Axis.
Value Axis Title	The title for the value axis.
Walls	The walls of a 3-D chart only (except 3-D pie charts).

UI choices for formatting

When a chart element is selected, you have some choices as to which UI method you can use to format the element:

➤ The Ribbon

➤ The Mini Toolbar

➤ The Format dialog box

Formatting by using the Ribbon

The controls in the Chart Tools ➜ Format tab are used to change the appearance of the selected chart element. For example, if you would like to change the color of a series in a column chart, one approach is to use one of the predefined styles in the Chart ➜ Tools ➜ Format ➜ Shape Styles group.

For a bit more control, follow these steps:

1. Click the series to select it.

2. Choose Chart Tools ➜ Format ➜ Shape Styles ➜ Shape Fill, and select a color.

3. Choose Chart Tools ➜ Format ➜ Shape Styles ➜ Shape Outline, and select a color for the outline of the columns.

    You can also modify the outline width and the type of dashes (if any).

4. Choose Chart Tools ➜ Format ➜ Shape Styles ➜ Shape Effects, and add one or more effects to the series.

Note that you can modify the Shape Fill, Shape Outline, and Shape Effects for almost every element in a chart.

Here's one way to change the formatting of a chart's title so that the text is white on a black background:

1. Click the chart title to select it.

2. Choose Chart Tools ➜ Format ➜ Shape Styles ➜ Shape Fill, and select black.

3. Choose Chart Tools ➜ Format ➜ WordArt Styles ➜ Text Fill, and select white.

Notice that some of the controls in the Home ➜ Font and Home ➜ Alignment groups are also available when a chart element is selected. An alternate way of changing a chart's title to white on black is as follows:

1. Click the chart title to select it.

2. Choose Insert ➜ Font ➜ Fill Color, and select black.

3. Choose Insert ➜ Font ➜ Font Color, and select white.

Note The Ribbon commands do not contain all possible formatting options for chart elements. In fact, the Ribbon controls contain only a small subset of the chart formatting commands. For optimal control, you need to use the Format dialog box (discussed later in this chapter).

Formatting by using the Mini Toolbar

When you right-click a chart element, Excel displays its shortcut menu, with the Mini Toolbar on top. Figure 6-2 shows the Mini Toolbar that appears when you right-click a chart title. Use the Mini Toolbar to make formatting changes to the selected element. Note that the Mini Toolbar also works if you've selected only some of the characters in the chart element. In such a case, the text formatting applies only to the selected characters.

Note In Excel 2007, the Mini Toolbar appears only when you right-click a chart element that contains text. In Excel 2010, the Mini Toolbar appears when you right-click any chart element. In addition, Excel 2010 displays another copy of the Chart Elements control in the Mini Toolbar.

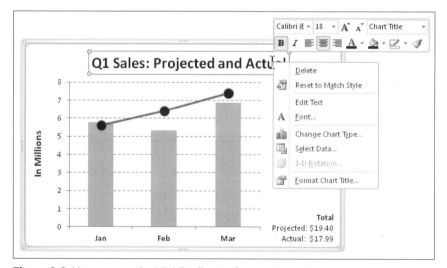

Figure 6-2: You can use the Mini Toolbar to format chart elements.

A few of the common keystroke combinations also work when a chart element that contains text is selected — specifically: Ctrl+B (bold), Ctrl+I (italic), and Ctrl+U (underline).

Formatting by using the Format dialog box

For complete control over text element formatting, use the Format dialog box. Each chart element has a unique Format dialog box, and the dialog box has several tabs.

You can access the Format dialog box by using either of the following methods:

> ➤ Select the chart element and press Ctrl+1.

> ➤ Right-click the chart element and choose Format *xxxx* from the shortcut menu (where *xxxx* is the chart element's name).

In addition, some of the Ribbon controls contain a menu item that, when clicked, opens the Format dialog box and displays a specific tab. For example, when you choose Chart Tools ➜ Format ➜ Shape Outline ➜ Weight, one of the options is More Lines. Click this option and Excel displays the Format dialog box with the Border Styles tab selected. This tab enables you to specify formatting that's not available on the Ribbon.

Figure 6-3 shows an example of a Format dialog box. Specifically, the figure shows the Legend Options tab of the Format Legend dialog box. As noted, each chart element has a different Format dialog box, which shows options that are relevant to the chart element.

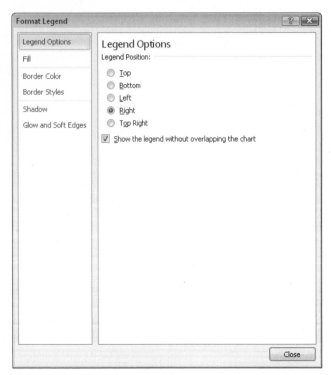

Figure 6-3: Each chart element has its own Format dialog box. This dialog box controls formatting for the chart's legend.

Note

The Format dialog box is a stay-on-top dialog box. In other words, you can keep this dialog box open while you're working on a chart. It's not necessary to close the dialog box to see the changes on the chart. In some cases, however, you need to activate a different control in the dialog box to see the changes you've specified. Usually, pressing Tab will move to the next control in the dialog box and force Excel to update the chart.

Adjusting Fills and Borders: General Procedures

Many of the Format dialog boxes for chart elements include a tab named Fill as well as other tabs that deal with border formatting. These tabs are used to change the interior and border of the selected element.

About the Fill tab

Figure 6-4 shows the Fill tab in the Format Chart Area dialog box when the Solid Fill option is selected. The controls on this tab change, depending on which option is selected.

Figure 6-4: The Fill tab of the Format Chart Area dialog box.

Although the Fill tabs of the various Format dialog boxes are similar, they are not identical. Depending on the chart element, the dialog box may have additional options that are relevant for the selected item.

Not all chart elements can be filled. For example, the Format Major Gridlines dialog box does not have a Fill tab because filling a line makes no sense. You can, however, change the gridline formatting by using the tabs that *are* displayed.

The main Fill tab options are as follows:

> ➤ **No Fill:** Makes the chart element transparent.
>
> ➤ **Solid Fill:** Displays a color selector so that you can choose a single color. You can also specify the transparency level for the color.
>
> ➤ **Gradient Fill:** Displays several additional controls that allow you to select a preset gradient or construct your own gradient. A gradient consists of from two to ten colors that are blended together in various ways. You have literally millions of possibilities.
>
> ➤ **Picture or Texture Fill:** Enables you to select from 24 built-in textures, choose an image file, or use clip art for the fill. This feature can often be useful in applying special effects to a data series. See the section "Formatting Chart Series," later in this chapter.
>
> ➤ **Pattern Fill:** Lets you specify a two-color pattern. This option is not available in Excel 2007.
>
> ➤ **Automatic:** Sets the fill to the default color. All chart elements start out with Automatic fill.

As a general rule, it's best to use these fill options sparingly. Using too much fill formatting can subdue your data, hindering the chart's ability to communicate the data. For example, Figure 6-5 shows a very ugly chart with various types of fill formatting applied. The column data series uses clip art, in the form of stacked monkeys. The plot area uses a texture, the chart area uses a gradient fill, and the axis labels use a solid black fill.

Formatting borders

A *border* is the line around an object. Excel offers four general choices for formatting a border:

> ➤ **No Line:** The chart element has no line.
>
> ➤ **Solid Line:** The chart element has a solid line. You can specify the color, the transparency, and a variety of other settings.
>
> ➤ **Gradient Line:** The chart element has a line that consists of a color gradient.
>
> ➤ **Automatic:** The default setting. Excel decides the border settings automatically.

Figure 6-6 shows the Border Styles tab of the Format Chart Area dialog box. If you explore this dialog box, you'll soon discover that a border can have a huge number of variations. Keep in mind that all settings are not available for all chart elements. For example, the Arrow Settings are disabled when a chart element that can't display an arrow is selected.

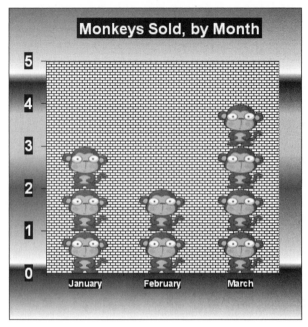

Figure 6-5: Using too many fill types can be quickly lead to ugly charts that are difficult to read.

Figure 6-6: Some of the settings available for a chart element border.

Formatting Chart Background Elements

Every chart has two key components that play a role in the chart's overall appearance:

> ➤ **The chart area:** The background area of the chart object
> ➤ **The plot area:** The area (within the chart area) that contains the actual chart

The default colors of the chart area and the plot area depend on which chart style you choose from the Chart Tools ➜ Design ➜ Chart Styles gallery.

Working with the chart area

The chart area is an object that contains all other elements on the chart. You can think of it as a chart's master background. The chart area is always the same size as the chart object (the chart's container).

Tip

When the chart area is selected, you can adjust the font for all the chart elements that display text. In other words, if you want to make all text in a chart 12 point, select the chart area and then apply the font formatting.

In some cases, you may want to make the chart area transparent so that the underlying worksheet shows through. Figure 6-7 shows a column chart with a transparent chart area. You can accomplish this by setting the chart area's fill to No Fill, or set it to a Solid Fill and make it 100% transparent.

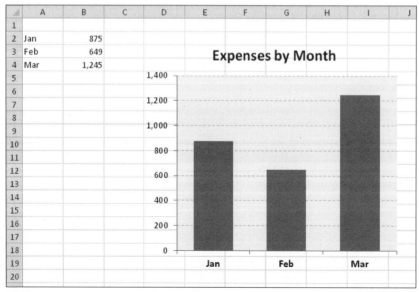

Figure 6-7: The chart area for this chart is transparent. The plot area, however, contains a fill color.

Working with the plot area

The plot area is the part of the chart that contains the actual chart. The plot area contains all chart elements except the chart title and the legend.

Although the plot area consists of elements such as axes and axis labels, when you change the fill of the plot area, these "outside" elements are not affected.

Tip

If you set the Fill option to No Fill, the plot area will be transparent. Therefore, the color and patterns applied to the chart area will show through. You can also set the plot area to a solid color and adjust the Transparency setting so that the chart area shows through partially.

In some situations, you may want to insert an image into the plot area. To do so, use the Fill tab of the Format Plot Area dialog box, and choose the Picture or Texture Fill option. The image can come from a file, the clipboard, or clip art. Figure 6-8 shows a column chart that uses a graphic in the plot area. In addition, the column series is partially transparent.

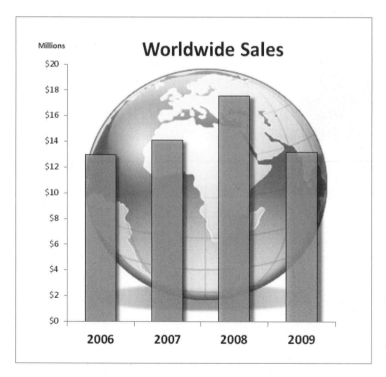

Figure 6-8: The plot area for this chart uses a graphic image.

To reposition the plot area within the chart area, select the plot area and then drag a border to move it. To change the size of the plot area, drag one of the corner "handles." If you like, you can expand the plot area so that it fills the entire chart area.

Copying chart formatting

You created a killer chart and spent hours customizing it. Now you need to create another one just like it. What are your options? You have several choices:

- **Copy the formatting.** Create a standard chart with the default formatting. Then select your original chart and press Ctrl+C. Click your new chart and choose Home ➜ Clipboard ➜ Paste ➜ Paste Special. In the Paste Special dialog box, select Formats.

- **Copy the chart; change the data sources.** Select the original chart and press Ctrl+C. Then, activate any cell and press Ctrl+V. This creates an exact copy of your chart. Activate a series in the new chart and drag the range highlights to the new ranges (and repeat for each series). Or, you can choose Chart Tools ➜ Design ➜ Data ➜ Select Data to display the Select Data Source dialog box.

- **Create a chart template.** Select your chart and then choose Chart Tools ➜ Design ➜ Type ➜ Save as Template. In the Save Chart Template dialog box, provide a descriptive filename. When you create your next chart, choose Insert ➜ Charts ➜ Other Charts ➜ All Chart Types, and select the Templates tab. Then, specify the template you created.

You'll find that different chart types vary in how they respond to changes in the plot area dimensions. For example, you cannot change the relative dimensions of the plot area of a pie chart or a radar chart (it's always square). But with other chart types, you can change the aspect ratio of the plot area by changing either the height or the width.

Also, be aware that the size of the plot area can be changed automatically when you adjust other elements of your chart. For example, if you add a legend or title to a chart, the size of the plot area may be reduced to accommodate the legend.

Tip

Remember to think of the purpose and utility of your chart before adding images to the plot area. Images may be appropriate for charts used as marketing or sales tools where visual components and eye candy help attract attention. Although in an analytical environment where the data is the primary product of your chart, there is no be a need to dress up your data with superfluous images.

Formatting Chart Series

Making a few simple formatting changes to a chart series can make a huge difference in the readability of your chart. When you create a chart, Excel uses its default colors and marker styles for the series. In many cases, you'll want to modify these colors or marker styles for clarity (basic formatting). In other cases, you may want to make some drastic changes for impact.

You can apply formatting to the entire series or to a single data point within the series — for example, make one column a different color to draw attention to it.

On the Web

This workbook, named `series.xlsx`, **is available at** `www.wiley.com/go/exceldr` **with the other example files for this book.**

Basic series formatting

Basic series formatting is very straightforward: Just select the data series on your chart and use the tools in the Chart Tools → Format → Shape Styles group to make changes. For more control, press Ctrl+1 and use the Format Data Series dialog box.

Using pictures and graphics for series formatting

You can add a picture to several chart elements, including data markers on line charts and series fills for column, bar, area, bubble, and filled radar charts. Figure 6-9 shows a column chart that uses a clip art image of a car. The picture was added using the Fill tab of the Format Data Series dialog box (select the Picture or Texture Fill option, then click the Clip Art button to select the image). In addition, the image is scaled so that each car represents 20 units.

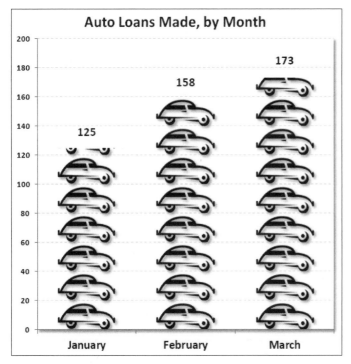

Figure 6-9: This column chart uses a clip art image.

Figure 6-10 shows another example. The data markers in this line chart display a shape that was inserted in the worksheet and then copied to the clipboard. Select the line series, press Ctrl+V to paste the shape.

You can also use the Marker Fill tab of the Format Data Series dialog box to specify Picture or Texture Fill. However, the result is very different. If you use the Clipboard button to paste the copied shape, the pasted image will fill the existing marker (not replace it). You'll probably need to increase the marker size, and also hide the marker borders.

Figure 6-10: The data markers use a shape that was copied to the clipboard.

Tip

Again, the purpose and utility of your chart should dictate whether pictures and graphics are appropriate. Charts for sales presentations, for example, can benefit from pictures and graphics given that visual enhancements can increase the possibility of prospective buyers paying attention to you. But in boardroom presentations where data is king, images will just get in the way. Think of it as selecting the right outfit for the right occasion. You wouldn't give a serious a speech in a Roman general's uniform. How well will you get your point across when your audience is thinking, "What's the deal with Tiberius"?

Additional series options

Chart series offer a number of additional options. These options are located in the Series Options tab of the Format Data Series dialog box. The set of options varies, depending on the chart type of the series. In most cases, the options are self-explanatory. But, if you are unsure about a particular series option, try it! If the result isn't satisfactory, change the setting to its original value or press Ctrl+Z to undo the change.

About those fancy effects

Excel 2007 introduced several new formatting options, which are known as *effects.* Access these effects by choosing Chart Tools ➜ Format ➜ Shape Styles ➜ Shape Effects. For more options, use the Format dialog box. Note that not all effects work with all chart elements.

Following is a general description of the effect types:

- **Shadow:** Adds a highly customizable shadow to the selected chart element. Choose from a number of preset shadows, or create your own using the Shadow tab of the Format dialog box. Shadows, when used tastefully, can improve the appearance of a chart by adding depth.

- **Glow:** Adds a color glow around the element. Charts are rarely improved by adding a glow to any element.

- **Soft Edges:** Makes the edges of the element softer. Extreme settings make the element appear to be out of focus, smaller, or even disappear.

- **Bevel:** Adds a 3-D bevel look to the element. This effect is highly customizable, and you can use it to create a frame for your chart (see the accompanying figure).

- **3-D Rotation:** This effect does not work with any chart elements.

The best advice regarding these effects is to use them sparingly with charts. Generally, a chart's formatting shouldn't draw attention away from the point you're trying to make with the chart.

Figure 6-11 shows an example of modifying series settings. The chart on the left uses the default settings (Series Overlap of 0% and Gap Width of 150%). The chart on the right uses a Series Overlap of 50% and a Gap Width of 28%.

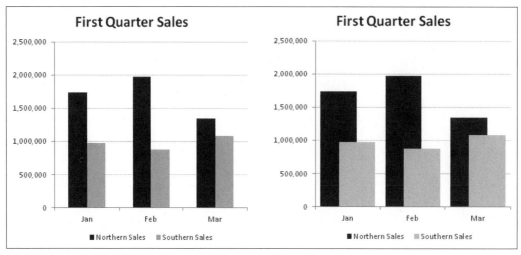

Figure 6-11: A column chart, before and after adjusting the Series Overlap and Gap Width settings

Working with Chart Titles

A chart can have as many as five different titles:

> ➤ Chart title

> ➤ Category axis title

> ➤ Value axis title

> ➤ Secondary category axis title

> ➤ Secondary value axis title

The number of titles depends on the chart type. For example, a pie chart supports only a chart title because it has no axes. Figure 6-12 shows a chart that contains four titles: the chart title, the horizontal category axis title, the vertical value axis title, and the secondary vertical axis title.

On the Web

> **This workbook, named** `titles.xlsx`**, is available at** `www.wiley.com/go/exceldr` **with the other example files for this book.**

Adding titles to a chart

To add a chart title to a chart, activate the chart and use the Chart Tools ➜ Layout ➜ Labels ➜ Chart Title control. This control drops down to display placement options.

To add axis titles to a chart, activate the chart and use the Chart Tools ➜ Layout ➜ Labels ➜ Axis Titles control. This control drops down to display placement options. Keep in mind that the options include only those that are appropriate for the chart. For example, if the chart doesn't have a secondary value axis, you don't have an option to add a title to the nonexistent axis.

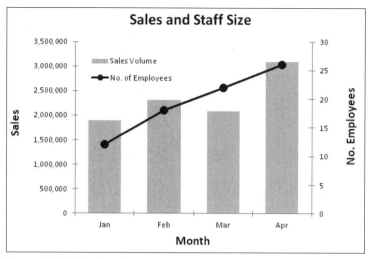

Figure 6-12: This chart has four titles.

Note

Contrary to what you might expect, you cannot resize a chart title. When you select a title, it displays the characteristic border and handles — but the handles cannot be dragged to change the size of the object. The only way to change the size is to change the size of the font used in the title. For more control over a chart's title, you can use a text box instead of an official title.

Changing title text

When you add a title to a chart, Excel inserts generic text to help you identify the title. To edit the text used in a chart title, click the title once to select it; then click a second time inside the text area. If the title has a vertical orientation, things get a bit tricky, because you need to use the up- and down-arrow keys rather than the left- and right- arrow keys.

Tip

For lengthy titles, Excel handles the line breaks automatically. To force a line break in the title, press Enter. To add a line break within existing title text, press Ctrl+Shift+Enter.

Formatting title text

Unfortunately, Excel does not provide a "one-stop" place to change all aspects of a chart title. The Format Chart Title dialog box provides options for changing the fill, border, shadows, 3-D format, and alignment. If you want to change anything related to the font, you need to use the Ribbon (or right-click and use the Mini Toolbar). Yet another option is to right-click the chart element and choose Font from the shortcut menu. This displays the Font dialog box, with options that aren't available elsewhere. For example, the Font dialog box lets you control the character spacing of the text.

Most of the font changes you make will use the tools in the Home ➜ Font group. You may be tempted to use the controls in the Chart Tools ➜ Format ➜ WordArt Styles group, but these controls are primarily for special effects.

Tip

You can easily modify the formatting for individual characters within a title. Select the title, highlight the characters that you want to modify, and apply the formatting. The formatting changes you make will affect only the selected characters.

Linking title text to a cell

When you create a chart, you might like to have some of the chart's text elements linked to cells. That way, when you change the text in the cell, the corresponding chart element updates. And, of course, you can even link chart text elements to cells that contain a formula. For example, you might link the chart title to a cell that contains a formula that returns the current date.

You can create a link to a cell for the chart title or any of the axis titles. Follow these steps:

1. Select the chart element that will contain the cell link. Make sure that the text element itself is selected (don't select text within the element).

2. Click the Formula bar.

3. Type an equal sign (=).

4. Click the cell that will be linked to the chart element.

5. Press Enter

Figure 6-13 shows a chart that has links for the following elements: chart title, the vertical axis title, and the horizontal axis title.

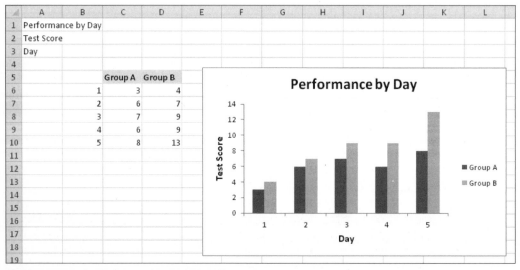

Figure 6-13: The titles in this chart are linked to cells.

Adding free-floating text to a chart

Text in a chart is not limited to titles. In fact, you can add free-floating text anywhere you want by inserting a text box into the chart. To do so, follow these steps:

1. Select the chart.
2. Choose Chart Tools ➜ Layout ➜ Insert ➜ Text Box.
3. Click and drag within the chart to create the text box.
4. Start typing the text.

You can click and drag the text box to change its size or location. And when the text box is selected, you can access the formatting tools using the controls on the Drawing Tools ➜ Format tab.

The accompanying figure shows a chart with a text box that contains quite a bit of formatted text. The chart's plot area was reduced in size to accommodate the text box.

There's nothing special about a text box. A text box is actually a rectangular shape object that contains text. You can change it to a different shape, if you like. Select the text box and choose Drawing Tools ➜ Format ➜ Insert Shapes ➜ Edit Shape ➜ Change Shape, and select a shape from the list. The Format Shape dialog box gives you lots of options for changing the look of the text box.

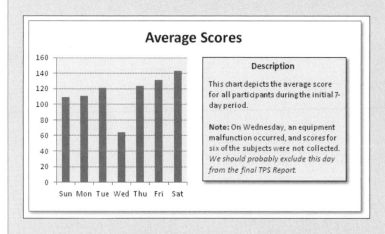

If you would like to link the text box to a cell, follow these steps:

1. Select the text box.
2. Click the Formula bar.
3. Type an equal sign (=).
4. Click the cell that will be linked to the chart element.

After you create the link, the text box will always display the contents of the cell it's linked to.

Some people prefer to use a text box in place of a chart's title because a text box provides much more control over formatting. When a text box is selected, its Format Shape dialog box provides several additional options, compared to the Format Chart Title dialog box.

Working with a Chart's Legend

A chart legend identifies the series in the chart and consists of text and keys. A *key* is a small graphic image that corresponds to the appearance of the corresponding chart series. The text displayed in a legend corresponds to the series names. The order of the items within a legend varies, depending on the chart type.

Adding or removing a legend

To add a legend to your chart, choose Chart Tools ➜ Layout ➜ Labels ➜ Legend. This drop-down control contains several options for the legend placement. After you've added a legend, you can drag it to move it anywhere you like.

The quickest way to remove a legend is to select it and press Delete.

Moving or resizing a legend

To move a legend, click it and drag it to the desired location. Or, you can use one of the options in the Chart Tools ➜ Layout ➜ Labels ➜ Legend control.

If you move a legend from its default position, you may want to change the size of the plot area to fill in the gap left by the legend. Just select the plot area and drag a border to make it the desired size.

To change the size of a legend, select it and drag any of its corners. Excel will adjust the legend automatically and may display it in multiple columns.

Formatting a legend

You can select an individual legend entry within a legend and format it separately. For example, you may want to make the text bold to draw attention to a particular data series. To select an element in the legend, first select the legend and then click the desired entry.

You can't change the formatting of individual characters in a legend entry. For example, if you'd like the legend to display a superscript or subscript character, you're out of luck.

When a single legend entry is selected, you can use the Format Legend Entry dialog box to format the entry. When a legend entry is selected and you apply any type of formatting except text formatting, the formatting affects the legend key and the corresponding series. In other words, the appearance of the legend key will *always* correspond to the data series.

Note

You can't use the Chart Elements drop-down list to select a legend entry. You must either click the item or select the legend itself, and then press the right-arrow key until the desired element is selected.

Changing the legend text

The legend text corresponds to the names of the series on the chart. If you didn't include series names when you originally selected the cells to create the chart, Excel displays a default series name (Series 1, Series 2, and so on) in the legend.

To add series names, choose Chart Tools ➜ Design ➜ Select Data to display the Select Data Source dialog box. Select the series name and click the Edit button. In the Edit Series dialog box, type the series name or enter a cell reference that contains the series name. Repeat for each series that needs naming. Alternatively, you can edit the SERIES formula, as described in Chapter 5.

Deleting a legend entry

For some charts, you may prefer that one or more of the data series not appear in the legend. To delete a legend entry, just select it and press Delete. The legend entry will be deleted, but the data series will remain intact.

If you've deleted one or more legend entries, you can restore the legend to its original state by deleting the entire legend and then adding it back.

Identifying series without using a legend

Legends are appropriate for charts that have at least two series. But even then, all charts do not require a legend. You may prefer to identify relevant data using other methods, such as a data label, a text box, or a shape with text. Figure 6-14 shows a chart in which the data series are identified by using text in shapes, which were added to the chart using Insert ➜ Illustrations ➜ Shapes.

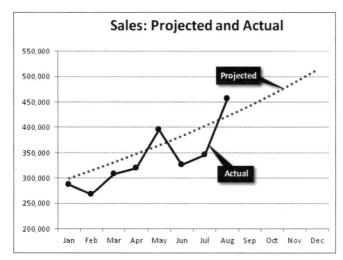

Figure 6-14: This chart uses shapes as an alternative to a legend.

Working with Chart Axes

As you know, charts vary in the number of axes that they use. Pie and doughnut charts have no axes. All 2-D charts have at least two axes, and they can have three (if you use a secondary value or category axis) or four (if you use a secondary category axis and a secondary value axis). Three-dimensional charts have three axes — the "depth" axis is known as the series axis.

Excel provides you with a great deal of control over the look of chart axes. To modify any aspect of an axis, access its Format Axis dialog box. The dialog box varies, depending on which type of axis is selected.

On the Web

This workbook, named `axes.xlsx`, **is available at** `www.wiley.com/go/exceldr` **with the other example files for this book.**

All aspects of axis formatting are covered in the sections that follow.

Value axis versus category axis

Before getting into the details of formatting, it's important to understand the difference between a category axis and a value axis. A category axis displays arbitrary text, whereas a value axis displays numerical intervals. Figure 6-15 shows a simple column chart with two series. The horizontal category axis displays labels that represent the categories. The vertical value axis, on the other hand, is a value axis which has a numerical scale.

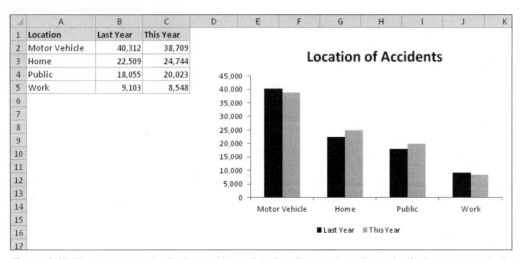

Figure 6-15: The category axis displays arbitrary labels, whereas the value axis displays a numerical scale.

In this example, the category labels happen to be text. Alternatively, the categories *could* be numbers. Figure 6-16 shows the same chart after replacing the category labels with numbers. Even though the chart becomes meaningless, it should be clear that the category axis does not display a true numeric scale. The numbers displayed are completely arbitrary, and the chart itself was not affected by changing these labels.

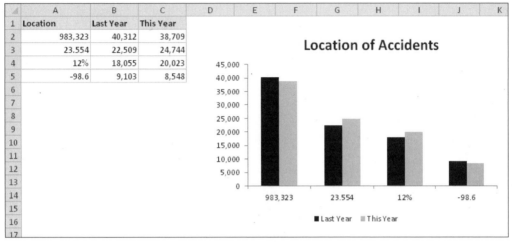

Figure 6-16: The category labels have been replaced with numbers — but the numbers do not function as numbers.

Two of Excel's chart types are different from the other chart types in one important respect. Scatter charts and bubble charts use *two* value axes. For these chart types, both axes represent numeric scales.

Figure 6-17 shows two charts (a scatter chart and a line chart) that use the same data. The data shows world population estimates for various years. Note that the interval between the years in column A is not consistent.

The scatter chart, which uses two value axes, plots the years as numeric values. The line chart, on the other hand, uses a (non-numeric) category axis, and it assumes that the categories (the years) are equally spaced. This, of course, is not a valid assumption, and the line chart presents a very inaccurate picture of the population growth: It appears to be linear, but it's definitely not.

Cross-Ref

For more information about time-based axes, refer to the "Using time-scale axes" section later in this chapter.

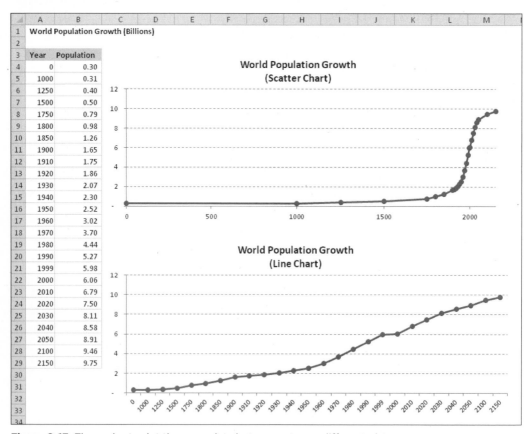

Figure 6-17: These charts plot the same data but present very different pictures.

Value axis scales

The numerical range of a value axis represents the axis's scale. By default, Excel automatically scales each value axis. It determines the minimum and maximum scale values for the axis, based on the numeric range of the data. Excel also automatically calculates a major unit and a minor unit for each axis scale. These settings determine how many intervals (or tick marks) are displayed on the axis and determine how many gridlines are displayed. In addition, the value at which the axis crosses the category axis is also calculated automatically.

You can, of course, override this automatic behavior and specify your own minimum, maximum, major unit, minor unit, and cross-over for any value axis. You set these specifications on the Axis Options tab of the Format Axis dialog box (see Figure 6-18).

Note

A category axis does not have a scale because it displays arbitrary category names. For a category axis, the Axis Options tab of the Format Axis dialog box displays a number of other options that determine the appearance and layout of the axis.

Figure 6-18: The Axis Options tab of the Format Axis dialog box.

On the Axis Options tab, the four sets of option buttons at the top determine the scale of the axis (its minimum, maximum, and intervals). By default, Excel determines these values based on the numerical range of the data, and the default setting is Auto. You can override Excel's choice and set any or all of them to Fixed and then enter your own values.

Adjusting the scale of a value axis can dramatically affect the chart's appearance. Manipulating the scale, in some cases, can present a false picture of the data. Figure 6-19 shows two line charts that depict the same data. The top chart uses Excel's default axis scale values, which extend from 8,000 to 9,200. In the bottom chart, the Minimum scale value was set to 0, and the Maximum scale value was set to 10,000. A casual viewer might draw two very different conclusions from these charts. The top chart makes the differences in the data seem more prominent. The lower chart gives the impression that not much change has occurred over time.

The actual scale that you use depends on the situation. There are no hard-and-fast rules regarding setting scale values, except that you shouldn't misrepresent data by manipulating the chart to prove a point that doesn't exist. In addition, most agree that the value axis of a bar or column chart should always start at zero (and even Excel follows that rule).

If you're preparing several charts that use similarly scaled data, keeping the scales constant across all charts facilitates comparisons across charts. The charts in Figure 6-20 show the distribution of responses for two survey questions. For the top chart, the value axis scale ranges from 0% to 50%. For the bottom chart, the value axis scale extends from 0% to 35%. Because the same scale was not used on the value axes, however, comparing the responses across survey items is difficult.

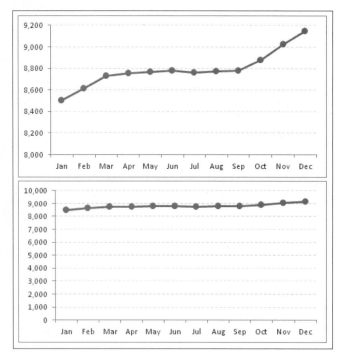

Figure 6-19: These two charts show the same data, but they use different value axis scales.

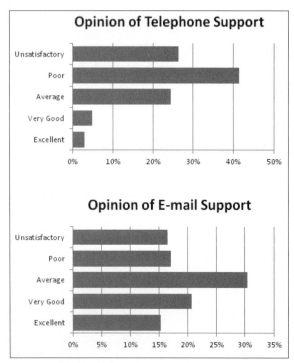

Figure 6-20: These charts use different scales on the value axis, making a comparison between the two difficult.

Another option in the Format Axis dialog box is Values in Reverse Order. The top chart in Figure 6-21 uses default axis settings. The bottom chart uses the Values in Reverse Order option, which reverses the scale's direction. Notice that the category axis is at the top. If you would prefer that it remain at the bottom of the chart, select the Maximum Axis Value option for the Horizontal Axis Crosses setting.

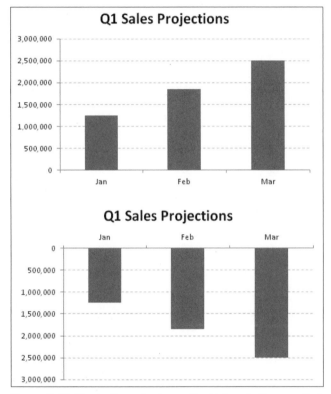

Figure 6-21: The bottom chart uses the Values in Reverse Order option.

If the values to be plotted cover a very large range, you may want to use a logarithmic scale for the value axis. A log scale is most often used for scientific applications. Figure 6-22 shows two charts. The top chart uses a standard scale, and the bottom chart uses a logarithmic scale. Note that the base is 10, so each scale value in the chart is 10 times greater than the one below it. Increasing the base unit to 100 would result in a scale in which each tick mark value is 100 times greater than the one below.

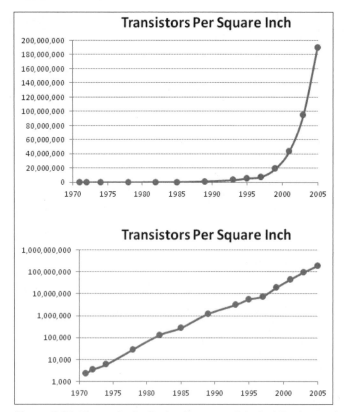

Figure 6-22: These charts display the same data, but the lower chart uses a logarithmic scale.

If your chart uses very large numbers, you may want to change the Display Units settings. Figure 6-23 shows a chart that uses very large numbers. The lower chart uses the Display Units as Millions setting, with the option to Show Display Units Label on Chart. Excel inserted the label "Millions," which was edited to display as "Millions of Miles."

Tip

Another way to change the number display is to use a custom number format for the axis values. For example, to display the values in millions, click the Number tab of the Format Axis dialog box, select the Custom category, and then enter this format code:

```
#,##0,,
```

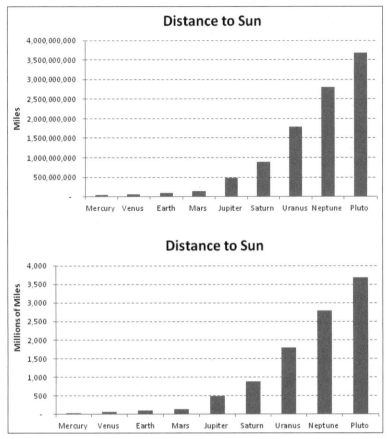

Figure 6-23: The lower chart uses display units of millions.

An axis also has tick marks — the short lines that depict the scale units and are perpendicular to the axis. In the Axis Options dialog box, you can select the type of tick mark for the major units and the minor units. The options are as follows:

➤ **None:** No tick marks

➤ **Inside:** Tick marks on the inside of the axis only

➤ **Outside:** Tick marks on the outside of the axis only

➤ **Cross:** Tick marks on both sides of the axis

You can also control the position of the tick mark labels. The options are as follows:

> ➤ **None:** No labels.

> ➤ **Low:** For a horizontal axis, labels appear at the bottom of the plot area; for a vertical axis, labels appear to the left of the plot area.

> ➤ **High:** For a horizontal axis, labels appear at the top of the plot area; for a vertical axis, labels appear to the right of the plot area.

> ➤ **Next to axis:** Labels appear next to the axis (the default setting).

Note

Major tick marks are the axis tick marks that normally have labels next to them. Minor tick marks are between the major tick marks.

When you combine these settings with the Axis Crosses At option, you have a great deal of flexibility, as shown in Figure 6-24. These charts all display the same data, but the axes are formatted differently.

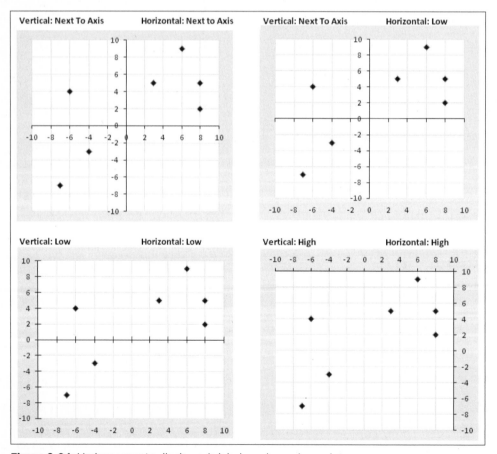

Figure 6-24: Various ways to display axis labels and crossing points.

Using time-scale axes

When you create a chart, Excel attempts to determine whether your category axis contains date or time values. If so, it creates a time-series chart. Figure 6-25 shows a simple example. Column A contains dates, and column B contains the values plotted on the column chart. The data consists of values for only ten dates, yet Excel created the chart with 31 intervals on the category axis. It recognized that the category axis values were dates, and created an equal-interval scale.

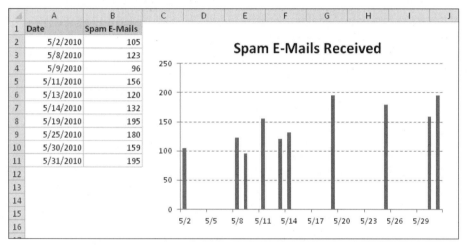

Figure 6-25: Excel recognizes the dates and creates a time-based category axis.

If you would like to override Excel's decision to use a time-based category axis, you need to access the Axes Options tab of the Format Axis dialog box. There, you'll discover that the default category axis option is Automatically Select Based on Data. Change this option to Text Axis, and the chart will resemble Figure 6-26. On this chart, the dates are treated as arbitrary text labels.

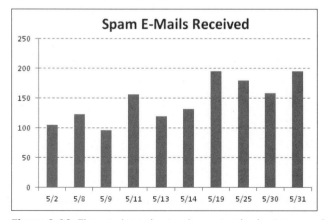

Figure 6-26: The previous chart, using a standard category axis.

Note **A time-scale axis option is available only for the category axis (not the value axis).**

When a category axis uses dates, the Axis Options tab of the Format Axis dialog box lets you specify the Base Unit, the Major Unit, and the Minor Unit — each in terms of days, months, or years.

If you need a time-scale axis for smaller units (such as hours), you need to use a scatter chart. That's because a date-scale axis treats all values as integers. Therefore, every time value is plotted as midnight of that day. Figure 6-27 shows a scatter chart that plots scheduled versus actual arrival times for flights. Note that both of the value axes display times, in one-hour increments.

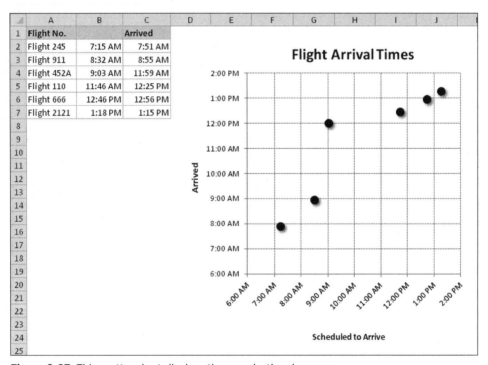

Figure 6-27: This scatter chart displays times on both value axes.

Unfortunately, Excel does not allow you to specify time values on the Axis Options tab of the Format Axis dialog box. If you want to override the default minimum, maximum, or major unit values, you must manually convert the time value to a decimal value.

This chart uses the following scale values:

➤ Minimum axis scale value: .25 (6:00 am)

➤ Maximum axis scale value: .58333 (2:00 pm)

➤ Major unit: .041666 (1:00:00)

To convert a time value to a decimal number, enter the time value into a cell. Then apply General number formatting to the cell. Time values are expressed as a percentage of a 24-hour day. For example, 12:00 noon is 0.50.

Creating a multiline category axis

Most of the time, the labels on a category axis consist of data from a single column or row. You can, however, create multiline category labels, as shown in Figure 6-28. This chart uses the text in columns A:C for the category axis labels.

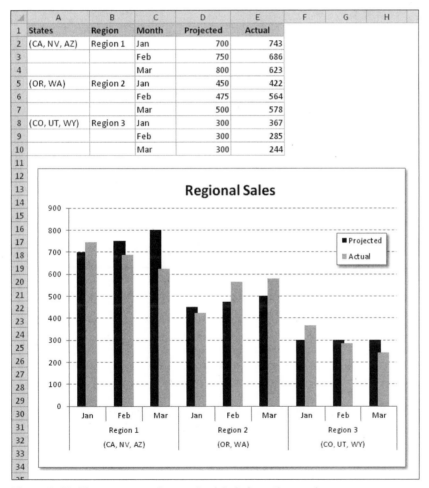

Figure 6-28: The category axis contains labels from three columns.

When this chart was created, range A1:E10 was selected. Excel determined automatically that the first three columns would be used for the category axis labels.

Note This type of data layout is common when you work with pivot table, and pivot charts often use multiline category axes.

Removing axes

To change the visibility of an axis from the chart, use the Chart Tools ➜ Layout ➜ Axes ➜ Axes command. This drop-down control also contains a number of display options for the axis — the same options that are available in the Format Axis dialog box.

A more direct way to remove an axis is to select it and then press Delete.

Figure 6-29 shows three charts with no axes displayed. Using data labels makes the value axis superfluous, and it is assumed that the reader understands what the horizontal axis represents.

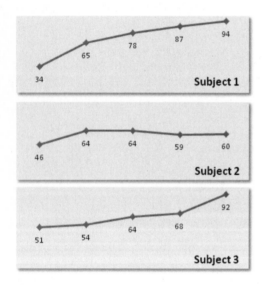

Figure 6-29: Three line charts with no axes.

Axis number formats

A value axis, by default, displays its values using the same number format that's used by the chart's data. You can provide a different number format, if you like, by using the Number tab of the Format Axis dialog box. Changing the number format for a category axis that displays text will have no effect.

Don't forget about custom number formats. Figure 6-30 shows a chart that uses the following custom number format for the value axis:

```
General " mph"
```

This number format causes the text *mph* to be appended to each value.

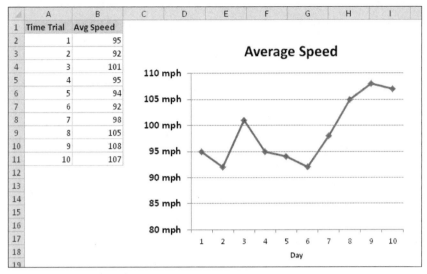

Figure 6-30: The value axis uses a custom number format to provide units for the values.

Working with Gridlines

Gridlines can help the viewer determine the values represented by the series on the chart. Gridlines are optional, and you have quite a bit of control over the appearance of gridlines. Gridlines simply extend the tick marks on the axes. The tick marks are determined by the major unit and minor unit specified for the axis.

Note   Gridlines are applicable to all chart types except pie charts and doughnut charts.

Some charts look better with gridlines; others appear more cluttered. It's up to you to decide whether gridlines can enhance your chart. Sometimes, horizontal gridlines alone are enough, although scatter charts often benefit from both horizontal and vertical gridlines. In many cases, gridlines will be less overpowering if you make them dashed lines, with a gray color.

Adding or removing gridlines

To add or remove gridlines, use the Chart Tools ➜ Layout ➜ Axes ➜ Gridlines command. Each axis has two sets of gridlines: major and minor. Major units are the ones that display a label. Minor units are those in between the labels. If you're working with a chart that has a secondary category axis, a secondary value axis, or a series axis (for a 3-D chart), the dialog box has additional options for three sets of gridlines.

A more direct way to remove a set of gridlines is to select the gridlines and press Delete.

Note

If a chart uses a secondary axis, you can specify either or both value axes to display gridlines. As you might expect, displaying two sets of gridlines in the same direction can be confusing and result in additional clutter.

To modify the properties of a set of gridlines, select one gridline in the set (which selects all in the set) and access the Format Gridlines dialog box. Or, use the controls in the Chart Tools ➜ Format ➜ Shape Styles group.

Note

You can't apply different formatting to individual gridlines within a set of gridlines. All gridlines in a set are always formatted identically.

Working with Data Labels

For some charts, you may want to identify the individual data points in a series by displaying data labels.

Adding or removing data labels

Some of the layouts in the Chart Tools ➜ Design ➜ Chart Layouts gallery include data labels. To add data labels to a chart, select the chart and choose Chart Tools ➜ Layout ➜ Labels ➜ Data Labels. This control is a drop-down list, which displays placement options.

Note

If a chart series is selected, the Chart Tools ➜ Layout ➜ Labels ➜ Data Labels command adds data labels only to the selected series. If a single point is selected, this commands adds a data label only to the selected point. If a chart element other than a series (or single point) is selected, the command adds data labels to all series in the chart.

To remove data labels from a particular series, select the data labels and press Delete. To remove a single data label, select the individual label and press Delete. To remove the data labels from all series in a chart, select an element other than data labels and choose Chart Tools ➜ Layout ➜ Labels ➜ Data Labels ➜ None.

Note

This workbook, named `data labels.xlsx`, is available at www.wiley.com/go/exceldr with the other example files for this book.

Editing data labels

After adding data labels to a series, you can apply formatting to the labels by using the Ribbon, the Mini Toolbar, or the Format Data Labels dialog box. To specify the contents of the data labels, use the Label Options tab of the Format Data Labels dialog box. Figure 6-31 shows this dialog box for a pie chart.

Note

When you click a data label, the labels for the entire series are selected. If you click a second time (on a single label), only that data label is selected. In other words, Excel lets you format all data labels at once or format just a single data label.

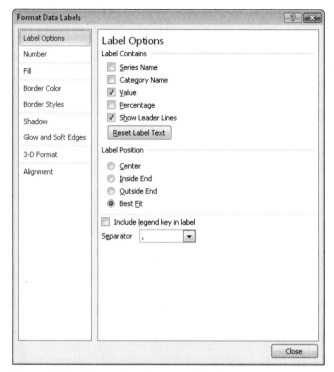

Figure 6-31: Options for displaying data labels.

The types of information that can be displayed in data labels are as follows:

➤ The series name

➤ The category name

➤ The numeric value

➤ The value as a percentage of the sum of the values in the series (for pie charts and doughnut charts only)

➤ The bubble size (for bubble charts only)

Other options are as follows. Keep in mind that not all options are available for all chart types.

➤ **Show Leader Lines:** If selected, Excel displays a line that connects the data label with the chart series data point.

➤ **Label Position:** Specifies the location of the data labels, relative to each data point.

➤ **Include Legend Key in Label:** If selected, each data label displays its legend key image next to it.

➤ **Separator:** If you specify multiple contents for the data labels, this control enables you to specify the character that separates the elements (a comma, a semicolon, a period, a space, or a line break).

The Format Data Labels dialog box also lets you specify a variety of other formatting options for your data labels.

The column chart in Figure 6-32 contains data labels that display category names and their values. These labels are positioned to appear on the Outside End. These data labels use the New Line separator option, so the value appears on a separate line. Because the category name is included in the data labels, the horizontal category axis labels aren't necessary.

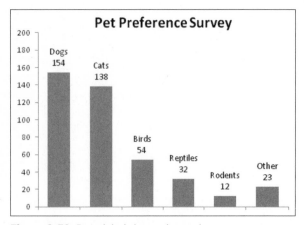

Figure 6-32: Data labels in a column chart.

Note

The data labels display the values for each data point. For this particular chart, it would be preferable to display the value as a percentage of the total. Unfortunately, the Percent option is available only for a pie or doughnut chart. The alternative is to calculate the percentages using formulas and then plot the percentage data rather than the actual value data.

Figure 6-33 shows a line chart in which the data labels are positioned on top of the (large) markers. The data labels were positioned using the Center option.

Figure 6-33: Positioning data labels on series markers.

To override a particular data label with other text, select the label and enter the new text. To select an individual data label, click once to select all the data labels; then click the specific data label to select it.

To link a selected data label to a cell, follow these steps:

1. Click in the Formula bar.

2. Type an equal sign (**=**).

3. Click the cell that contains the text.

4. Press Enter.

After adding data labels, you'll often find that the data labels aren't positioned optimally. For example, one or more of the labels may be obscured by another data point or a gridline. If you select an individual label, you can drag the label to a better location.

Problems and limitations with data labels

As you work with data labels, you will probably discover that Excel's Data Labels feature leaves a bit to be desired. For example, it would be nice to be able to specify a range of text to be used for the data labels. This would be particularly useful in scatter charts in which you want to identify each data point with a particular text item. Figure 6-34 shows a scatter chart. If you would like to apply data labels to identify the student for each data point, you're out of luck.

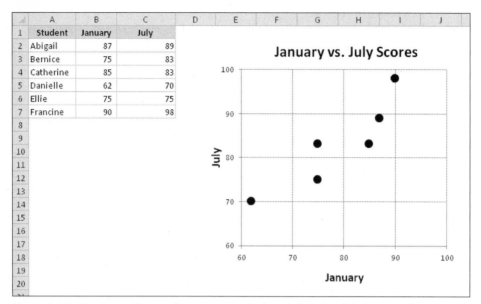

Figure 6-34: Excel provides no direct way to add descriptive data labels to the data points.

Despite what must amount to thousands of requests, Microsoft still has not added this feature to Excel! You need to add data labels and then manually edit each label.

Note A few utility add-ins are available which all you to specify an arbitrary range of text to be used for data labels. One such product is Power Utility Pak, available from John Walkenbach's Web site (http://spreadsheetpage.com).

As you work with data labels, you'll find that this feature works best for series that contain a relatively small number of data points. The chart in Figure 6-35, for example, contains 24 data points. You can't display all the data labels on this chart and keep the chart legible.

One option is to delete some of the individual data labels. For example, you might want to delete all the data labels except those at the high and low points of the series. Deleting only certain data labels is, however, a manual process. To delete an individual data label, select it and press Delete. Using gridlines provides another way to let the reader discern the values for the data points. Yet another alternative is to use a data table, which is described in the next section.

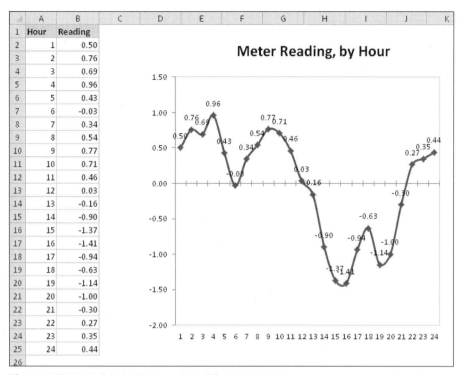

	A	B
1	**Hour**	**Reading**
2	1	0.50
3	2	0.76
4	3	0.69
5	4	0.96
6	5	0.43
7	6	-0.03
8	7	0.34
9	8	0.54
10	9	0.77
11	10	0.71
12	11	0.46
13	12	0.03
14	13	-0.16
15	14	-0.90
16	15	-1.37
17	16	-1.41
18	17	-0.94
19	18	-0.63
20	19	-1.14
21	20	-1.00
22	21	-0.30
23	22	0.27
24	23	0.35
25	24	0.44
26		

Figure 6-35: Data labels don't work well for this chart.

Working with a Chart Data Table

There may be situations where it's valuable to show all the data values along with the plotted data points. However, you've adding data labels can inundate your audience with a bevy of numbers that muddle the chart.

Instead of using data labels, you can attach a *Data Table* to your Excel chart. A data table allows you to see the data values for each plotted data point, beneath the chart, showing the data without overcrowding the chart itself. Figure 6-36 shows a chart that includes a data table.

Note

This workbook, named `data table.xlsx`**, is available at** www.wiley.com/go/
exceldr **with the example files for this book.**

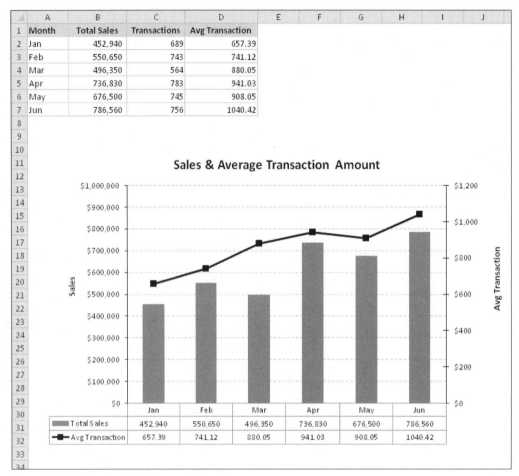

Figure 6-36: This chart includes a data table.

Adding and removing a data table

To add a data table to a chart, select the chart and choose Chart Tools ➜ Layout ➜ Labels ➜ Data Table ➜ Show Data Table.

To remove a data table from a chart, select the chart and choose Chart Tools ➜ Layout ➜ Labels ➜ Data Table ➜ None. Or, select the data table element in the chart and press Delete.

Problems and limitations with data tables

One problem with data tables, as noted previously, is that this feature is available for only a few chart types. Formatting options for a data table are relatively limited. Data table formatting changes are made in the Format Data Table dialog box.

The Fill tab is a bit misleading because it does not actually allow you to change the fill color for the data table. Rather, you are limited to formatting the background of the text and numbers in the data table.

Unfortunately, you cannot apply different font formatting to individual cells or rows within the data table. You also can't change the number formatting. The numbers displayed in a data table always use the same number formatting as the source data.

When you add a data table to a chart, the data table essentially replaces the axis labels on the horizontal axis. The first row of the data table contains these labels, so losing them isn't a major problem. However, you will not be able to apply separate formatting to the axis labels — they will have the same formatting as the other parts of the data table.

Note

An exception to the behavior described in the preceding paragraph occurs with bar charts and charts with a time-scale category axis. For these types of charts, the data table is positioned below the chart and does not replace any axis labels.

Another potential problem with data tables occurs when they are used with embedded charts. If you resize the chart to make it smaller, the data table may not show all the data.

Using a data table is probably best suited for charts on chart sheets. If you need to show the data used in an embedded chart, you can do so using data in cells, which provides you with much more flexibility in terms of formatting.

PART III

Going Beyond Tables and Charts

Using Pivot Tables

In This Chapter

- Using pivot tables as your data model

- Creating and modifying a pivot table

- Customizing pivot table fields, formats, and functions

- Filtering data using Pivot Table views

In Chapter 2, we discuss using a data model as the foundation for your dashboards and reports. This data model helps you to organize your information into three logical layers: data, analysis, and presentation. As you'll discover in this chapter, pivot tables lend themselves nicely to this data model concept. With pivot tables, you can build data models that are not only easy to set up, but can then be updated with a simple press of a button. So you can spend less time maintaining your dashboards and reports and more time doing other things. No utility in Excel enables you to achieve a more efficient data model than a pivot table.

Introducing the Pivot Table

A pivot table is a tool that allows you to create an interactive view of your source data (commonly referred to as a pivot table report). A pivot table can help transform endless rows and columns of numbers into a meaningful presentation of data. You can easily create groupings of summary items: for example, combine Northern Region totals with Western Region totals, filter that data using a variety of views, and insert special formulas that perform new calculations.

Pivot tables get their namesake from your ability to interactively drag and drop fields within the pivot table to dynamically change (or pivot) the perspective, giving you an entirely new view using the same source data. You can then display subtotals and interactively drill down to any level of detail that you want. Note that the data itself doesn't change, and is not connected to the pivot table. The reason a pivot table is so well suited to a dashboard is that you can quickly update the view of your pivot table by changing the source data that it points to. This allows you to set up both your analysis and presentation layers at one time. You can then simply press a button to update your presentation.

Anatomy of a pivot table

A pivot table is comprised of four areas: Values, Row Labels, Column Labels, and Report Filters. The data you place in these areas defines both the use and presentation of the data in your pivot table. We now discuss the function of each of these four areas.

Values area

The Values area allows you to calculate and count the source data. In Figure 7-1, it is the large rectangular area below and to the right of the column and row headings. In this example, the Values area contains a sum of the values in the Sales Amount field.

The data fields that you drag and drop here are typically those that you want to measure — fields, such as the sum of revenue, a count of the units, or an average of the prices.

Region	(All)			
Sales Amount	**Segment**			
Market	Accessories	Bikes	Clothing	Components
Australia	23,974	1,351,873	43,232	203,791
Canada	119,303	11,714,700	383,022	2,246,255
Central	46,551	6,782,978	155,874	947,448
France	48,942	3,597,879	129,508	871,125
Germany	35,681	1,602,487	75,593	337,787
Northeast	51,246	5,690,285	163,442	1,051,702
Northwest	53,308	10,484,495	201,052	1,784,207
Southeast	45,736	6,737,556	165,689	959,337
Southwest	110,080	15,430,281	364,099	2,693,568
United Kingdom	43,180	3,435,134	120,225	712,588

Values Area

Figure 7-1: The Values area of a pivot table calculates and counts the data.

Row Labels area

The Row Labels area is shown in Figure 7-2. Dragging a data field into the Row Labels area displays the unique values from that field down the rows of the left side of the pivot table. The Row Labels area typically has at least one field, although it's possible to have no fields.

The types of data fields that you would drop here include those that you want to group and categorize, such as, products, names, and locations.

Region	(All) ▾		

Sales Amount	Segment ▾		
Market ▾	Accessories	Bikes	Clothing Components
Australia	23,974	1,351,873	43,232 203,791
Canada	119,303	11,714,700	383,022 2,246,255
Central	46,551	6,782,978	155,874 947,448
France	48,942	3,597,879	129,508 871,125
Germany	35,681	1,602,487	75,593 337,787
Northeast	51,246	5,690,285	163,442 1,051,702
Northwest	53,308	10,484,495	201,052 1,784,207
Southeast	45,736	6,737,556	165,689 959,337
Southwest	110,080	15,430,281	364,099 2,693,568
United Kingdom	43,180	3,435,134	120,225 712,588

Row Area

Figure 7-2: The Row Labels area of a pivot table gives you a row-oriented perspective.

Column Labels area

The Column Labels area contains headings that stretch across the top of columns in the pivot table, as you can see in Figure 7-3. In this example, the Column Labels area contains the unique list of business segments.

Column Area

Region	(All) ▾		

Sales Amount	Segment ▾		
Market ▾	Accessories	Bikes	Clothing Components
Australia	23,974	1,351,873	43,232 203,791
Canada	119,303	11,714,700	383,022 2,246,255
Central	46,551	6,782,978	155,874 947,448
France	48,942	3,597,879	129,508 871,125
Germany	35,681	1,602,487	75,593 337,787
Northeast	51,246	5,690,285	163,442 1,051,702
Northwest	53,308	10,484,495	201,052 1,784,207
Southeast	45,736	6,737,556	165,689 959,337
Southwest	110,080	15,430,281	364,099 2,693,568
United Kingdom	43,180	3,435,134	120,225 712,588

Figure 7-3: The Column Labels area of a pivot table gives you a column-oriented perspective.

Placing a data field into the Column Labels area displays the unique values from that field in a column-oriented perspective. The Column Labels area is ideal for creating a data matrix or showing trends over time.

Report Filter area

At the top of the pivot table, the Report Filter area is an optional set of one or more drop-down controls. In Figure 7-4, the Report Filter area contains the Region field, and the pivot table is set to show all regions.

Placing data fields into the Report Filter area allows you to change the views for the entire pivot table based on your selection. The types of data fields that you'd drop here include those that you want to isolate and focus on; for example, region, line of business, and employees.

Filter Area

Region		(All)	▼		
Sales Amount		Segment ▼			
Market	▼	Accessories	Bikes	Clothing	Components
Australia		23,974	1,351,873	43,232	203,791
Canada		119,303	11,714,700	383,022	2,246,255
Central		46,551	6,782,978	155,874	947,448
France		48,942	3,597,879	129,508	871,125
Germany		35,681	1,602,487	75,593	337,787
Northeast		51,246	5,690,285	163,442	1,051,702
Northwest		53,308	10,484,495	201,052	1,784,207
Southeast		45,736	6,737,556	165,689	959,337
Southwest		110,080	15,430,281	364,099	2,693,568
United Kingdom		43,180	3,435,134	120,225	712,588

Figure 7-4: The Report Filter area allows you to easily apply filters to your pivot table, focusing on specific data items.

Creating the basic pivot table

Now that you have a good understanding of the structure of a pivot table, let's follow these steps to create your first pivot table.

On the Web

You can find the example file for this chapter on this book's companion Web site at `www.wiley.com/go/exceldr` **in the workbook named** `Chapter 7 Sample Data. xlsx.`

1. Click any single cell inside your source data (the table you'll use to feed the pivot table).

2. Click the Insert tab on the Ribbon.

    Find the PivotTable icon, as shown in Figure 7-5.

3. From the drop-down list under the PivotTable icon, select PivotTable.

Figure 7-5: Create a pivot table using the Insert tab.

This opens the Create PivotTable dialog box, as shown in Figure 7-6.

4. Specify the location of your source data.

5. Specify the worksheet where you want to put the pivot table.

In Figure 7-6, note that the default location for a new pivot table is New Worksheet. This means your pivot table will be placed in a new worksheet within the current workbook. To change this, select the Existing Worksheet option and specify the worksheet in which you want to place the pivot table.

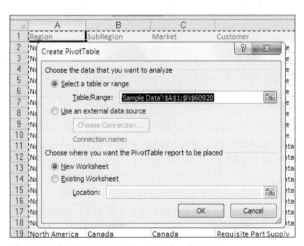

Figure 7-6: The Create PivotTable dialog box.

6. Click OK.

At this point, you have an empty pivot table report on a new worksheet.

Laying out the pivot table

Next to the empty pivot table, you see the PivotTable Field List dialog box, as shown in Figure 7-7.

You can add the fields you need into the pivot table by dragging and dropping the field names to one of the four areas found in the PivotTable Field List — Report Filter, Column Labels, Row Labels, and Values.

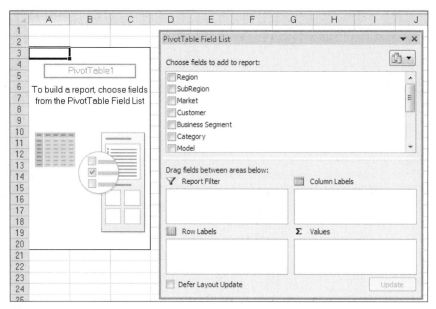

Figure 7-7: The PivotTable Field List dialog box.

Note

If clicking the pivot table doesn't activate the PivotTable Field List dialog box, you can manually activate it by right-clicking anywhere inside the pivot table and selecting Show Field List. Alternatively, you can go to the Ribbon, click Option, and then select Field List in the Show group.

Now before you start dropping fields into the various areas, ask yourself two questions: "What am I measuring?" and "How do I want to see it?." The answer to these questions gives you some guidance in determining which fields go where.

For your first pivot table example, we want to measure the dollar sales by market. This tells you that you need to work with the Sales Amount field and the Market field.

How do we want to view that? We want markets to go down the left side of the report and the sales amount to be calculated next to each market. You'll need to add the Market field to the Row Labels area, and the Sales Amount field to the Values area.

1. In the field list, select the Market field (see Figure 7-8).

   Now that you have regions in your pivot table, it's time to add the dollar sales.

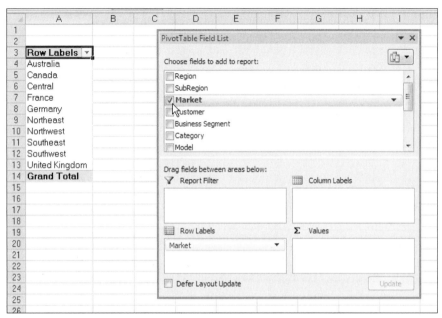

Figure 7-8: Select the Market field to add it to the field selector list.

2. In the field selector area, select the Sales Amount field (see Figure 7-9).

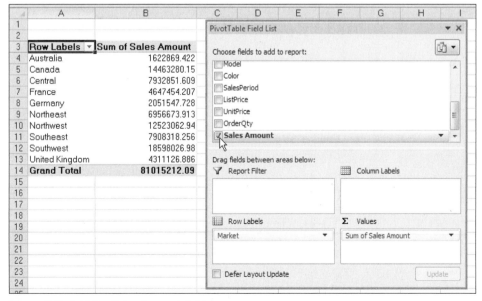

Figure 7-9: Add the Sales Amount field.

Note

Placing a check next to any field that is non-numeric (text or date) automatically places that field into the Row Labels area of the pivot table. Placing a check next to any field that is numeric automatically places that field in the Values area of the pivot table.

One more thing: when you add new fields, you may find it difficult to see all the fields in the box for each area. You can expand the PivotTable Field List dialog box by clicking and dragging the borders of the dialog box to avoid that problem.

As you can see, you have just analyzed the sales for each market in just five steps! That's an amazing feat considering you start with over 60,000 rows of data. With a little formatting, this modest pivot table can become the starting point for a dashboard or report.

Modifying the pivot table

Now here's the wonderful thing about pivot tables. For your data model, you can add as many analysis layers as possible by changing or rearranging the fields in your source data table. Say that you want to show the dollar sales each market earned by business segment. Because your pivot table already contains the Market and Sales Amount fields, all you have to add is the Business Segment field.

So simply click anywhere on your pivot table to reactivate the PivotTable Field List dialog box and then select the Business Segment field. Figure 7-10 illustrates what your pivot table now looks like.

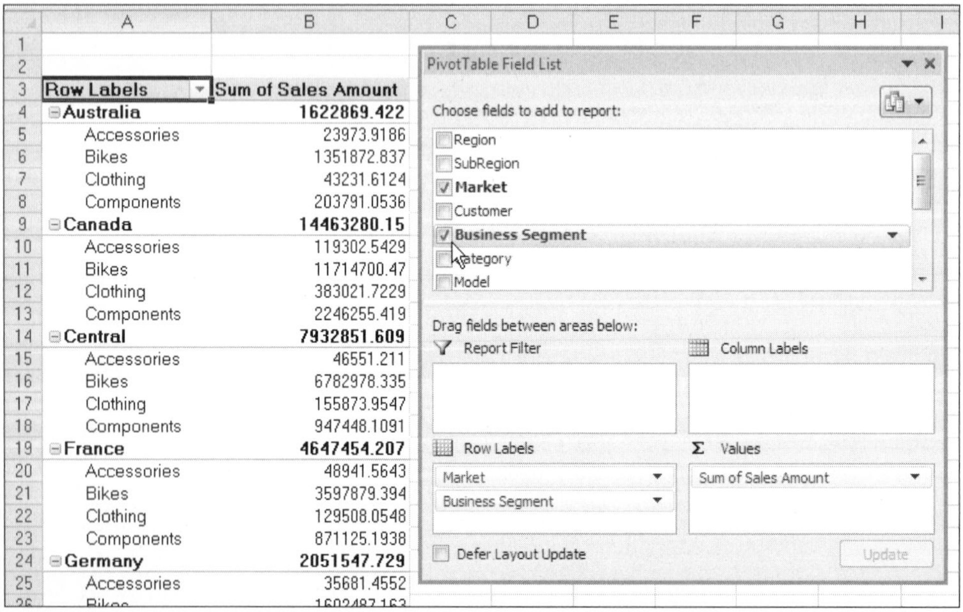

Figure 7-10: Adding a new analysis layer to your data model is as easy as selecting another field.

Note

If clicking the pivot table doesn't activate the PivotTable Field List dialog box, you can manually activate it by right-clicking anywhere inside the pivot table and selecting Show Field List.

What if this layout doesn't work for you? Maybe you want to see business segments listed at the top of the pivot table results. No problem. Simply drag the Business Segment field from the Row Labels area to the Column Labels area. As you can see in Figure 7-11, this instantly restructures the pivot table.

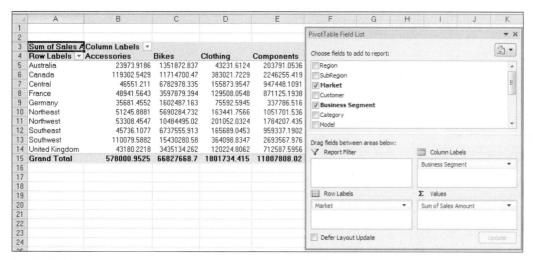

Figure 7-11: Your business segments are now column oriented.

Changing the pivot table view

Often you're asked to produce reports for one particular region, market, product, and so on. Instead of working hours and hours building separate pivot tables for every possible scenario, you can leverage pivot tables to help create multiple views of the same data. For example, you can do so by creating a region filter in your pivot table.

Click anywhere on your pivot table to reactivate the PivotTable Field List dialog box and then drag the Region field to the Report Filter area. This adds a drop-down control to your pivot table, as shown in Figure 7-12. You can then use this control to view one particular region at a time.

Updating your pivot table

As time goes by, your data may change and grow with newly added rows and columns. The action of updating your pivot table with these changes is to use the Refresh command for your pivot table. To update the pivot table, simply right-click inside your pivot table and select Refresh, as demonstrated in Figure 7-13.

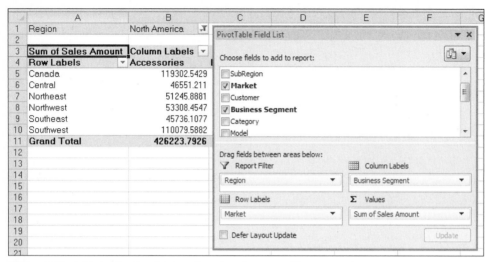

Figure 7-12: Add the Region field to view data for a specific geographic area.

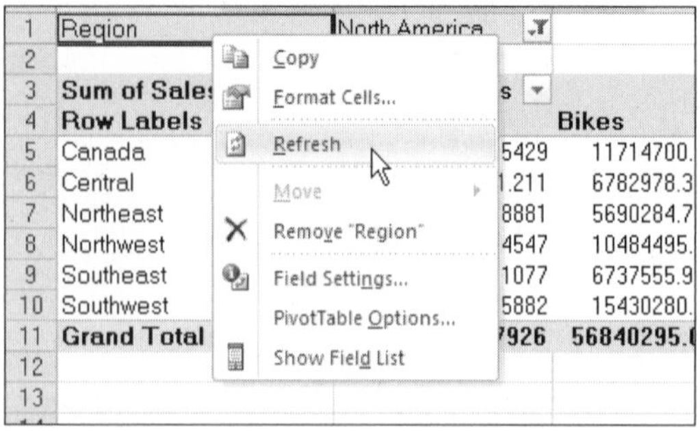

Figure 7-13: Use the Refresh command to update the data in your pivot table.

Sometimes, the source data that feeds your pivot table changes in structure. For example, you may want to add or delete rows or columns from your data table. These types of changes then affect the range of your data source, not just a few data items in the table.

In this case, a simple update of your pivot table data won't do. You have to update the range that is captured by the pivot table. Here's how:

1. Click anywhere inside your pivot table to activate the PivotTable Tools context tab on the Ribbon.

2. Click the Options tab.

3. Click the Change Data Source button, as demonstrated in Figure 7-14.

4. Change the range selection to include any new rows or columns (see Figure 7-15).

5. Click OK.

Figure 7-14: Changing the data range that feeds your pivot table.

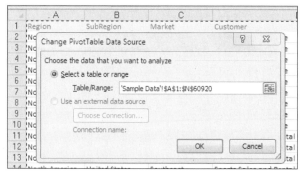

Figure 7-15: Select the new range that feeds your pivot table.

Pivot tables and worksheet bloat

It's important to understand that pivot tables do come with space and memory implications for your dashboards and reports. When you create a pivot table, Excel takes a snapshot of your source data and stores it in a pivot cache. A pivot cache is essentially a memory container that holds this snapshot of your data. Each pivot table that you create from a separate data source creates its own pivot cache, which increases your workbook's memory usage and file size. The increase in memory usage and file size depends on the size of the original data source that Excel duplicates to create the pivot cache.

Simple enough, right? Well here's the rub: You often need to create separate pivot tables from the same data source in order to create two distinct analysis layers in your data model. If you create two pivot tables from the data source, Excel automatically creates a new pivot cache even though one may already exist for the same data source. This means that you're bloating your worksheet with redundant data each time you create a new pivot table using the same data source.

To work around this potential problem, you can use the copy and paste commands. That's right; simply copying a pivot table and pasting it somewhere else creates another pivot table, without duplicating the pivot cache. This enables you to create multiple pivot tables that use the same source data, with negligible increase in memory and file size.

Customizing Your Pivot Table

The pivot tables you create often need to be tweaked in order to get the look and feel that you're looking for. In this section, we cover some of the ways that you can customize your pivot tables to suit your dashboard's needs.

Renaming the fields

Notice that every field in your pivot table has a name. The fields in the row, column, and filter areas inherit their names from the data labels in your source data. For example, the fields in the Values area are given a name, such as Sum of Sales Amount.

Now you might prefer the name Total Sales instead of the unattractive default name, like Sum of Sales Amount. In this situation, the ability to change your field name is handy. To change a field name, perform the following steps:

1. Right-click any value within the target field.

   For example, if you want to change the name of the field Sum of Sales Amount, you right-click any value under that field.

2. Select Value Field Settings (see Figure 7-16).

   This opens the Value Field Settings dialog box.

3. Type the new name in the Custom Name box (see Figure 7-17).

4. Click OK.

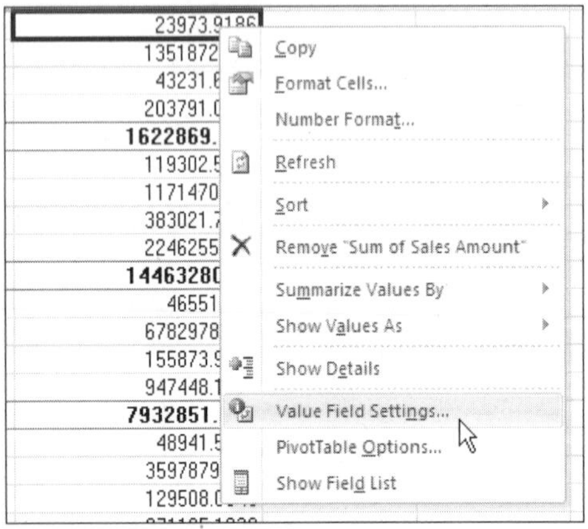

Figure 7-16: Right-click any value in the target field to select the Value Field Settings option.

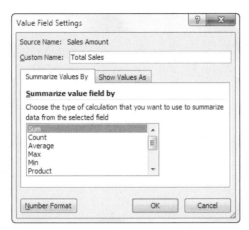

Figure 7-17: Use the Custom Name box to change the name.

Note

If you use the same name of the data label that you specified in your source data, you receive an error. In our example, if you try to rename the Sum of Sales Amount field as Sales Amount, you do get an error message. To get around this, you can add a space to the end of any field name. Excel considers Sales Amount (followed by a space) to be different from Sales Amount. This way you can use the name that you want, and no one will notice any difference.

Formatting numbers

You can format numbers in a pivot table to fit your needs (such as currency, percent, or number). For example, you can control the numeric formatting of a field using the Value Field Settings dialog box. Here's how:

1. Right-click any value within the target field.

   For example, if you want to change the format of the values in the Sales Amount field, right-click any value under that field.

2. To display the Select Value Field Settings dialog box, select Value Field Settings.

3. To display the Format Cells dialog box, click Number Format.

4. Indicate the number format you desire, just as you normally would on your worksheet.

5. Click OK.

After you set a new format for a field, the applied formatting will persist even if you refresh or rearrange your pivot table.

Changing summary calculations

When you create your pivot table, Excel, by default, summarizes your data by either counting or summing the items. Instead of Sum or Count, you might want to choose other functions, such as Average, Min, Max, and so on. In all, 11 options are available, including:

➤ **Sum:** Adds all numeric data.

➤ **Count:** Counts all data items within a given field, including numeric-, text-, and date-formatted cells.

➤ **Average:** Calculates an average for the target data items.

➤ **Max:** Displays the largest value in the target data items.

➤ **Min:** Displays the smallest value in the target data items.

➤ **Product:** Multiplies all target data items together.

➤ **Count Nums:** Counts only the numeric cells in the target data items.

➤ **StdDevP and StdDev:** Calculates the standard deviation for the target data items. Use StdDevP if your data source contains the complete population. Use StdDev if your data source contains a sample of the population.

➤ **VarP and Var:** Calculates the statistical variance for the target data items. Use VarP if your data contains a complete population. If your data contains only a sampling of the complete population, use Var to estimate the variance.

To change the summary calculation for any given field, perform the following steps:

1. Right-click any value within the target field.

2. To display the Value Field settings dialog box, select Value Field Settings.

3. Select the type of calculation you want to use from the list of calculations (see Figure 7-18).

4. Click OK.

Note

Did you know that a single blank cell causes Excel to count instead of sum? That's right. If all the cells in a column contain numeric data, Excel chooses Sum. If just one cell is either blank or contains text, Excel chooses Count. Be sure to pay attention to the fields that you place into the Values area of the pivot table. If the field name starts with Count Of, Excel's counting the items in the field instead of summing the values.

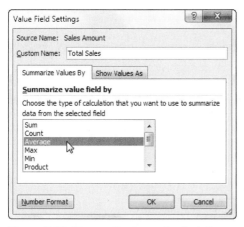

Figure 7-18: Change the type of calculation used in for a field.

Suppressing subtotals

Notice that each time you add a field to your pivot table, Excel adds a subtotal for that field. There may be, however, times when the inclusion of subtotals either doesn't make sense or just hinders a clear view of your pivot table report. For example, Figure 7-19 shows a pivot table where the subtotals inundate the report with totals that serve only to hide the real data you're trying to report.

	A	B	C	D	E
2					
3	Region	SubRegion	Market	Business Segment	Sum of Sales Amount
4	North America	United States	Central	Accessories	$46,551
5				Bikes	$6,782,978
6				Clothing	$155,874
7				Components	$947,448
8			Central Total		$7,932,852
9			Northeast	Accessories	$51,246
10				Bikes	$5,690,285
11				Clothing	$163,442
12				Components	$1,051,702
13			Northeast Total		$6,956,674
14			Northwest	Accessories	$53,308
15				Bikes	$10,484,495
16				Clothing	$201,052
17				Components	$1,784,207
18			Northwest Total		$12,523,063
19			Southeast	Accessories	$45,736
20				Bikes	$6,737,556
21				Clothing	$165,689
22				Components	$959,337
23			Southeast Total		$7,908,318
24			Southwest	Accessories	$110,080
25				Bikes	$15,430,281
26				Clothing	$364,099
27				Components	$2,693,568
28			Southwest Total		$18,598,027
29		United States Total			$53,918,934
30	North America Total				$53,918,934
31	Grand Total				$53,918,934

Figure 7-19: Subtotals sometimes muddle the data you're trying to show.

Removing all subtotals at one time

You can remove all subtotals at once by performing these steps:

1. To activate the PivotTable Tools context tab on the Ribbon, click anywhere inside your pivot table.

2. Click the Design tab.

3. Select the Subtotals icon and select Do Not Show Subtotals (see Figure 7-20).

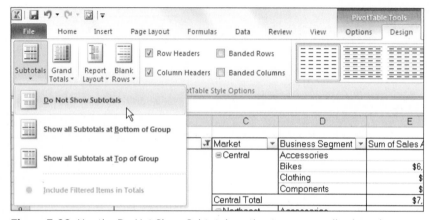

Figure 7-20: Use the Do Not Show Subtotals option to remove all subtotals at once.

As you can see in Figure 7-21, the same report without subtotals is much more pleasant to review.

	A	B	C	D	E
2					
3	Region	SubRegion	Market	Business Segment	Sum of Sales Amount
4	North America	United States	Central	Accessories	$46,551
5				Bikes	$6,782,978
6				Clothing	$155,874
7				Components	$947,448
8			Northeast	Accessories	$51,246
9				Bikes	$5,690,285
10				Clothing	$163,442
11				Components	$1,051,702
12			Northwest	Accessories	$53,308
13				Bikes	$10,484,495
14				Clothing	$201,052
15				Components	$1,784,207
16			Southeast	Accessories	$45,736
17				Bikes	$6,737,556
18				Clothing	$165,689
19				Components	$959,337
20			Southwest	Accessories	$110,080
21				Bikes	$15,430,281
22				Clothing	$364,099
23				Components	$2,693,568
24	Grand Total				$53,918,934

Figure 7-21: The same report without subtotals.

Removing the subtotals for only one field

Maybe you want to remove the subtotals for only one field? In such a case, you can perform the following steps:

1. Right-click any value within the target field.

2. To display the Field Settings dialog box, select Field Settings.

3. Select None under the Subtotals option (see Figure 7-22).

4. Click OK.

Figure 7-22: Select the None option to remove subtotals for one field.

Removing grand totals

You may want to remove the Grand Totals field from your pivot table.

1. Right-click anywhere on your pivot table.

2. To display the Options dialog box, select PivotTable Options.

3. Click the Totals & Filters tab.

4. Deselect Show Grand Totals for Rows.

5. Deselect Show Grand Totals for Columns.

Hiding and showing data items

A pivot table summarizes and displays all the information in your source data. There may, how-ever, be situations when you want to inhibit certain data items from being included in your pivot table summary. In these situations, you can choose to hide a data item.

In terms of pivot tables, hiding doesn't just mean preventing the data item from displaying on the dashboard, hiding a data item also prevents it from being factored into the summary calculations.

In the pivot table shown in Figure 7-23, we show sales amounts for all Business Segments by Market. In this example, however, we want to show totals without taking sales from the Bikes segment into consideration. In other words, we want to hide the Bikes segment.

	A	B	C
2			
3	**Market** ▾	**Business Segment** ▾	**Sum of Sales Amount**
4	⊟Australia	Accessories	$23,974
5		Bikes	$1,351,873
6		Clothing	$43,232
7		Components	$203,791
8	**Australia Total**		**$1,622,869**
9	⊟Canada	Accessories	$119,303
10		Bikes	$11,714,700
11		Clothing	$383,022
12		Components	$2,246,255
13	**Canada Total**		**$14,463,280**
14	⊟Central	Accessories	$46,551
15		Bikes	$6,782,978
16		Clothing	$155,874
17		Components	$947,448
18	Central Total		$7,932,852

Figure 7-23: We want to remove Bikes from this analysis.

To hide the Bikes Business Segment, in the Business Segment drop-down list, deselect Bikes (see Figure 7-24).

After clicking OK, the pivot table instantly recalculates, leaving out the Bikes segment. As you can see in Figure 7-25, the Market totals sales now reflect the sales without Bikes.

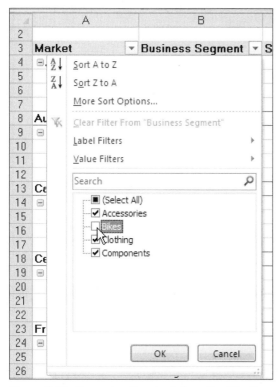

Figure 7-24: Removing the check from the Bike items hides the Bikes segment.

	A	B	C
2			
3	**Market** ▼	**Business Segment** ⌐T	**Sum of Sales Amount**
4	⊟Australia	Accessories	$23,974
5		Clothing	$43,232
6		Components	$203,791
7	**Australia Total**		**$270,997**
8	⊟Canada	Accessories	$119,303
9		Clothing	$383,022
10		Components	$2,246,255
11	**Canada Total**		**$2,748,580**
12	⊟Central	Accessories	$46,551
13		Clothing	$155,874
14		Components	$947,448
15	**Central Total**		**$1,149,873**

Figure 7-25: Segment analysis without the Bikes segment.

We can just as quickly reinstate all hidden data items for the field. Simply click the Business Segment drop-down list and select Select All (see Figure 7-26).

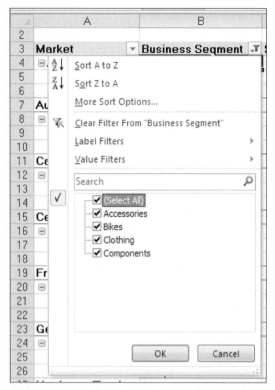

Figure 7-26: Placing a check next to Select All forces all data items in that field to become unhidden.

Hiding or showing items without data

By default, your pivot table shows only data items that have data. This may cause unintended problems for your data.

Look at Figure 7-27, which shows a pivot table with the SalesPeriod field in the Row Labels area and the Region field in the Report Filter area. Note that the Region field is set to (All), and every sales period appears in the report.

	A	B
1	Region	(All)
2		
3	SalesPeriod	Sum of Sales Amount
4	01/01/08	$713,230
5	02/01/08	$1,900,797
6	03/01/08	$1,455,282
7	04/01/08	$883,011
8	05/01/08	$2,269,722
9	06/01/08	$1,137,250
10	07/01/08	$2,411,569
11	08/01/08	$3,615,926
12	09/01/08	$2,894,658
13	10/01/08	$1,804,184

Figure 7-27: All sales periods are showing.

If you display only Europe in the filter area, only a portion of all the sales periods now show (see Figure 7-28).

	A	B
1	Region	Europe ⫯
2		
3	SalesPeriod ▾	Sum of Sales Amount
4	07/01/08	$180,241
5	08/01/08	$448,373
6	09/01/08	$373,122
7	10/01/08	$119,384
8	11/01/08	$330,026
9	12/01/08	$254,011
10	01/01/09	$71,313
11	02/01/09	$264,487
12	03/01/09	$177,006
13	04/01/09	$105,153

Figure 7-28: Filtering for the Europe region causes some of the sales periods to not display.

But displaying only those items with data could cause trouble if I plan on using this pivot table as the source for my charts or other dashboard components. With that in mind, it isn't ideal if half the year disappears each time a customer selects Europe.

Here's how you can prevent Excel from hiding pivot items without data:

1. Right-click any value within the target field.

   In this example, the target field is the SalesPeriod field.

2. To display the Field Settings dialog box, select Field Settings.

3. Click the Layout & Print tab in the Field Settings dialog box.

4. Select Show Items with No Data (see Figure 7-29).

5. Click OK.

As you can see in Figure 7-30, after you select the Show Items with No Data option, all the sales periods appear whether the selected region had sales that period or not.

Now that we're confident that the structure of the pivot table is locked, we can use it as the source for all charts and other components in our dashboard.

Figure 7-29: Select the Show Items with No Data option to display all data items.

	A	B
1	Region	Europe
2		
3	SalesPeriod	Sum of Sales Amount
4	01/01/08	
5	02/01/08	
6	03/01/08	
7	04/01/08	
8	05/01/08	
9	06/01/08	
10	07/01/08	$180,241
11	08/01/08	$448,373
12	09/01/08	$373,122
13	10/01/08	$119,384
14	11/01/08	$330,026

Figure 7-30: All sales periods display even if there is no data.

Sorting your pivot table

By default, items in each pivot field are sorted in ascending sequence based on the item name. Excel gives you the freedom to change the sort order of the items in your pivot table.

Like many actions that you can perform in Excel, lots of different ways exists to sort data within a pivot table. The easiest way, and the way that we use the most, is to apply the sort directly in the pivot table. Here's how:

1. **Right-click any value within the target field (the field you need to sort).**

   In the example shown in Figure 7-31, we want to sort by Sales Amount.

2. **Select Sort and then select the sort direction.**

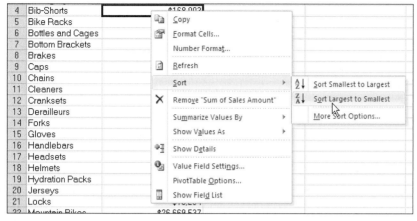

Figure 7-31: Applying a sort to a pivot table field.

The changes take effect immediately and persist while you work with your pivot table.

Examples of Filtering Your Data

At this point in your exploration of pivot tables, you know enough to start creating your own pivot table and specifying unique views. In this section, we share a few ways we like to view our data. Although you could specify these views by hand, using the pivot table feature saves you hours of work and allows you to more easily update and maintain your information.

Producing top and bottom views

You'll often find that people are interested in the top and bottom measurement of things: for example, the top 50 customers, the bottom five sales reps, the top ten products. Although you may think this is because they have the attention span of a four-year-old, there's a more logical reason for focusing on the outliers.

Effective dashboards and reports are often about showing actionable data. If you, as a manager, know who the bottom ten revenue-generating accounts are, you could apply your effort and resources in building up those accounts. Because you most likely wouldn't have the resources to focus on all accounts, viewing a manageable subset of accounts would be more useful.

Luckily, pivot tables make it easy to filter your data for the top five, the bottom ten, or any conceivable combination of top or bottom records. Here's an example.

Imagine that in your company, the Accessories Business Segment is a high-margin business — you make the most profit for each dollar of sales in the Accessories segment. To increase sales, your manager wants to focus on the 50 customers who spend the least amount of money on Accessories. He obviously wants to spend his time and resources on getting those customers to buy more accessories. Here's what to do:

1. Build a pivot table with Business Segment in the Report Filter area, Customer in the Row Labels area, and Sales Amount in the Values area (see Figure 7-32.) For cosmetic value, change the layout to Tabular Form.

	A	B	
1	Business Segment	(All)	▼
2			
3	**Customer** ▼	**Sum of Sales Amount**	
4	A Bike Store	85177.0812	
5	A Great Bicycle Company	9055.2903	
6	A Typical Bike Shop	83457.1089	
7	Acceptable Sales & Service	1258.3767	
8	Accessories Network	2215.8975	
9	Acclaimed Bicycle Company	7682.28	
10	Ace Bicycle Supply	3749.1338	
11	Action Bicycle Specialists	328503.1613	
12	Active Cycling	1805.454	
13	Active Life Toys	200013.366	
14	Active Systems	643.3457	
15	Active Transport Inc.	88245.8727	
16	Activity Center	42804.2561	
17	Advanced Bike Components	363131.3817	
18	Aerobic Exercise Company	2676.654	
19	Affordable Sports Equipment	311446.431	
20	All Cycle Shop	2028.7111	

Figure 7-32: Build this pivot table to start.

2. Right-click any customer name in the Customer field and select Filter, and then select Top 10 (see Figure 7-33).

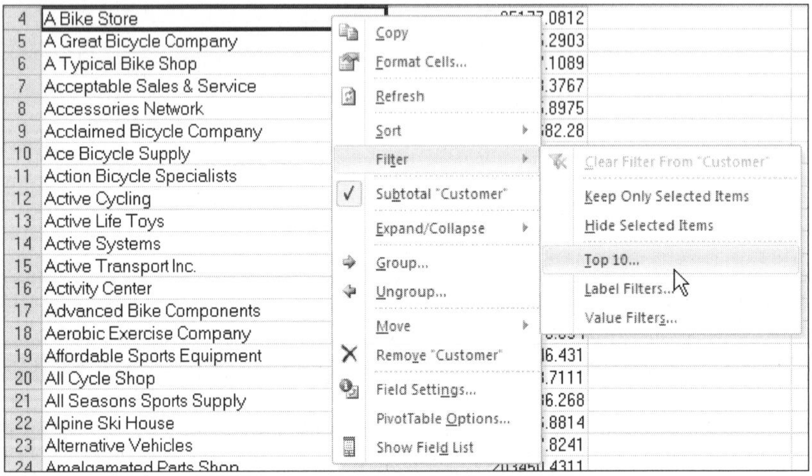

Figure 7-33: Select the Top 10 filter option.

3. In the Top 10 Filter dialog box (see Figure 7-34), define the view you're looking for.

In this example, you want the Bottom 50 Items (Customers), as defined by the Sum of Sales Amount field.

Figure 7-34: Specify the filter you want to apply.

4. Click OK.

5. In the Report Filter area, click the drop-down list for the Business Segment field and select Change the Filter area (see Figure 7-35).

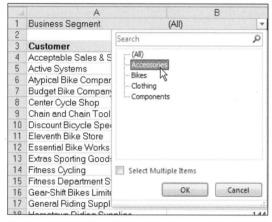

Figure 7-35: Filter your pivot table report to show Accessories.

At this point, you have exactly what you need — the 50 customers who spend the least amount of money on accessories. You can go a step further and format the report a bit by sorting on the Sum of Sales Amount and applying a currency format to the numbers (see Figure 7-36).

	A	B
1	Business Segment	Accessories
2		
3	**Customer**	**Sum of Sales Amount**
4	Mobile Outlet	$1.374
5	Efficient Cycling	$1.374
6	Racing Bike Outlet	$1.374
7	Bike Goods	$1.374
8	Cycle Merchants	$1.374
9	Purchase Mart	$1.374
10	Vigorous Sports Store	$2.748
11	Closest Bicycle Store	$2.994
12	This Area Sporting Goods	$2.994
13	The Bicycle Accessories Company	$2.994
14	Novelty Bikes	$4.122
15	Bike Products and Accessories	$4.122
16	Roadway Bicycle Supply	$4.77
17	Transport Bikes	$4.77

Figure 7-36: Your final report.

Note that because you built this view using a pivot table, you can now filter according to any new field. For example, you can add the Market field to the Report Filter area to get the 50 United Kingdom customers who spend the least amount of money on accessories. This, my friends, is the power of using pivot tables for the basis of your dashboards and reports. Continue to play around with the Top 10 filter option to see what kind of reports you can come up with (see Figure 7-37).

	A	B
1	SubRegion	United Kingdom
2	Business Segment	Accessories
3		
4	**Customer**	**Sum of Sales Amount**
5	Vigorous Sports Store	$2.75
6	Closest Bicycle Store	$2.99
7	Exclusive Bicycle Mart	$15.00
8	Extended Tours	$20.19
9	Instruments and Parts Company	$20.99
10	Tachometers and Accessories	$23.18
11	Metropolitan Bicycle Supply	$25.76
12	Number One Bike Co.	$29.73
13	Nearby Cycle Shop	$35.99
14	Metro Metals Co.	$46.11
15	Cycles Wholesaler & Mfg.	$375.53
16	Cycling Goods	$432.54
17	Exceptional Cycle Services	$757.72
18	Channel Outlet	$918.44
19	Express Bike Services	$1,718.19
20	Downhill Bicycle Specialists	$1,915.21
21	Uttermost Bike Shop	$3,806.93
22	Bulk Discount Store	$4,067.01
23	Commerce Bicycle Specialists	$4,435.70
24	Action Bicycle Specialists	$4,861.49
25	Exhibition Showroom	$5,723.12
26	Riding Cycles	$6,459.01
27	Prosperous Tours	$7,486.63
28	**Grand Total**	**$43,180.22**

Figure 7-37: You can easily adapt this report to produce any combination of views.

Note

You may notice that in Figure 7-37, the bottom 50 view is showing only 23 records. This is because there are fewer than 50 customers in the United Kingdom market that have accessories sales. Because I asked for the bottom 50, Excel shows up to 50 accounts; but fewer if there are fewer than 50. If there's a tie for any rank in the bottom 50, Excel shows you all the tied records.

You can remove the applied filters in your pivot tables by taking these actions:

1. Click anywhere inside your pivot table to activate the PivotTable Tools context tab in the Ribbon.

2. Click the Options tab.

3. Select the Clear icon and select Clear Filters, as shown in Figure 7-38.

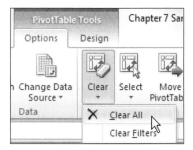

Figure 7-38: Select Clear Filters to remove the applied filters in a field.

Creating views by month, quarter, and year

Raw transactional data is rarely aggregated by month, quarter, or year for you. This type of data is often captured by the day. However, people often want reports by month or quarters instead of detail by day. Fortunately, pivot tables make it easy to group date fields into various time dimensions. Here's how:

1. Build a pivot table with Sales Date in the Row Labels area and Sales Amount in the Values area, similar to the one in Figure 7-39.

	A	B
1	Region	(All) ▾
2		
3	**SalesDate** ▾	**Sum of Sales Amount**
4	01/01/08	$22,889
5	01/02/08	$26,794
6	01/03/08	$14,118
7	01/04/08	$19,905
8	01/05/08	$26,170
9	01/06/08	$11,550
10	01/07/08	$47,136
11	01/08/08	$9,646
12	01/09/08	$25,337
13	01/10/08	$12,577
14	01/11/08	$31,988
15	01/12/08	$33,923
16	01/13/08	$27,343

Figure 7-39: Build this pivot table to start.

2. Right-click any date and select Group, as shown in Figure 7-40.

   The Grouping dialog box appears, as shown in Figure 7-41.

3. Select the time dimensions that you want.

   In this example, you can select Months, Quarters, and Years.

4. Click OK.

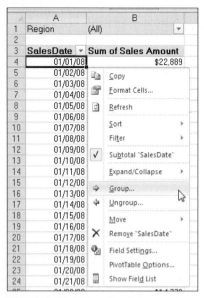

Figure 7-40: Select the Group option.

Figure 7-41: Select the time dimensions that suit your needs.

Here are several interesting things to note about the resulting pivot table. First, notice that Quarters and Years has been added to your field list. Keep in mind that your source data hasn't changed to include these new fields; instead, these fields are now part of your pivot table. Another interesting thing to note is that by default, the Years and Quarters fields are automatically added next to the original date field in the pivot table layout, as shown in Figure 7-42.

	A	B	C	D
1	Region	(All)		
2				
3	Years	Quarters	SalesDate	Sum of Sales Amount
4	⊟2008	⊟Qtr1	Jan	$713,230
5			Feb	$1,682,318
6			Mar	$1,673,760
7		⊟Qtr2	Apr	$872,568
8			May	$2,280,165
9			Jun	$1,102,021
10		⊟Qtr3	Jul	$2,446,798
11			Aug	$3,615,926
12			Sep	$2,826,440
13		⊟Qtr4	Oct	$1,872,402
14			Nov	$2,939,785
15			Dec	$2,303,436
16	⊟2009	⊟Qtr1	Jan	$1,318,597
17			Feb	$2,166,151
18			Mar	$1,784,231
19		⊟Qtr2	Apr	$1,829,387
20			May	$2,921,701
21			Jun	$1,932,251
22		⊟Qtr3	Jul	$2,788,963

Figure 7-42: Your pivot table is now grouped by Years and Quarters.

After your date field is grouped, you can use each added time grouping just as you would any other field in your pivot table. In Figure 7-43, I use the newly created time groupings to show sales for each market by quarter for 2009.

	A	B	C	D	E	F	G
1	Region	(All)					
2							
3	Sum of Sales Amount	Years	Quarters				
4		⊟2008				⊟2009	
5	Market	Qtr1	Qtr2	Qtr3	Qtr4	Qtr1	Qtr2
6	Australia						
7	Canada	$775,872	$815,729	$1,865,639	$1,404,792	$1,009,221	$1,339
8	Central	$465,867	$601,948	$845,727	$722,191	$561,981	$68
9	France			$523,411	$337,497	$238,879	$330
10	Germany						
11	Northeast	$287,219	$329,247	$973,594	$863,718	$669,898	$849
12	Northwest	$859,414	$724,407	$1,024,777	$893,999	$683,557	$79
13	Southeast	$670,885	$755,142	$777,236	$635,278	$477,565	$59
14	Southwest	$1,010,051	$1,028,280	$2,406,226	$1,886,450	$1,353,951	$1,80
15	United Kingdom			$472,553	$371,696	$273,927	$28
16	Grand Total	$4,069,309	$4,254,754	$8,889,163	$7,115,622	$5,268,979	$6,683

Figure 7-43: You can use your newly created time dimensions just like a normal pivot field.

Creating a percent distribution view

A percent distribution (or percent contribution) view allows you to see how much of the total is made up of a specific data item. This view is useful when you're trying to measure the general impact of a particular item.

The pivot table, as shown in Figure 7-44, gives you a view into the percent of sales that comes from each business segment. Here, you can tell that bikes make up 81 percent of Canada's sales whereas only 77 percent of France's sales come from bikes.

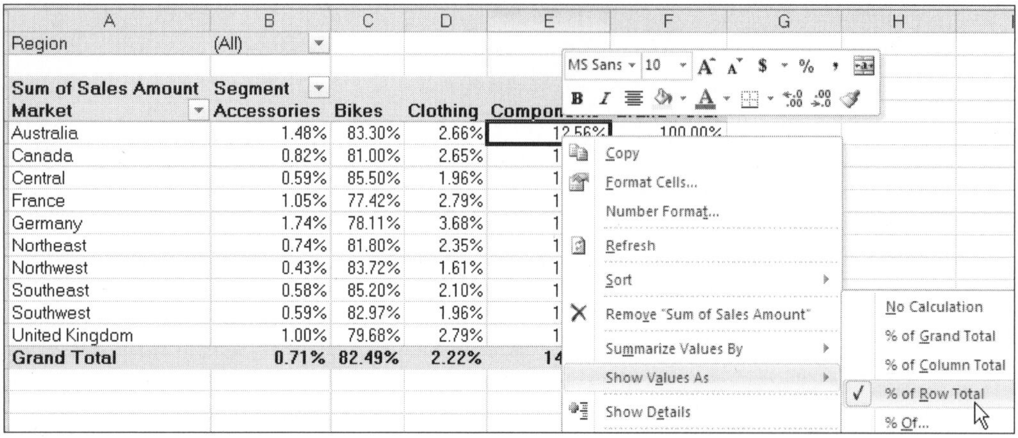

	A	B	C	D	E	F	G	H
Region	(All)							
Sum of Sales Amount	Segment							
Market	Accessories	Bikes	Clothing	Compon...				
Australia	1.48%	83.30%	2.66%	12.56%	100.00%			
Canada	0.82%	81.00%	2.65%	1		Copy		
Central	0.59%	85.50%	1.96%	1		Format Cells...		
France	1.05%	77.42%	2.79%	1		Number Format...		
Germany	1.74%	78.11%	3.68%	1				
Northeast	0.74%	81.80%	2.35%	1		Refresh		
Northwest	0.43%	83.72%	1.61%	1				
Southeast	0.58%	85.20%	2.10%	1		Sort		
Southwest	0.59%	82.97%	1.96%	1		Remove "Sum of Sales Amount"		No Calculation
United Kingdom	1.00%	79.68%	2.79%	1				% of Grand Total
Grand Total	0.71%	82.49%	2.22%	14		Summarize Values By		% of Column Total
						Show Values As		% of Row Total
						Show Details		% Of...

Figure 7-44: This view shows percent of total for the row.

You'll also notice in Figure 7-44 that this view was created by selecting the % of Row option in the Value Field Settings dialog box. Here are the steps to create this type of view:

1. Right-click any value within the target field.

   For example, if you want to change the settings for the Sales Amount field, right-click any value under that field.

2. Select Show Values As.

3. Select % of Row.

The pivot table in Figure 7-45 gives you a view into the percent of sales that comes from each market. Here, you have the same type of view, but this time, you use the % of Column option.

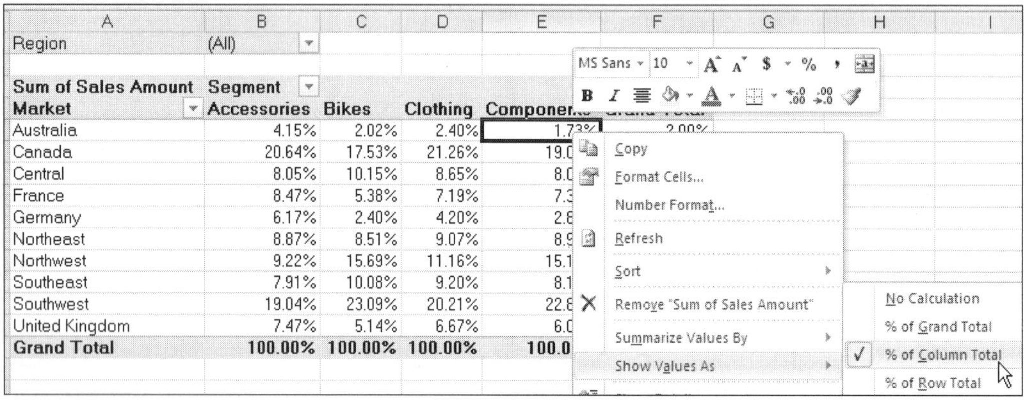

	A	B	C	D	E	F	G	H	I
Region	(All)								
Sum of Sales Amount	Segment								
Market	Accessories	Bikes	Clothing	Componen...					
Australia	4.15%	2.02%	2.40%	1.73%	2.00%				
Canada	20.64%	17.53%	21.26%	19.0		Copy			
Central	8.05%	10.15%	8.65%	8.0		Format Cells...			
France	8.47%	5.38%	7.19%	7.3		Number Format...			
Germany	6.17%	2.40%	4.20%	2.8					
Northeast	8.87%	8.51%	9.07%	8.9		Refresh			
Northwest	9.22%	15.69%	11.16%	15.1					
Southeast	7.91%	10.08%	9.20%	8.1		Sort			
Southwest	19.04%	23.09%	20.21%	22.8		Remove "Sum of Sales Amount"		No Calculation
United Kingdom	7.47%	5.14%	6.67%	6.0				% of Grand Total
Grand Total	100.00%	100.00%	100.00%	100.0		Summarize Values By		% of Column Total
						Show Values As		% of Row Total

Figure 7-45: This view shows percent of total for the column.

Again, remember that because you built these views in a pivot table, you have the flexibility to slice the data by region, bring in new fields, rearrange data, and most importantly, refresh this view when new data comes in.

Creating a YTD totals view

Sometimes, it's useful to capture a running totals view to analyze the movement of numbers on a year-to-date (YTD) basis. Figure 7-46 illustrates a pivot table that shows a running total of revenue by month for each year. In this view, you can see where the YTD sales stand at any given month in each year. For example, you can see that in August 2010, revenues were about a million dollars lower than the same point in 2009.

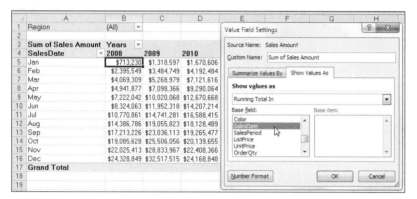

Figure 7-46: This view shows a running total of sales for each month.

Note In the sample data for this chapter, you don't see Months and Years. You have to create them by grouping the SalesDate field. Feel free to review the "Creating views by month, quarter, and year" section earlier in this chapter to find out how.

To create this type of view, follow these steps:

1. Right-click any value within the target field.

   For example, if you want to change the settings for the Sales Amount field, right-click any value under that field.

2. Select Value Field Settings.

   The Value Field Settings dialog box appears.

3. Click the Show Values As tab.

4. Select Running Total In from the drop-down list.

5. In the Base Field list, select the field that you want the running totals to be calculated against.

   In most cases, this would be a time series such as, in this example, the SalesDate field.

6. Click OK.

Creating a month-over-month variance view

Another commonly requested view is a month-over-month variance. How did this month's sales compare to last month's sales? The best way to create these types of views is to show the raw number and the percent variance together.

In that light, you can start creating this view by building a pivot table similar to the one shown in Figure 7-47. Notice that you bring in the Sales Amount field twice. One of these remains untouched, showing the raw data. The other is changed to show the month-over-month variance.

	A	B	C
1	Years	2010	
2			
3		Values	
4	SalesDate	Sum of Sales Amount	Sum of Sales Amount2
5	Jan	$1,670,606	$1,670,606
6	Feb	$2,521,878	$2,521,878
7	Mar	$2,929,133	$2,929,133
8	Apr	$2,168,448	$2,168,448
9	May	$3,380,604	$3,380,604
10	Jun	$1,536,545	$1,536,545
11	Jul	$2,381,202	$2,381,202
12	Aug	$1,540,073	$1,540,073
13	Sep	$1,136,989	$1,136,989
14	Oct	$874,178	$874,178
15	Nov	$2,268,711	$2,268,711
16	Dec	$1,760,483	$1,760,483
17	Grand Total	$24,168,848	$24,168,848

Figure 7-47: Build a pivot table that contains the Sum of Sales Amount twice.

Figure 7-48 illustrates the settings that convert the second Sum of Sales Amount field into a month-over-month variance calculation.

As you can see, after applying these settings, the pivot table gives you a nice view of raw sales dollar and the variance over last month. You can obviously change the field names (see the "Renaming the fields" section earlier in this chapter) to reflect the appropriate labels for each column.

Note

In the sample data for this chapter, you don't see Months and Years. You have to create them by grouping the SalesDate field. Feel free to review the section, "Creating views by month, quarter, and year," earlier in this chapter to find out how.

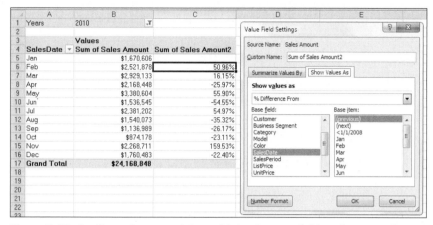

Figure 7-48: Configure the second Sum of Sales Amount field to show month-over-month variance.

To create the view in Figure 7-48, follow these steps:

1. Right-click any value within the target field.

   In this case, the target field is the second Sum of Sales Amount field.

2. Select Value Field Settings.

   The Value Field Settings dialog box appears.

3. Click the Show Values As tab.

4. Select % Difference From from the drop-down list.

5. In the Base Field list, select the field that you want the running totals to be calculated against.

   In most cases, this is a time series like, in this example, the SalesDate field.

6. In the Base Item list, select the item you want to compare against when calculating the percent variance. In this example, you want to calculate each month's variance to the previous month. Therefore, select the (previous) item.

8

Using Pivot Charts

In This Chapter

- Creating a pivot chart from a pivot table
- Specifying pivot chart commands
- Adding Excel's new slicers feature
- Viewing pivot chart examples

Chapter 7 introduces you to pivot tables. And this chapter covers a spin-off feature: pivot charts. The discussion here assumes that you're familiar with the material presented in Chapter 7.

A *pivot chart* is a graphical representation of a data summary displayed in a pivot table. A pivot chart is always based on a pivot table. Excel lets you create a pivot table and a pivot chart at the same time, but you can't create a pivot chart without a pivot table.

Getting Started with Pivot Charts

If you're familiar with creating charts in Excel, you'll have no problem creating and customizing pivot charts. Most of Excel's charting features are available in a pivot chart. But, as you'll see, pivot charts enable a few extra tricks — most notably, the ability to filter the data that's displayed.

 For an introduction to Excel chart basics, refer to Part II.

Cross-Ref

Creating a pivot chart

Excel provides three ways to create a pivot chart:

> Select any cell in an existing pivot table and choose PivotTable Tools → Options → Tools → Pivot Chart.

> Choose Insert → Tables → Pivot Table → Pivot Chart. Excel creates a pivot table and a pivot chart.

➤ Select any cell in an existing pivot table and select a chart type from the Insert ➔ Charts group.

Tip

A pivot chart cannot be a scatter chart, a bubble chart, or a stock chart. If you specify any of these chart types, Excel displays an error message.

The method you choose to create a PivotChart is up to you. Most people create the pivot table first, and then create a pivot chart from the pivot table. If you create the pivot table and pivot chart at the same time, the chart may get in the way while you're constructing the pivot table.

Note

A pivot chart is always based on a pivot table. You can't create a pivot chart without an underlying pivot table. Also, a pivot chart always reflects the current layout of the pivot table. If you change the layout of a pivot table, the layout of its corresponding pivot chart also changes. And it works in the opposite direction. If you apply filtering to a pivot chart, its corresponding pivot table displays the same filtering.

You can create multiple pivot charts from a single pivot table, and you can manipulate and format the charts separately. However, all the charts display the same data.

If you have a pivot chart and you delete the underlying pivot table, the pivot chart remains intact. The chart's SERIES formulas contain the original data, stored in arrays.

A pivot chart example

Figure 8-1 shows a pivot table created from the data used in Chapter 7. This pivot table summarizes total sales by Market. The pivot table layout is:

➤ Region: A Report Filter

➤ Segment: A Report Filter

➤ Market: Row Labels

➤ Sales Amount: Values

The two report filters in this figure are set to display all data. In other words, no filtering is in effect.

On the Web

You can find the example file for this section on the book's companion Web site at `wiley.com/go/exceldr` **in the workbook named** `Chapter 7 Sample Data.xlsx`.

	A	B	C	D
1				
2		Region	(All)	▼
3		Segment	(All)	▼
4				
5		**Market**	▼	**Sales Amount**
6		Australia	1,622,869	
7		Canada	14,463,280	
8		Central	7,932,852	
9		France	4,647,454	
10		Germany	2,051,548	
11		Northeast	6,956,674	
12		Northwest	12,523,063	
13		Southeast	7,908,318	
14		Southwest	18,598,027	
15		United Kingdom	4,311,127	
16				
17				
18				

Figure 8-1: A pivot table that you'll use to create a pivot chart.

To create a pivot chart, select any cell in the pivot table and choose PivotTable Tools ➜ Options ➜ Tools ➜ Pivot Chart. Excel displays its Insert Chart dialog box, from which you can choose a chart type (see Figure 8-2). For this example, select a standard bar chart and click OK. Excel creates the pivot chart shown in Figure 8-3.

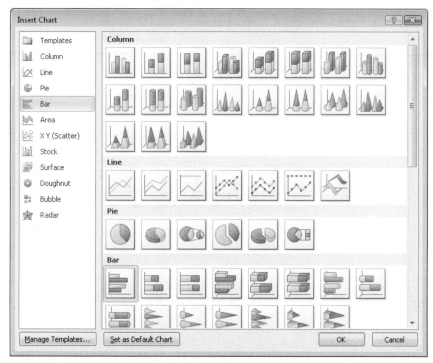

Figure 8-2: Selecting a chart type for the pivot chart.

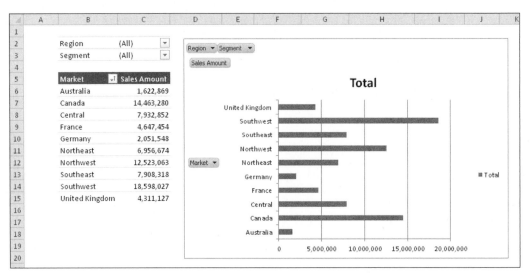

Figure 8-3: The pivot chart uses the data displayed in the pivot table.

The chart displays the values from the pivot table. But, unlike a standard chart, the pivot chart includes some field buttons, used to filter the data. The field buttons in the pivot chart correspond to the filtering controls in the pivot table.

As you might expect, you can use the field buttons to change the data displayed in the chart. These drop-down controls work just like the drop-down lists in a pivot table. Figure 8-4 shows the pivot chart after applying two filter operations: Region is Europe, and Segment is Bikes. Notice that the filtering is also shown in the pivot table. This is an example of how a pivot table and a pivot chart work together. You could also perform the filtering in the pivot table, rather than in the chart. The result would be the same.

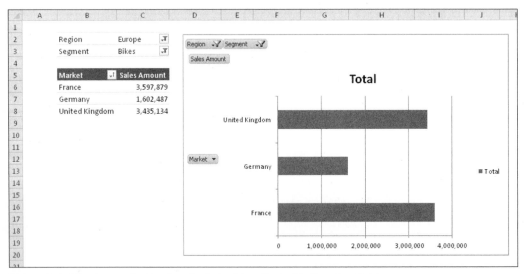

Figure 8-4: Filtering applied to the pivot chart is reflected in the pivot table.

Working with Pivot Charts

When you select a pivot chart, the Ribbon displays a contextual tab: PivotChart Tools. The commands in the Design, Layout, and Format tabs are virtually identical to those for a standard chart, so you're in familiar territory. The commands in the Analyze tab contain a few commands specific to pivot charts.

Hiding field buttons

The field buttons on a pivot chart may seem a bit redundant if the pivot chart is next to the pivot table. The filters in the pivot table display exactly the same information.

If you prefer not to see the field buttons, you can turn them off. Use the PivotChart Tools ➜ Analyze ➜ Show/Hide ➜ Field Buttons command. This command displays a drop-down list, so you can choose which field buttons to hide. Or, just right-click a field button and choose Hide from the shortcut menu. Figure 8-5 shows a pivot chart with the field buttons hidden.

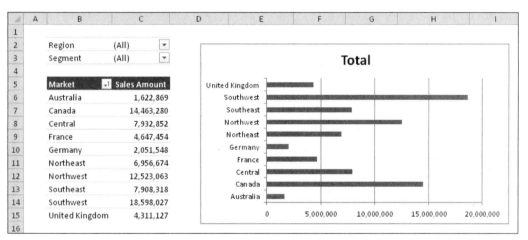

Figure 8-5: A pivot chart, sans field buttons.

Moving a pivot chart

By default, pivot charts are embedded in the worksheet that contains the pivot table. To move the pivot chart to a different worksheet (or to a chart sheet), choose PivotChart ➜ Tools ➜ Design ➜ Location ➜ Move Chart. In the Move Chart dialog box, specify the new location for the pivot chart.

If you move a pivot chart to a chart sheet, you probably want to keep the field buttons visible. Otherwise, filtering the pivot chart requires re-activating the worksheet that contains the pivot table.

Working with slicers

Excel 2010 introduced a new pivot table feature called slicers.

A *slicer* is an interactive control that simplifies filtering data in a pivot table (and in a pivot chart). Figure 8-6 shows a pivot table and pivot chart with two slicers. The slicers are positioned below the chart. Each slicer represents a particular field. In this case, the slicers represent the Region and the Segment fields. The pivot table (and pivot chart) show the sales for the North America region, for the Bikes and Clothing segments.

You can use slicers to create an attractive and interactive interface for people who might not understand how to filter data in a pivot table.

Tip

The same type of filtering can be accomplished by using the field buttons in the pivot table or the pivot chart.

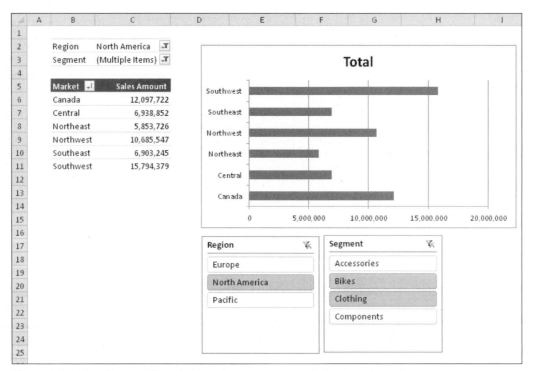

Figure 8-6: Using slicers to filter the data that you want to display in a pivot chart.

Adding slicers

To add one or more slicers to a worksheet, start by selecting any cell in a pivot table. Then choose PivotTable Tools ➜ Options ➜ Sort & Filter ➜ Insert Slicer. The Insert Slicers dialog box appears, with a list of all the fields in the pivot table (see Figure 8-7). Select the slicers that you want, and then click OK.

Figure 8-7: Selecting slicers for a pivot table.

Customizing slicers

Slicers are essentially graphic objects that float on the worksheet. They can be moved and resized, and you can change their appearance. When you select a slicer, Excel displays the Slicer Tools contextual tab. Use the tools on this tab to change the style and make other adjustments to the slicers.

Filtering slicers

The number of buttons on a slicer depends on the number of items in the field. To filter the data, just click a button in the slicer. To filter by multiple values, press and hold Ctrl while you click.

To remove the effects of filtering by a particular slicer, select the Clear Filter icon in the slicer's upper-right corner (or press Alt+C while the slicer is selected).

More Pivot Chart Examples

The following sections contain a variety of pivot chart examples that use account data from a bank. A portion of the data is shown in Figure 8-8.

This table consists of a month's worth of new account information for a three-branch bank. The table contains 712 rows, and each row represents a new account. The table has the following columns:

➤ The date the account was opened

➤ The day of the week the account was opened

➤ The opening amount

➤ The account type (CD, checking, savings, or IRA)

➤ Who opened the account (a teller or a new-account representative)

➤ The branch at which it was opened (Central, Westside, or North County)

➤ The type of customer (an existing customer or a new customer)

	A	B	C	D	E	F	G
1	Date	Weekday	Amount	AcctType	OpenedBy	Branch	Customer
2	Oct-01	Friday	5,000	IRA	New Accts	Central	Existing
3	Oct-01	Friday	14,571	CD	Teller	Central	New
4	Oct-01	Friday	500	Checking	New Accts	Central	Existing
5	Oct-01	Friday	15,000	CD	New Accts	Central	Existing
6	Oct-01	Friday	4,623	Savings	New Accts	North County	Existing
7	Oct-01	Friday	8,721	Savings	New Accts	Westside	New
8	Oct-01	Friday	15,276	Savings	New Accts	North County	Existing
9	Oct-01	Friday	5,000	Savings	New Accts	Westside	Existing
10	Oct-01	Friday	15,759	CD	Teller	Westside	Existing
11	Oct-01	Friday	12,000	CD	New Accts	Westside	Existing
12	Oct-01	Friday	7,177	Savings	Teller	North County	Existing
13	Oct-01	Friday	6,837	Savings	New Accts	Westside	Existing
14	Oct-01	Friday	3,171	Checking	New Accts	Westside	Existing
15	Oct-01	Friday	50,000	Savings	New Accts	Central	Existing
16	Oct-01	Friday	4,690	Checking	New Accts	North County	New
17	Oct-01	Friday	12,438	Checking	New Accts	Central	Existing
18	Oct-01	Friday	5,000	Checking	New Accts	North County	Existing
19	Oct-01	Friday	7,000	Savings	New Accts	North County	New
20	Oct-01	Friday	11,957	Checking	New Accts	Central	Existing
21	Oct-01	Friday	13,636	CD	New Accts	North County	Existing
22	Oct-01	Friday	16,000	CD	New Accts	Central	New
23	Oct-01	Friday	5,879	Checking	New Accts	Central	Existing
24	Oct-01	Friday	4,000	Savings	New Accts	Central	Existing
25	Oct-01	Friday	10,000	CD	Teller	North County	Existing
26	Oct-01	Friday	7,427	Checking	New Accts	North County	Existing
27	Oct-01	Friday	4,500	Checking	New Accts	North County	New
28	Oct-01	Friday	12,962	Checking	Teller	Central	Existing
29	Oct-01	Friday	500	Checking	New Accts	Central	New
30	Oct-01	Friday	5,364	Checking	Teller	Central	New
31	Oct-01	Friday	45,000	CD	Teller	North County	Existing
32	Oct-01	Friday	14,867	Checking	Teller	North County	Existing
33	Oct-01	Friday	13,061	Checking	Teller	Central	New
34	Oct-01	Friday	11,779	CD	Teller	Central	New
35	Oct-02	Saturday	4,995	Checking	New Accts	Central	New
36	Oct-02	Saturday	10,096	Savings	New Accts	Central	New
37	Oct-02	Saturday	14,861	Savings	New Accts	Central	New
38	Oct-02	Saturday	500	Checking	Teller	Central	New
39	Oct-02	Saturday	5,524	Checking	New Accts	Central	Existing
40	Oct-02	Saturday	5,863	Savings	Teller	North County	New

Figure 8-8: Bank account data to demonstrate pivot tables and pivot charts.

On the Web **The examples in the following sections are available on the companion Web site for this book at** www.wiley.com/go/exceldr **in the workbook named** bank account examples.xlsx.

The bank accounts table contains quite a bit of information. In its current form, though, the data doesn't reveal much. To make the data more useful, you need to summarize it. Summarizing a table is essentially the process of answering questions about the data. Following are a few questions that may be of interest to the bank's management:

> ➤ What is the daily total new deposit amount for each branch?

> ➤ Which day of the week accounts for the most deposits?

> ➤ How many accounts were opened at each branch, broken down by account type?

> ➤ What's the dollar distribution of the different account types?

> ➤ What types of accounts do tellers open most often?

> ➤ How does the Central branch compare with the other two branches?

> ➤ In which branch do tellers open the most checking accounts for new customers?

You can, of course, spend time sorting the data and creating formulas to answer these questions. But almost always, a pivot table is a better choice. Creating a pivot table takes only a few seconds, doesn't require a single formula, and produces a nice-looking report. In addition, pivot tables are much less prone to error than creating formulas.

The sections that follow use pivot tables to answer these questions, and each pivot table has an accompanying pivot chart to better display the data.

Question 1

What is the daily total new deposit amount for each branch?

Figure 8-9 shows the pivot table and pivot chart that answers this question.

> ➤ The Branch field is in the Column Labels area.

> ➤ The Date field is in the Row Labels area.

> ➤ The Amount field is in the Values area and is summarized by Sum.

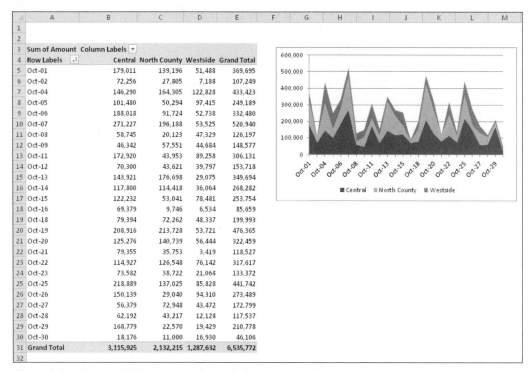

	Central	North County	Westside	Grand Total
Sum of Amount Column Labels				
Row Labels	Central	North County	Westside	Grand Total
Oct-01	179,011	139,196	51,488	369,695
Oct-02	72,256	27,805	7,188	107,249
Oct-04	146,290	164,305	122,828	433,423
Oct-05	101,480	50,294	97,415	249,189
Oct-06	188,018	91,724	52,738	332,480
Oct-07	271,227	196,188	53,525	520,940
Oct-08	58,745	20,123	47,329	126,197
Oct-09	46,342	57,551	44,684	148,577
Oct-11	172,920	43,953	89,258	306,131
Oct-12	70,300	43,621	39,797	153,718
Oct-13	143,921	176,698	29,075	349,694
Oct-14	117,800	114,418	36,064	268,282
Oct-15	122,232	53,041	78,481	253,754
Oct-16	69,379	9,746	6,534	85,659
Oct-18	79,394	72,262	48,337	199,993
Oct-19	208,916	213,728	53,721	476,365
Oct-20	125,276	140,739	56,444	322,459
Oct-21	79,355	35,753	3,419	118,527
Oct-22	114,927	126,548	76,142	317,617
Oct-23	73,582	38,722	21,068	133,372
Oct-25	218,889	137,025	85,828	441,742
Oct-26	150,139	29,040	94,310	273,489
Oct-27	56,379	72,948	43,472	172,799
Oct-28	62,192	43,217	12,128	117,537
Oct-29	168,779	22,570	19,429	210,778
Oct-30	18,176	11,000	16,930	46,106
Grand Total	**3,115,925**	**2,132,215**	**1,287,632**	**6,535,772**

Figure 8-9: This pivot table shows daily totals for each branch.

The pivot chart is a stacked area chart. However, it's not a very good chart because there's just too much data. This is a perfect candidate for filtering — and adding a slicer makes it very easy to filter the data to show only one branch at a time. Figure 8-10 shows the chart after adding a slicer, positioned below the pivot chart. The daily data for one branch (Central) is displayed.

Also, note that you can sort the pivot table by any column. For example, you can sort the Grand Total column in descending order to find out which day of the month had the largest amount of new funds. To sort, just right-click any cell in the column to sort and choose Sort from the short-cut menu. Note that this change to the pivot table also changes the pivot chart.

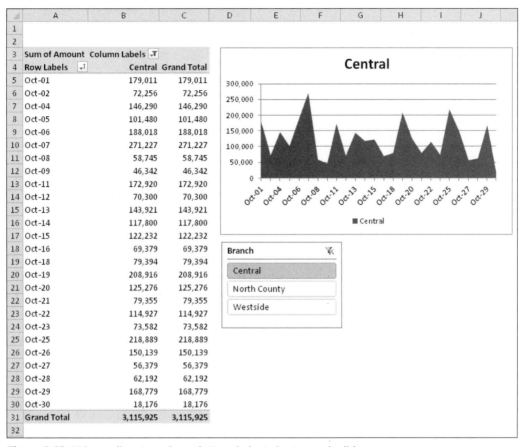

	A	B	C
3	Sum of Amount	Column Labels	
4	Row Labels	Central	Grand Total
5	Oct-01	179,011	179,011
6	Oct-02	72,256	72,256
7	Oct-04	146,290	146,290
8	Oct-05	101,480	101,480
9	Oct-06	188,018	188,018
10	Oct-07	271,227	271,227
11	Oct-08	58,745	58,745
12	Oct-09	46,342	46,342
13	Oct-11	172,920	172,920
14	Oct-12	70,300	70,300
15	Oct-13	143,921	143,921
16	Oct-14	117,800	117,800
17	Oct-15	122,232	122,232
18	Oct-16	69,379	69,379
19	Oct-18	79,394	79,394
20	Oct-19	208,916	208,916
21	Oct-20	125,276	125,276
22	Oct-21	79,355	79,355
23	Oct-22	114,927	114,927
24	Oct-23	73,582	73,582
25	Oct-25	218,889	218,889
26	Oct-26	150,139	150,139
27	Oct-27	56,379	56,379
28	Oct-28	62,192	62,192
29	Oct-29	168,779	168,779
30	Oct-30	18,176	18,176
31	Grand Total	3,115,925	3,115,925

Figure 8-10: Using a slicer to make a cluttered pivot chart more legible.

Question 2

How many accounts were opened at each branch, broken down by account type?

Figure 8-11 shows a pivot table that answers this question with numbers, and a pivot chart that answers it graphically.

> ➤ The AcctType field is in the Column Labels area.
> ➤ The Branch field is in the Row Labels area.
> ➤ The Amount field is in the Values area and is summarized by Count.

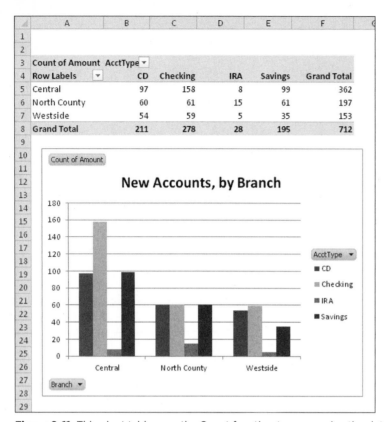

Row Labels	CD	Checking	IRA	Savings	Grand Total
Central	97	158	8	99	362
North County	60	61	15	61	197
Westside	54	59	5	35	153
Grand Total	211	278	28	195	712

Figure 8-11: This pivot table uses the Count function to summarize the data.

Notice that the summary function for the Amount fields is Count, not Sum. To change the summary function to Count, right-click any cell in the Value area and choose Summarize Data By ➔ Count from the shortcut menu.

What if you wanted a second chart (a pie chart) to show the data in the Grand Total column? You can't create a pivot chart from only a portion of the pivot table. To create this pie chart, you need to remove the Branch field from the pivot table and move the AcctType field to the Row Labels area. If you would like to show both charts together, you must create a second pivot table (or make a copy of the original one) and generate the pie chart from the second pivot table. Figure 8-12 shows the pivot table and pivot chart that show the number of accounts by account type.

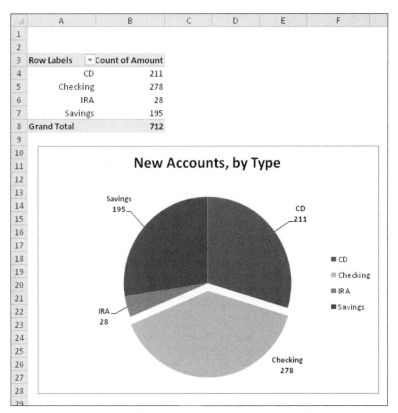

Figure 8-12: This pivot table and pivot chart show the number of new accounts by type, across all branches.

Question 3

What's the dollar distribution of the different account types?

Figure 8-13 shows a pivot table that answers this question. For example, 234 of the new accounts were for an amount of $4,999 or less.

This pivot table uses only one field: Amount.

> ➤ The Amount field is in the Row Labels area (grouped).

> ➤ The Amount field is also in the Values area and is summarized by Count.

When the Amount field was added to the Row Labels section, the pivot table showed a row for each unique dollar amount. To group the values, right-click one of the row labels and select Group. Then use the Grouping dialog box to set up bins of $5,000 increments.

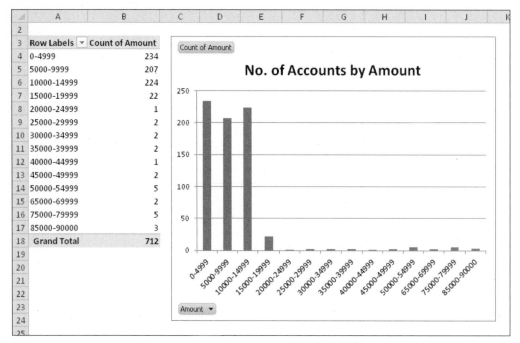

Figure 8-13: This pivot table counts the number of accounts that fall into each value range.

The second instance of the Amount field (in the Values area) was originally summarized by Count. To change the summarize method, right-click a value and choose Summarize Values By ➜ Count.

Notice that the number of accounts for the larger dollar amounts is small. You may prefer to change the grouping so the larger amounts are in a single bin of 20,001 or more. To do so, right-click any cell in the Row Labels column and select Group. In the Grouping dialog box, specify 1 for the Start At value, 20,000 for the Ending At value, and 5,000 for the By value. Figure 8-14 shows the result. Notice that Excel incorrectly labels the last column as >20001. Technically, it should be >20000.

Question 4

What types of accounts do tellers open most often?

Figure 8-15 shows that the most common account opened by tellers is a checking account.

➤ The OpenedBy field is in the Report Filters area.

➤ The AcctType field is in the Row Labels area.

➤ The Amount field is in the Values area (summarized by Count).

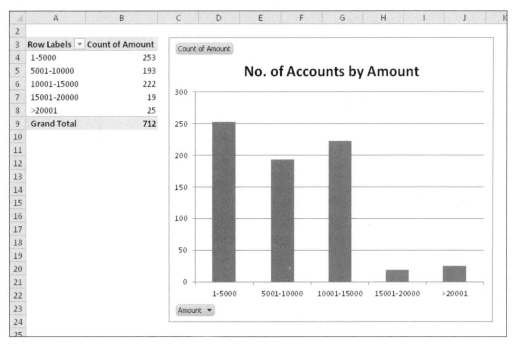

Figure 8-14: The pivot table and pivot chart after changing the grouping parameters.

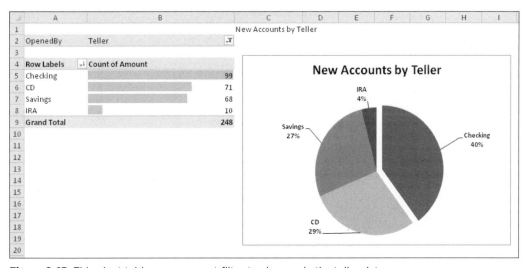

Figure 8-15: This pivot table uses a report filter to show only the teller data.

This pivot table uses the OpenedBy field as a report filter and is showing the data only for tellers. The pivot table rows are sorted so that the largest value is at the top. Column B used conditional formatting data bars as another way to display the counts graphically.

Note that the pivot chart's title is linked to cell C1, which contains this formula:

```
="New Accounts By "&B2
```

Using a linked formula enables you to make the chart's title more descriptive. If you select a different value for the Report Filter field, the chart's title updates accordingly. Without the linked formula, the pivot chart's title would always display "Total".

Question 5

How does the Central branch compare to the other two branches?

Figure 8-16 shows a pivot table that sheds some light on this rather vague question. It simply shows how the Central branch compares to the other two branches combined.

➤ The AcctType field is in the Row Labels area.

➤ The Branch field is in the Column Labels area.

➤ The Amount field is in the Values area, summarized by Sum.

The North County and Westside branches are grouped together and named Other Branches. The pivot table (and pivot chart) shows the amount, by account type.

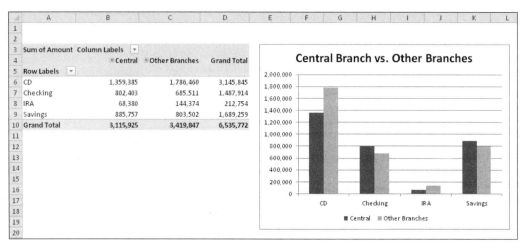

Figure 8-16: This pivot table (and pivot chart) compares the Central branch with the other two branches combined.

Question 6

In which branch do tellers open the most checking accounts for new customers?

Figure 8-17 shows a pivot table that answers this question. At the Central branch, tellers opened 23 checking accounts for new customers.

> ➤ The Customer field is in the Report Filters area.

> ➤ The OpenedBy field is in the Report Filters area.

> ➤ The AcctType field is in the Report Filters area.

> ➤ The Branch field is in the Row Labels area.

> ➤ The Amount field is in the Values area, summarized by Count.

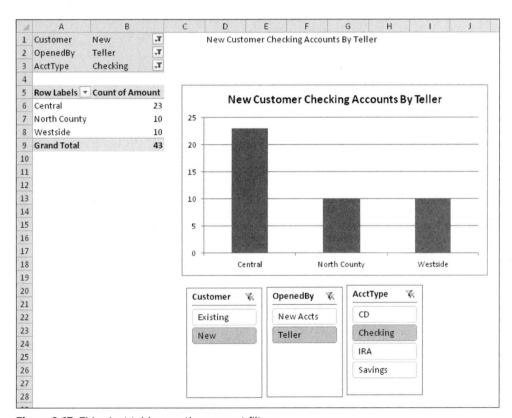

Figure 8-17: This pivot table uses three report filters.

This pivot table uses three report filters. The Customer field is filtered to show only New, the OpenedBy field is filtered to show only Teller, and the AcctType field is filtered to show only Checking. Three slicers have been added below the pivot chart, so the user has the option of changing the Report Filters directly, or clicking the buttons in the slicers.

The pivot table depicts the result graphically. Note that we used a linked formula for the pivot chart's title to make the title more descriptive. The title is linked to cell D1, which contains the following formula that gets information from the three report filters:

```
=B1&" Customer "&B3&" Accounts By "&B2
```

Creating a Frequency Distribution Chart

The example in this section describes how to use a pivot table to create a frequency distribution chart, sometimes known as a histogram. This technique works with values and text.

Figure 8-18 shows a workbook with ratings from a survey item. Column A consists of the respondent number and column B contains the rating. The goal is to create a frequency distribution chart that shows the number of each rating response. Note that column A is not actually required. A frequency distribution can be created from a single column of data.

	A	B	C	D	E	F	G
1	**Respondent**	**Rating**					
2	1	Good					
3	2	Very Good					
4	3	Very Good					
5	4	Good					
6	5	Good					
7	6	Poor					
8	7	Very Poor					
9	8	Good					
10	9	Excellent					
11	10	Very Good					
12	11	Very Good					
13	12	Good					
14	13	Poor					
15	14	Excellent					
16	15	Good					
17	16	Very Good					
18	17	Excellent					
19	18	Good					
20	19	Good					
21	20	Good					

Figure 8-18: A pivot chart can display the frequency of each response in column B.

The pivot table is very simple:

➤ The Rating field is in the Row Labels area.

➤ Another instance of the Rating field is in the Values area, summarized by Count.

Figure 8-19 shows the pivot table and pivot chart.

Figure 8-19: The pivot chart displays the frequency of each response.

Notice that the Rating items are listed in alphabetical order in the pivot table, and on the category axis of the pivot chart. Normally, you would want the items to be ordered from worst to best. To change the order of the items, click and drag the left or right border of an item in the pivot table, and drag it to a new position. The pivot chart will adjust accordingly. Figure 8-20 shows the pivot chart after rearranging the items in the pivot table.

Tip

Another way to change the order of items is to just type the name of an item (for example, "Good") in the cell where you want it to be. Excel will rearrange the items.

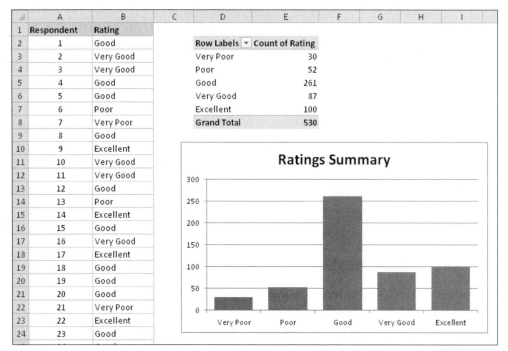

Figure 8-20: The pivot chart, after rearranging the items.

If the data consists of numerical values, you might want to create groups (or bins). To do so, right-click the field button in the pivot table and choose Group. Then specify the parameters for the grouping.

Figure 8-21 shows a frequency distribution for numeric data, with the results grouped. Note that the pivot table displays a count of the values. By default, the pivot table displays the sum. You'll need to change this by right-clicking a value in the pivot table and choosing Summarize Values By ➜ Count.

Specifying which rows to plot

This section describes how to enable the user to determine which pivot table rows to display in a pivot chart. In other words, it's an interactive chart. Figure 8-22 shows a range of data — results from a customer survey. Each of the 450 customers responded to 14 survey items. Responses are coded as numbers:

1. Strongly Disagree

2. Disagree

3. Undecided

4. Agree

5. Strongly Agree

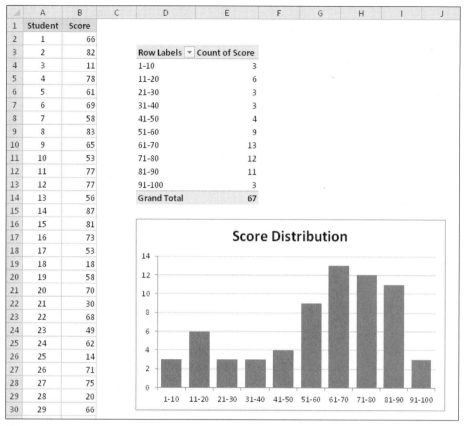

Figure 8-21: This pivot chart displays a frequency distribution for the data in column B, in groups of 10.

The examples in this section can be found at www.wiley.com/go/exceldr **in the workbook named** survey results.xlsx.

The goal is to tabulate the survey results and display a chart that depicts the results for one or more of the survey items. The first step is to create the pivot table.

➤ The Rating field is in the Column Labels area.

➤ The Item field is in the Row Labels area

➤ The Rating field is in the Values area, summarized by Count. The values are displayed as % of Row Total.

	A	B	C
1	Respondent	Item	Rating
2	1	Employees are friendly	5
3	1	Employees are helpful	2
4	1	Employees are knowledgeable	3
5	1	I like your TV ads	4
6	1	I like your web site	1
7	1	I would recommend your company	3
8	1	Overall, I am satisfied	1
9	1	Pricing is competitive	2
10	1	Store hours are convenient	3
11	1	Store locations are convenient	1
12	1	Stores are well-maintained	3
13	1	You are easy to reach by phone	1
14	1	You have a good selection of products	1
15	1	You sell quality products	2
16	2	Employees are friendly	5
17	2	Employees are helpful	3
18	2	Employees are knowledgeable	5
19	2	I like your TV ads	2
20	2	I like your web site	3
21	2	I would recommend your company	5
22	2	Overall, I am satisfied	1
23	2	Pricing is competitive	2
24	2	Store hours are convenient	3
25	2	Store locations are convenient	5
26	2	Stores are well-maintained	5
27	2	You are easy to reach by phone	3
28	2	You have a good selection of products	1

Figure 8-22: This survey data will be converted to a pivot table.

Figure 8-23 show the pivot table, along with a pivot chart.

The pivot table looks good, but the chart is a bit overwhelming. To limit the amount of information in the chart, use either of these methods:

> ➤ Select the drop-down list in the Item header in the pivot table and deselect the Select All check box. Then, select one or more items to display. The change is reflected in the pivot chart.

> ➤ Activate the pivot chart, and use the Item Field button. Deselect the Select All check box and then select one or more items to display. The change is reflected in the pivot table.

> ➤ Add a slicer for the Item field, and use the slicer to specify which item(s) to display. Slicers are available in Excel 2010 only.

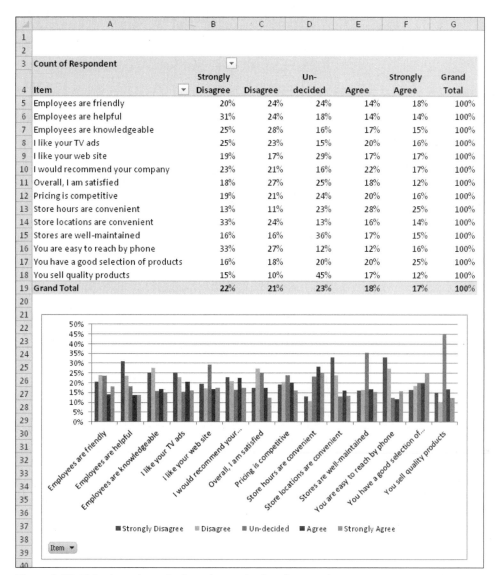

Count of Respondent						
Item	Strongly Disagree	Disagree	Un-decided	Agree	Strongly Agree	Grand Total
Employees are friendly	20%	24%	24%	14%	18%	100%
Employees are helpful	31%	24%	18%	14%	14%	100%
Employees are knowledgeable	25%	28%	16%	17%	15%	100%
I like your TV ads	25%	23%	15%	20%	16%	100%
I like your web site	19%	17%	29%	17%	17%	100%
I would recommend your company	23%	21%	16%	22%	17%	100%
Overall, I am satisfied	18%	27%	25%	18%	12%	100%
Pricing is competitive	19%	21%	24%	20%	16%	100%
Store hours are convenient	13%	11%	23%	28%	25%	100%
Store locations are convenient	33%	24%	13%	16%	14%	100%
Stores are well-maintained	16%	16%	36%	17%	15%	100%
You are easy to reach by phone	33%	27%	12%	12%	16%	100%
You have a good selection of products	16%	18%	20%	20%	25%	100%
You sell quality products	15%	10%	45%	17%	12%	100%
Grand Total	22%	21%	23%	18%	17%	100%

Figure 8-23: This pivot chart displays the results for all survey items.

Using this filtering capability, the user can show the results for any single survey item, and even compare multiple items side by side. Figure 8-24 shows the pivot table and pivot chart after adding a slicer, and filtering the data to show two survey items.

Notice that the slicer has two columns. To specify the number of columns, select the slicer and use the Columns control in the Slicer Tools ➜ Options ➜ Buttons group.

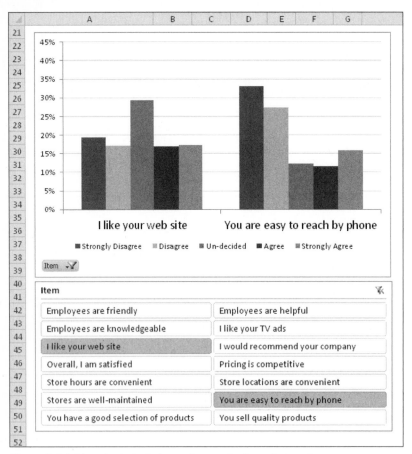

Figure 8-24: The pivot chart shows the results for only two items.

Using Excel Sparklines

In This Chapter

- Introducing the new Excel 2010 sparkline feature

- Adding sparklines to a worksheet

- Working with groups of sparklines

- Modifying your sparkline graphic

One of the new features in Excel 2010 is sparkline graphics. Sparklines were developed by visualization guru Edward Tufte. Tufte envisioned mini word-sized charts placed in and among the data that they represent. Sparklines enable you to see trends and patterns within your data at a glance using minimal space. Following the sparkline concept, Microsoft then implemented sparklines in Excel worksheets so that you can get visual context for data that does not take up a lot of real estate on your dashboard.

This chapter introduces you to sparklines, and demonstrates how you can use them as visualizations in your dashboard.

Note

Sparklines are new to Excel 2010. If you create a workbook that uses sparklines, and that workbook is opened using a previous version of Excel, the sparkline cells will be empty.

Sparklines alternatives

Sparklines is a new feature, and is available only in Excel 2010. If you don't use Excel 2010, you might want to check out some add-ins that bring sparkline features to earlier versions of Excel. Some of these products support additional sparkline types, and most have many additional customization options.

Search the Web for *sparklines excel*, and you'll find several add-ins to choose from.

Introducing Sparklines

Although sparklines look like miniature charts (and can sometimes take the place of a chart), this feature is completely separate from the Excel chart feature (for Excel chart basics, see Part II). For example, charts are placed on a worksheet's drawing layer, and a single chart can display several series of data. In contrast, a sparkline is displayed inside of a worksheet cell, and displays only one series of data.

Excel 2010 supports three types of sparklines: Line, Column, and Win/Loss. Figure 9-1 shows examples of each type of sparkline graphics, displayed in column H. Each sparkline depicts the six data points to the left.

> **Line**: Similar to a line chart, the line can display with a marker for each data point. The first group in Figure 9-1 shows Line sparklines with markers. A quick glance reveals that with the exception of Fund Number W-91, the funds have been losing value over the six-month period.

> **Column**: Similar to a column chart, the second group shows the same data with Column sparklines.

> **Win/Loss**: A binary type chart that displays each data point as a high block or a low block. The third group shows Win/Loss sparklines. Notice that the data is different. Each cell displays the *change* from the previous month. In the sparkline, each data point is depicted as a high block (win) or a low block (loss). In this example, a positive change from the previous month is a win, and a negative change from the previous month is a loss.

	A	B	C	D	E	F	G	H
1	**Line Sparklines**							
2								
3	**Fund Number**	**Jan**	**Feb**	**Mar**	**Apr**	**May**	**Jun**	**Sparklines**
4	A-13	103.98	98.92	88.12	86.34	75.58	71.2	
5	C-09	212.74	218.7	202.18	198.56	190.12	181.74	
6	K-88	75.74	73.68	69.86	60.34	64.92	59.46	
7	W-91	91.78	95.44	98.1	99.46	98.68	105.86	
8	M-03	324.48	309.14	313.1	287.82	276.24	260.9	
9								
10	**Column Sparklines**							
11								
12	**Fund Number**	**Jan**	**Feb**	**Mar**	**Apr**	**May**	**Jun**	**Sparklines**
13	A-13	103.98	98.92	88.12	86.34	75.58	71.2	
14	C-09	212.74	218.7	202.18	198.56	190.12	181.74	
15	K-88	75.74	73.68	69.86	60.34	64.92	59.46	
16	W-91	91.78	95.44	98.1	99.46	98.68	105.86	
17	M-03	324.48	309.14	313.1	287.82	276.24	260.9	
18								
19	**Win/Loss Sparklines**							
20								
21	**Fund Number**	**Jan**	**Feb**	**Mar**	**Apr**	**May**	**Jun**	**Sparklines**
22	A-13	#N/A	-5.06	-10.8	-1.78	-10.76	-4.38	
23	C-09	#N/A	5.96	-16.52	-3.62	-8.44	-8.38	
24	K-88	#N/A	-2.06	-3.82	-9.52	4.58	-5.46	
25	W-91	#N/A	3.66	2.66	1.36	-0.78	7.18	
26	M-03	#N/A	-15.34	3.96	-25.28	-11.58	-15.34	
27								

Figure 9-1: Three types of sparklines.

Creating Sparklines

Figure 9-2 shows some weather data that you can summarize with sparklines. To create sparkline graphics for the values in these nine rows, follow these steps:

1. Select the data range that you want to summarize. In this example, select B4:M12.

   If you are creating multiple sparklines, select all the data.

2. With the data selected, choose Insert ➜ Sparklines, and select one of the three sparkline types: Line, Column, or Win/Loss.

   Excel displays the Create Sparklines dialog box, as shown in Figure 9-3.

3. Specify the data range and the location for the sparklines. For this example, specify N4:N12 as the Location Range.

Typically, you'll put the sparklines next to the data, but that's not required. Most of the time, you'll use an empty range to hold the sparklines. However, Excel does not prevent you from inserting sparklines into non-empty cells. The sparkline location that you specify must match the source data in terms of number of rows or number of columns.

4. Click OK.

Excel creates the sparklines graphics of the type you specified.

	A	B	C	D	E	F	G	H	I	J	K	L	M
1	**Average Monthly Precipitation (Inches)**												
2													
3		Jan	Feb	Mar	Apr	May	Jun	Jul	Aug	Sep	Oct	Nov	Dec
4	ASHEVILLE, NC	4.06	3.83	4.59	3.50	4.41	4.38	3.87	4.30	3.72	3.17	3.82	3.39
5	BAKERSFIELD, CA	1.18	1.21	1.41	0.45	0.24	0.12	0.00	0.08	0.15	0.30	0.59	0.76
6	BATON ROUGE, LA	6.19	5.10	5.07	5.56	5.34	5.33	5.96	5.86	4.84	3.81	4.76	5.26
7	BILLINGS, MT	0.81	0.57	1.12	1.74	2.48	1.89	1.28	0.85	1.34	1.26	0.75	0.67
8	DAYTONA BEACH, FL	3.13	2.74	3.84	2.54	3.26	5.69	5.17	6.09	6.61	4.48	3.03	2.71
9	EUGENE, OR	7.65	6.35	5.80	3.66	2.66	1.53	0.64	0.99	1.54	3.35	8.44	8.29
10	HONOLULU, HI	2.73	2.35	1.89	1.11	0.78	0.43	0.50	0.46	0.74	2.18	2.26	2.85
11	ST. LOUIS, MO	2.14	2.28	3.60	3.69	4.11	3.76	3.90	2.98	2.96	2.76	3.71	2.86
12	TUCSON, AZ	0.99	0.88	0.81	0.28	0.24	0.24	2.07	2.30	1.45	1.21	0.67	1.03
13													

Figure 9-2: Data that you want to summarize with sparkline graphics.

Figure 9-3: Use the Create Sparklines dialog box to specify the data range and the location for the sparkline graphics.

The sparklines are linked to the data, so if you change any of the values in the data range, the sparkline graphic will update. If the sparkline data range contains the same number of rows and columns, Excel assumes that each sparkline uses data in a row. If you actually want the sparklines to show the data in columns, select a sparkline and choose Sparklines ➜ Design ➜ Sparklines ➜ Edit Data ➜ Switch Row/Column. Note that this command is available only when the data range contains the same number of rows and columns.

Tip

Most of the time, you'll create sparklines on the same sheet that contains the data. If you want to create sparklines on a different sheet, start by activating the sheet where the sparklines will be displayed. Then, in the Create Sparklines dialog box, specify the source data either by pointing or by typing the complete sheet reference (for example, Sheet1A1:C12). The Create Sparklines dialog box lets you specify a different sheet for the Data Range, but not for the Location Range.

Figure 9-4 shows column sparklines for the weather data.

	A	B	C	D	E	F	G	H	I	J	K	L	M	N
1	Average Monthly Precipitation (Inches)													
2														
3		Jan	Feb	Mar	Apr	May	Jun	Jul	Aug	Sep	Oct	Nov	Dec	
4	ASHEVILLE, NC	4.06	3.83	4.59	3.50	4.41	4.38	3.87	4.30	3.72	3.17	3.82	3.39	
5	BAKERSFIELD, CA	1.18	1.21	1.41	0.45	0.24	0.12	0.00	0.08	0.15	0.30	0.59	0.76	
6	BATON ROUGE, LA	6.19	5.10	5.07	5.56	5.34	5.33	5.96	5.86	4.84	3.81	4.76	5.26	
7	BILLINGS, MT	0.81	0.57	1.12	1.74	2.48	1.89	1.28	0.85	1.34	1.26	0.75	0.67	
8	DAYTONA BEACH, FL	3.13	2.74	3.84	2.54	3.26	5.69	5.17	6.09	6.61	4.48	3.03	2.71	
9	EUGENE, OR	7.65	6.35	5.80	3.66	2.66	1.53	0.64	0.99	1.54	3.35	8.44	8.29	
10	HONOLULU, HI	2.73	2.35	1.89	1.11	0.78	0.43	0.50	0.46	0.74	2.18	2.26	2.85	
11	ST. LOUIS, MO	2.14	2.28	3.60	3.69	4.11	3.76	3.90	2.98	2.96	2.76	3.71	2.86	
12	TUCSON, AZ	0.99	0.88	0.81	0.28	0.24	0.24	2.07	2.30	1.45	1.21	0.67	1.03	
13														
14														

Figure 9-4: Column sparklines summarize the precipitation data for nine cities.

▶ Understanding sparkline groups

Most of the time, you'll probably create a group of sparklines — one for each row or column of data. A worksheet can hold any number of sparkline groups. Excel remembers each group, and you can work with the group as a single unit. For example, you can select one sparkline in a group, and then modify the formatting of all sparklines in the group. When you select one sparkline cell, Excel displays an outline of all the other sparklines in the group.

You can, however, perform some operations on an individual sparkline in a group:

- **Change the sparkline's data source.** Click the sparkline cell and choose Sparkline Tools ➜ Design ➜ Sparkline ➜ Edit Data ➜ Edit Single Sparkline's Data. Excel displays a dialog box that lets you change the data source for the selected sparkline.

- **Delete the sparkline.** Click the sparkline cell and choose Sparkline Tools ➜ Design ➜ Group ➜ Clear ➜ Clear Selected Sparklines.

Both operations are available from the shortcut menu that appears when you right-click a sparkline cell.

You can also ungroup a set of sparklines. Select any sparkline in the group and choose Sparkline Tools ➜ Design ➜ Group ➜ Ungroup. After you ungroup a set of sparklines, you can work with each sparkline individually.

Customizing Sparklines

When you activate a cell that contains a sparkline, Excel displays an outline around all the spark-lines in its group. You can then use the commands on the Sparkline Tools ➔ Design tab to customize the group of sparklines.

Sizing and merging sparkline cells

When you change the width or height of a cell that contains a sparkline, the sparkline adjusts to fill the new cell size. In addition, you can put a sparkline into merged cells. To merge cells, select at least two cells and choose the Home ➔ Alignment ➔ Merge & Center.

Figure 9-5 shows the same sparkline, displayed at four sizes resulting from column width, row height, and merged cells.

Note If you merge cells, and the merged cells occupy more than one row or one column, Excel won't let you insert a group of sparklines into those merged cells. Rather, you need to insert the sparklines into a normal range (with no merged cells), and then merge the cells.

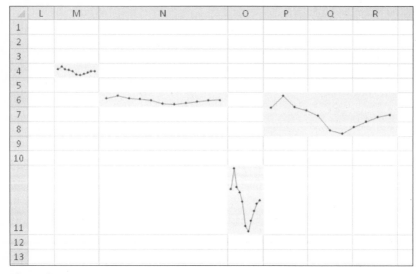

Figure 9-5: A sparkline at various sizes.

You can also put a sparkline in non-empty cells, including merged cells. Figure 9-6 shows two sparklines that occupy the same merged cells with text that describes the graphics.

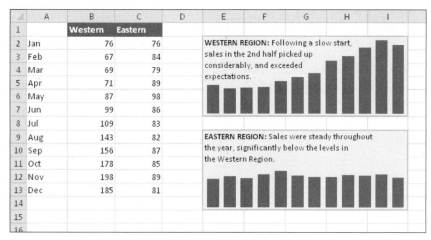

Figure 9-6: Sparklines in merged cells (E2:I7 and E9:I14).

Handling hidden or missing data

In some cases, you just want to present a top-level overview without the numbers. One way to do this is to hide the rows or columns that contain the data. Figure 9-7 shows a table with the values displayed, and the same table with the values hidden (by hiding the columns).

By default, if you hide rows or columns that contain data used in a sparkline graphic, the hidden data does not appear in the sparkline. In addition, blank cells are displayed as a gap in the graphic.

To change these default settings, choose Sparkline Tools → Design → Sparkline → Edit Data → Hidden & Empty Cells. In the Hidden and Empty Cell Settings dialog box, specify how to handle hidden data and empty cells.

Product Line	Jan	Feb	Mar	Apr	May	Jun	6-Month Trend		Product Line	6-Month Trend
Women's shoes	87	92	101	121	89	88			Women's shoes	
Men's shoes	67	66	73	59	54	61			Men's shoes	
Children's shoes	92	101	114	125	109	111			Children's shoes	
Women's hats	76	71	65	73	65	51			Women's hats	
Men's hats	12	15	18	26	13	12			Men's hats	
Children's hats	44	46	48	44	42	41			Children's hats	

Figure 9-7: Sparklines can use data in hidden rows or columns.

Changing the sparkline type

As mentioned earlier in this chapter, Excel supports three sparkline types: Line, Column, and Win/Loss. After you create a sparkline or group of sparklines, you can easily change the type by clicking the sparkline and selecting one of the three icons in the Sparkline Tools → Design → Type group. If the selected sparkline is part of a group, all sparklines in the group are changed to the new type.

Tip

If you've customized the appearance, Excel remembers your customization settings for each sparkline type if you switch among different sparkline types.

Changing sparkline colors and line width

After you create a sparkline, changing the color is easy. Use the controls in the Sparkline Tools ➜ Design ➜ Style group.

Note

Colors used in sparkline graphics are tied to the document theme. If you change the theme (by choosing Page Layout ➜ Themes ➜ Themes), the sparkline colors then change to the new theme colors.

For Line sparklines, you can also specify the line width. Choose Sparkline Tools ➜ Design ➜ Style ➜ Sparkline Color ➜ Weight.

Using color to emphasize key data points

Use the commands in the Sparkline Tools ➜ Design ➜ Show group to customize the sparklines to emphasize key aspects of the data. The options are

> **High Point:** Apply a different color to the highest data point in the sparkline.

> **Low Point:** Apply a different color to the lowest data point in the sparkline.

> **Negative Points:** Apply a different color to negative values in the sparkline.

> **First Point:** Apply a different color to the first data point in the sparkline.

> **Last Point:** Apply a different color to the last data point in the sparkline.

> **Markers:** Show data markers in the sparkline. This option is available only for Line sparklines.

You control the color of the sparkline by using the Marker Color control in the Sparkline Tools ➜ Design ➜ Style group. Unfortunately, you cannot change the size of the markers in Line sparklines.

Figure 9-8 shows some Line sparklines with various types of colors added.

Adjusting sparkline axis scaling

When you create one or more sparklines, they all use (by default) automatic axis scaling. In other words, Excel determines the minimum and maximum vertical axis values for each sparkline in the group, based on the numeric range of the sparkline data.

	A	B	C	D	E	F	G	H	I	J	K
1											
2											
3		12	9	-6	-12	2	8	16	14		Default
4		12	9	-6	-12	2	8	16	14		Markers
5		12	9	-6	-12	2	8	16	14		High Point, Low Point
6		12	9	-6	-12	2	8	16	14		First Point, Last Point
7		12	9	-6	-12	2	8	16	14		Negative Points
8											
9											

Figure 9-8: Using color to emphasize key data points for Line sparklines.

The Sparkline Tools ➔ Design ➔ Group ➔ Axis command lets you override this automatic behavior and control the minimum and maximum value for each sparkline, or for a group of sparklines. For even more control, you can use the Custom Value option and specify the minimum and maximum for the sparkline group.

Axis scaling can make a huge difference in the sparklines. Figure 9-9 shows two groups of sparklines. The group at the top uses the default axis settings (Automatic For Each Sparkline). Each sparkline in this group shows the six-month trend for the product, but there is no indication of the magnitude of the values.

The sparkline group at the bottom (which uses the same data), uses the Same For All Sparklines setting for the minimum and maximum axis values. With these settings in effect, the magnitude of the values *across* the products is apparent — but the trend across the months within a product is not apparent.

The axis scaling option you choose depends upon what aspect of the data you want to emphasize.

	A	B	C	D	E	F	G	H
1								
2		Jan	Feb	Mar	Apr	May	Jun	Sparklines
3	Product A	100	100	101	100	112	119	
4	Product B	300	300	312	310	323	327	
5	Product C	600	601	611	611	625	624	
6								
7								
8								
9		Jan	Feb	Mar	Apr	May	Jun	Sparklines
10	Product A	100	100	101	100	112	119	
11	Product B	300	300	312	310	323	327	
12	Product C	600	601	611	611	625	624	
13								

Figure 9-9: The bottom group of sparklines shows the effect of using the same axis minimum and maximum values for all sparklines in a group.

Faking a reference line

One useful feature that's missing in the Excel 2010 implementation of sparklines is a reference line. For example, it might be useful to show performance relative to a goal. If the goal is displayed as a reference line in a sparkline, the viewer can quickly see whether the performance for a period exceeded the goal.

One approach is to write formulas that transform the data, and then use a sparkline axis as a fake reference line. Figure 9-10 shows an example. Students have a monthly reading goal of 500 pages. The range of data shows the actual pages read, with sparklines in column H. The sparklines show the six-month page data, but it's impossible to tell who exceeded the goal, and when they did it.

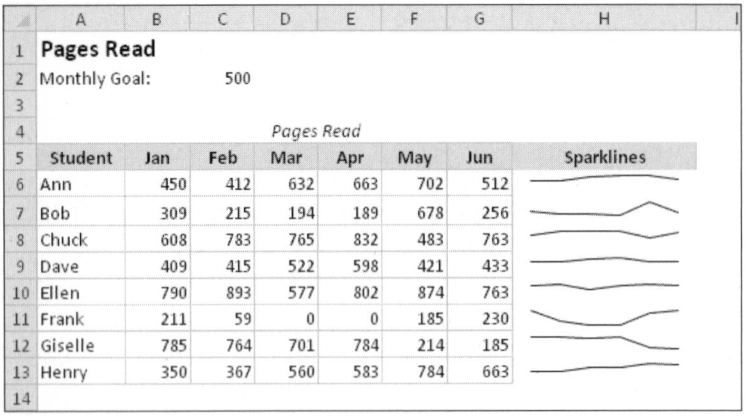

	A	B	C	D	E	F	G	H
1	**Pages Read**							
2	Monthly Goal:		500					
3								
4					Pages Read			
5	Student	Jan	Feb	Mar	Apr	May	Jun	Sparklines
6	Ann	450	412	632	663	702	512	
7	Bob	309	215	194	189	678	256	
8	Chuck	608	783	765	832	483	763	
9	Dave	409	415	522	598	421	433	
10	Ellen	790	893	577	802	874	763	
11	Frank	211	59	0	0	185	230	
12	Giselle	785	764	701	784	214	185	
13	Henry	350	367	560	583	784	663	
14								

Figure 9-10: Sparklines display the number of pages read per month.

The lower set of sparklines in Figure 9-11 shows another approach: Transforming the data such that meeting the goal is expressed as a 1, and failing to meet the goal is expressed as a –1. The following formula (in cell B18) transforms the original data:

```
=IF(B6>$C$2,1,-1)
```

This formula was copied to the other cells in B18:G25 range.

Using the transformed data, Win/Loss sparklines are used to visualize the results. This approach is better than the original, but it doesn't convey any magnitude differences. For example, you cannot tell whether the student missed the goal by 1 page or by 500 pages.

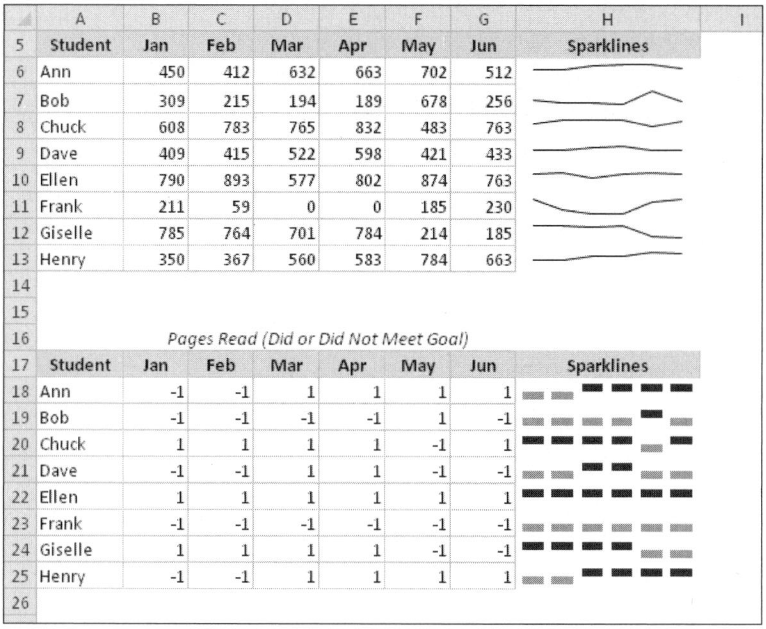

	A	B	C	D	E	F	G	H	I
5	Student	Jan	Feb	Mar	Apr	May	Jun	Sparklines	
6	Ann	450	412	632	663	702	512		
7	Bob	309	215	194	189	678	256		
8	Chuck	608	783	765	832	483	763		
9	Dave	409	415	522	598	421	433		
10	Ellen	790	893	577	802	874	763		
11	Frank	211	59	0	0	185	230		
12	Giselle	785	764	701	784	214	185		
13	Henry	350	367	560	583	784	663		
14									
15									
16				*Pages Read (Did or Did Not Meet Goal)*					
17	Student	Jan	Feb	Mar	Apr	May	Jun	Sparklines	
18	Ann	-1	-1	1	1	1	1		
19	Bob	-1	-1	-1	-1	1	-1		
20	Chuck	1	1	1	1	-1	1		
21	Dave	-1	-1	1	1	-1	-1		
22	Ellen	1	1	1	1	1	1		
23	Frank	-1	-1	-1	-1	-1	-1		
24	Giselle	1	1	1	1	-1	-1		
25	Henry	-1	-1	1	1	1	1		
26									

Figure 9-11: Using Win/Loss sparklines to display goal status.

Figure 9-12 shows a better approach. Here, the original data is transformed by subtracting the goal from the pages read. The formula in cell B31 is:

```
=B6-$C$2
```

This formula was copied to the other cells in the B31:G38 range, and a group of Line sparklines display the resulting values. This group has the Show Axis setting enabled, and also uses Negative Point markers so the negative values (failure to meet the goal) clearly stand out.

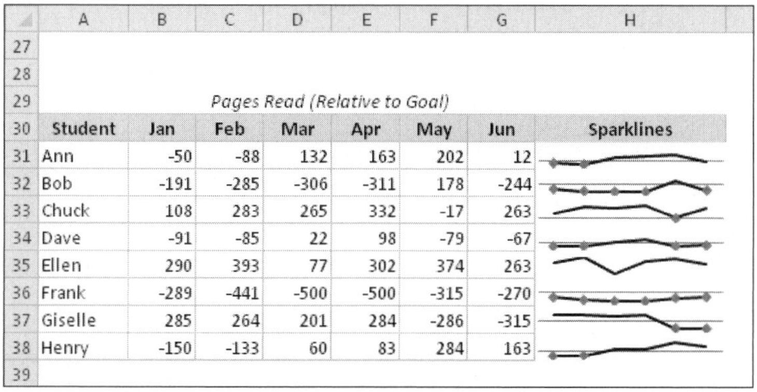

	A	B	C	D	E	F	G	H
27								
28								
29				*Pages Read (Relative to Goal)*				
30	Student	Jan	Feb	Mar	Apr	May	Jun	Sparklines
31	Ann	-50	-88	132	163	202	12	
32	Bob	-191	-285	-306	-311	178	-244	
33	Chuck	108	283	265	332	-17	263	
34	Dave	-91	-85	22	98	-79	-67	
35	Ellen	290	393	77	302	374	263	
36	Frank	-289	-441	-500	-500	-315	-270	
37	Giselle	285	264	201	284	-286	-315	
38	Henry	-150	-133	60	83	284	163	
39								

Figure 9-12: The axis in the sparklines represents the goal.

Specifying a date axis

By default, data displayed in a sparkline is assumed to be at equal intervals. For example, a sparkline might display a daily account balance, sales by month, or profits by year. But what if the data aren't at equal intervals?

Figure 9-13 shows data, by date, along with a sparklines graphic created from Column B. Notice that some dates are missing, but the sparkline shows the columns as if the values were spaced at equal intervals.

	A	B	C	D	E	F
1	Date	Amount				
2	1/1/2010	154				
3	1/2/2010	201				
4	1/3/2010	245				
5	1/4/2010	176				
6	1/11/2010	267				
7	1/12/2010	289				
8	1/13/2010	331				
9	1/14/2010	365				
10	1/18/2010	298				
11	1/19/2010	424				
12						
13						

Figure 9-13: The sparkline displays the values as if they are at equal time intervals.

To better depict this type of time-based data, the solution is to specify a date axis. Select the sparkline and choose Sparkline Tools ➜ Design ➜ Group ➜ Axis ➜ Date Axis Type. Excel displays a dialog box, asking for the range that contains the corresponding dates. In this example, specify range A2:A11. Click OK, and the sparkline displays gaps for the missing dates (see Figure 9-14).

	A	B	C	D	E	F
1	Date	Amount				
2	1/1/2010	154				
3	1/2/2010	201				
4	1/3/2010	245				
5	1/4/2010	176				
6	1/11/2010	267				
7	1/12/2010	289				
8	1/13/2010	331				
9	1/14/2010	365				
10	1/18/2010	298				
11	1/19/2010	424				
12						
13						

Figure 9-14: After specifying a date axis, the sparkline shows the values accurately.

Auto-updating sparkline ranges

If a sparkline uses data in a normal range of cells, adding new data to the beginning or end of the range does *not* force the sparkline to use the new data. You need to use the Edit Sparklines dialog box to update the data range (choose Sparkline Tools ➜ Design ➜ Sparkline ➜ Edit Data). But, if the sparkline data is in a column within a table (created by using Insert ➜ Tables ➜ Table), then the sparkline uses new data that's added to the end of the table.

Figure 9-15 shows an example. The sparkline was created using the data in the Rate column of the table. When you add the new rate for September, the sparkline will automatically update its Data Range.

	A	B	C	D	E	F
1		End of month interest rates				
2						
3		Month	Rate			
4		Jan	5.20%			
5		Feb	5.02%			
6		Mar	4.97%			
7		Apr	4.99%			
8		May	4.89%			
9		Jun	4.72%			
10		Jul	4.68%			
11		Aug	4.61%			
12						

Figure 9-15: Creating a sparkline from data in a table.

Displaying a sparkline for a dynamic range

The example in this section describes how to create a sparkline that displays only the most recent data points in a range. Figure 9-16 shows a worksheet that tracks daily sales. The sparkline displays only the seven most recent data points in column B.

The trick is to create a dynamic range name. Here's how:

1. Choose Formulas ➜ Defined Names ➜ Define Name, specify Last7 as the Name, and type the following formula in the Refers To field:

   ```
   =OFFSET($B$2,COUNTA($B:$B)-7-1,0,7,1)
   ```

   This formula calculates a range by using the OFFSET function.

   The first argument is the first cell in the range (B2). The second argument is the number of cells in the column (minus the number to be returned, and minus 1 to accommodate the label in B1).

   This name always refers to the last seven non-empty cells in column B. To display a different number of data points, change both instances of 7 to a different value.

2. Chose Insert ➜ Sparklines ➜ Line.

3. In the Data Range field, type **Last7** (the dynamic range name).

4. Specify cell E4 as the Location Range.

The sparkline shows the data in range B11:B17.

5. Add new data to column B.

The sparkline adjusts to display only the last seven data points.

	A	B	C	D	E	F
1	Day	Sales				
2	1	695				
3	2	687				
4	3	687		Last 7 Days:		
5	4	695				
6	5	708				
7	6	719				
8	7	726				
9	8	727				
10	9	735				
11	10	744				
12	11	765				
13	12	740				
14	13	782				
15	14	735				
16	15	890				
17	16	883				
18	17					
19	18					
20	19					

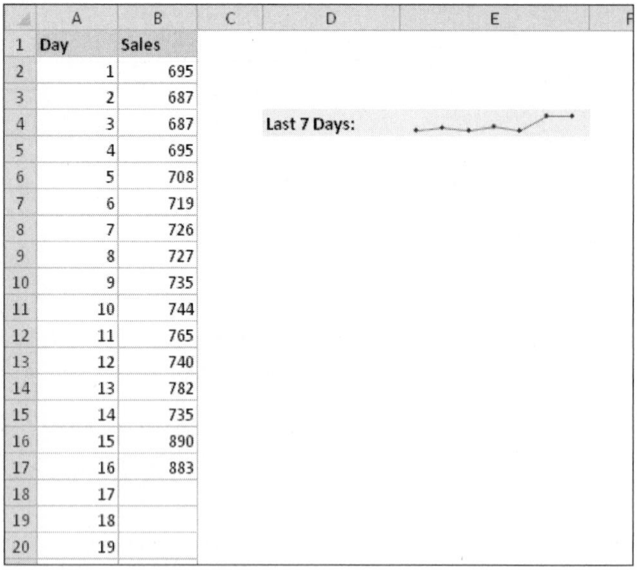

Figure 9-16: Using a dynamic range name to display only the last seven data points in a sparkline.

Chartless Visualization Techniques

In This Chapter

- Creating dynamic labels
- Using the Camera tool
- Working with formula-driven visualizations
- Using fancy fonts
- Leveraging symbols in formulas

Up to this point, we've discussed the tools that you can use to build basic dashboard components: charts, pivot tables, pivot charts, and sparklines. In this chapter, you'll focus on components that are less apparent — *chartless visualizations.*

In contrast to the previous topics, chartless visualization is less a feature specific to Excel than it is a concept that you can apply to your dashboard presentation. With these types of visualizations, you can easily add layers of interactivity to your dashboard and take advantage of some common worksheet features that can simplify your work.

Dynamic Labels

A common place to add dynamic labels is to an interactive chart. In Figure 10-1, I have a pivot chart that shows the Top 10 Categories of sports product sales organized by a geographic market. When a user changes the market location in the drop-down list, the chart updates accordingly. Now, it would be helpful to add a label to the chart that clearly states the market that the user is viewing.

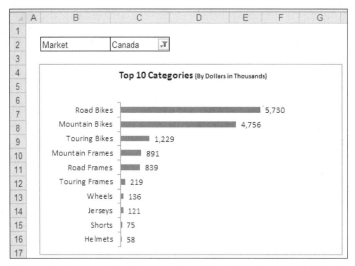

Figure 10-1: Interactive charts, such as this pivot chart, are ideal places to use a dynamic label that changes based on your current selection.

Cross-Ref

For a complete discussion of pivot charts, see Chapter 8.

To add a dynamic label within your chart, follow these steps:

1. On the Insert tab on the Ribbon, select the Text Box icon, as shown in Figure 10-2.

Figure 10-2: Select the Text Box icon.

2. Click inside the chart to create an empty text box.

3. While the text box is selected, go up to the Formula bar, type the equal sign (=), and then click the cell that contains the text for your dynamic label.

   In Figure 10-3, the text box is linked to cell C2. You'll notice that cell C2 contains the drop-down list for the pivot table.

4. Format the text box so that it looks like any other label.

   You can format the text box using the standard formatting options found on the Home tab.

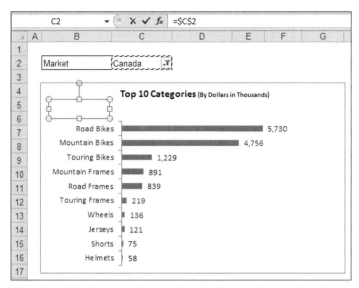

Figure 10-3: Link the text box to the cell that contains the text for your dynamic label.

Now, the label on your chart corresponds with the cell to which it's linked. Figure 10-4 illustrates how the dynamic label can blend in visually with your chart.

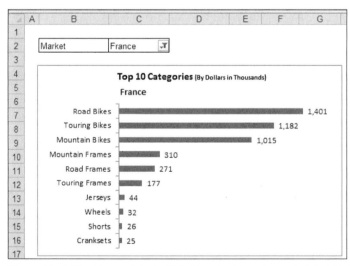

Figure 10-4: The France label within the chart is a dynamic label that changes when a new market is selected in the drop-down list.

Be aware that text boxes can't display any more than 255 characters.

Note

Linking Formulas to Text Boxes

When you link your text boxes to cells that contain formulas instead of simple labels, a whole new set of opportunities open up. With formulas, the label becomes even more interactive.

Figure 10-5 shows two views of the same pivot chart. On the top, the Northeast market is selected, and you see that a pivot chart label that focuses on the Q4 variance. On the bottom, the Southeast market is selected, and you can see that the label changes to correspond with the new data about the Q4 variance for the Southeast market.

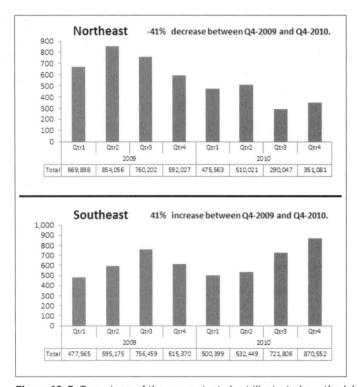

Figure 10-5: Two views of the same pivot chart illustrate how the label changes for each market.

 The example file named `Chapter 10 Sample File.xlsx` **is at** `www.wiley.com/ go/exceldr`.

On the Web

Figure 10-5 actually uses three dynamic labels: one to display the current selected market; one to display the actual calculation of Q4-2010 versus Q4-2009, and one to add some contextual text that describes the analysis.

Figure 10-6 illustrates the behind-the-scenes links. Take a moment to examine what's happening here. The label that shows how 41% links to cell B13, contains a formula that returns the variance analysis. The label that shows how the contextual text links to cell C13, contains an IF function that returns a different sentence, depending on whether the variance percent is an increase or decrease.

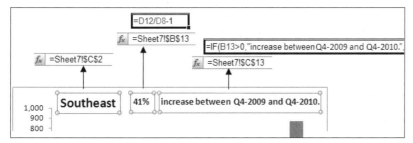

Figure 10-6: This pivot chart actually uses three dynamic labels; each links to a different cell.

Together, these labels provide your audience with a clear message about the variance for the selected market. This is one of countless ways you can implement this technique.

Excel's Camera Tool

Excel's Camera tool enables you to take a live picture of a range of cells that updates dynamically while the data in that range updates. If you haven't ever heard of it, don't feel too bad. This nifty tool has been hidden away in that last few versions of Excel. Although Microsoft has chosen not to include this tool in the mainstream Ribbon, it's actually quite useful for those of us building dashboards and reports.

Finding the Camera tool

Before you can use the Camera tool, you have to find it and add it to your Quick Access toolbar.

Tip

The Quick Access toolbar is a customizable toolbar in which you can store frequently used commands so that they're always accessible with just one click. You can add commands to the Quick Access toolbar by dragging them directly from the Ribbon or by going through the Customize menu.

Follow these steps to add the Camera tool to the Quick Access toolbar:

1. To go to Excel's Backstage View, on the Ribbon, click the File tab.

2. To open the Excel Options dialog box, click the Options button.

3. Click the Quick Access Toolbar button.

4. In the Choose Commands From drop-down list box, select Commands Not in the Ribbon.

5. Scroll down the alphabetical list of commands (see Figure 10-7) and find Camera; double-click to add it to Quick Access toolbar.

6. Click OK.

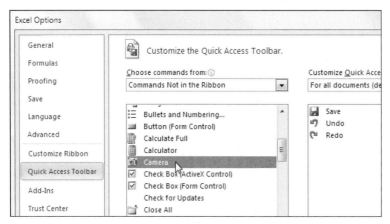

Figure 10-7: Add the Camera tool to the Quick Access toolbar.

When you've taken these steps, you'll see the Camera tool in your Quick Access toolbar, as shown in Figure 10-8.

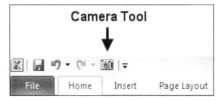

Figure 10-8: Not surprisingly, the icon for the Camera tool looks like a camera.

Using the Camera tool

To use the Camera tool, you simply highlight a range of cells to then capture everything in that range in a live picture. The cool thing about the Camera tool is that you're not limited to showing a single cell's value like you are with a linked text box. And because the picture is live, any updates made to the source range automatically changes the picture.

Take a moment to walk through this basic demonstration of the Camera tool. In Figure 10-9, you'll see some simple numbers and a chart based on those numbers. The goal here is to create a live picture of the range that holds both the numbers and the chart.

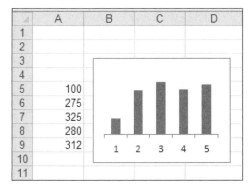

Figure 10-9: Enter some simple numbers in a range and create a basic chart from those numbers.

1. Highlight the range that contains the information you want to capture. In this scenario, we selected A3:D11.

2. Select the Camera tool icon in the Quick Access toolbar.

   We added the Camera tool to the Quick Access toolbar in the preceding section.

3. Click the worksheet in the location where you want to place the picture.

   Excel immediately creates a live picture of the entire range, as shown in Figure 10-10.

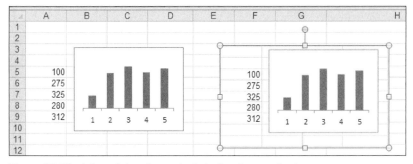

Figure 10-10: A live picture is created via the Camera tool.

Changing any number in the original range automatically causes the picture to update.

Tip

By default, the picture that's created has a border around it. To remove the border, right-click the picture and select Format Picture. This opens the Format Picture dialog box. In the Colors and Lines tab, you see a Line Color drop-down list. Here you can select No Color, thereby removing the border. On a similar note, to get a picture without gridlines, simply remove the gridlines from the source range.

Creating a live picture without the Camera tool

Did you know you can create a live picture without actually using the Camera tool? That's right. Excel 2010 has made it relatively easy to manually mimic the Camera tool's functionality.

1. Select the target range and copy it.

2. Go to the Home tab on the Ribbon and click the drop-down control under the Paste command

3. Under the Other Paste Options group, select Linked Picture.

Of course, the advantage of using the Camera tool is that you can do the same thing with two clicks.

Enhancing a dashboard with the Camera tool

Here are a few ways to go beyond the basics and use the Camera tool to enhance your dashboards and reports.

➤ Consolidate varied ranges from different sources into one print area.

➤ Rotate objects to simplify your work.

➤ Create small charts.

Consolidating disparate ranges into one print area

Sometimes a data model gets so complex that it's difficult to keep all the final data in one printable area. This often forces the printing of multiple pages that are inconsistent in layout and size. Given that dashboards are most effective when contained in a compact area that can be printed in a page or two, complex data models prove to be problematic when it comes to layout and design.

You can use the Camera tool in these situations to create live pictures of various ranges that you can place on a single page. Figure 10-11 shows a workbook that contains data from various worksheets. The secret here is that these are nothing more than linked pictures created by the Camera tool.

When you create pictures with the Camera Tool, you can resize and move the pictures around freely. This gives you the freedom to test different layouts without the need to work about column widths, hidden rows, or other such nonsense. In short, you can create and manage multiple analyses on different tabs and then bring together all your presentation pieces into a nicely formatted presentation layer.

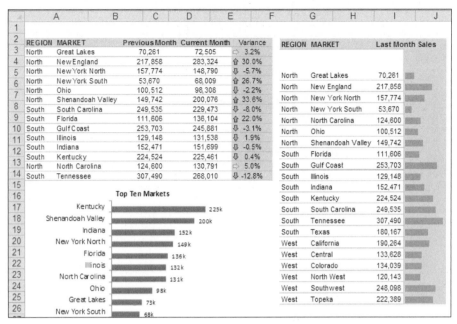

Figure 10-11: Use the Camera tool to get multiple source ranges into a compact area.

Rotating objects to save time

Again, because the Camera tool outputs pictures, you can rotate the pictures in situations where placing the copied range on its side can help save time. A great example is a chart. Certain charts are relatively easy to create in a vertical orientation but extremely difficult to create in a horizontal orientation.

Figure 10-12 shows a vertical bullet graph (on the left). Whereas creating a horizontal bullet graph involves lots of intricate steps with multiple chart types, this graph is relatively easy to create in this vertical format.

The Camera tool to the rescue! When the live picture of the chart is created, all you have to do is rotate the picture using the rotate handle to create a horizontal version.

Creating small charts

Although you can resize charts easily enough through other means, you typically would have to spend time tweaking the scale, font, and other elements on the chart until you make the chart small enough. Because the Camera tool creates a picture that keeps its pixel ratios intact while you resize, it allows you to achieve small chart sizes without tweaking a single chart element.

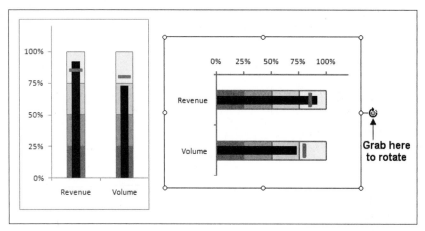

Figure 10-12: You can use the rotation handle to rotate your live pictures to a horizontal orientation, as seen here on the right.

Formula-Driven Labels

A *formula-driven label* is a label or text resulting from a formula, which you can use for further analysis and reporting. The idea here is that you build some logic into a formula and then use the resulting value as a new dimension of data which can sort, conditionally format, and add a chart to a dashboard.

Take a look at the example in Figure 10-13. Beside each number is a cell that contains a formula. The formula determines whether the number is above 300. If it is, the word *Above* is displayed, if not, the word *Below* is displayed.

100	=IF(G4>300,"Above","Below")
275	Below
325	Above
280	Below
312	Above

Figure 10-13: The results of the formula adds an additional dimension of data for each number.

This is a good starting point to adding a visual element to your formulas, thereby creating a *formula-driven visualization.* That is, creating formulas which return visualizations instead of just text.

In-cell charting

Figure 10-14 shows a table that contains an in-cell chart, providing a visualization of the numbers shown. The cool thing is that the in-cell chart achieved here is the result of a simple formula.

	A	B	C	D
1	REGION	MARKET	Last Month Sales	
2	North	Great Lakes	70,261	
3	North	New England	217,858	
4	North	New York North	157,774	
5	North	New York South	53,670	
6	North	North Carolina	124,600	
7	North	Ohio	100,512	
8	North	Shenandoah Valley	149,742	
9	South	Florida	111,606	
10	South	Gulf Coast	253,703	
11	South	Illinois	129,148	
12	South	Indiana	152,471	
13	South	Kentucky	224,524	
14	South	South Carolina	249,535	
15	South	Tennessee	307,490	
16	South	Texas	180,167	
17	West	California	190,264	
18	West	Central	133,628	
19	West	Colorado	134,039	
20	West	North West	120,143	
21	West	Southwest	248,098	
22	West	Topeka	222,389	

Figure 10-14: The in-cell chart that you see is nothing more than a formula.

This effect was achieved by using Excel's REPT function. The REPT repeats a given character a specified number of times. For example, if you went to a cell and entered **=REPT("s",10)**, the returned value would be sssssssssss (the "s" character repeated ten times).

The idea is instead of using a letter, you use a character that, when repeated, looks kind of like a chart. The *pipe character* (the | shown above the backslash on your keyboard) is a good character for this kind of thing. If you went to a cell and typed **=REPT("|",10)**, the returned value would be ||||||||||. That looks very similar to a bar in a chart.

Note

You may be wondering why you'd even use this. Why would you not just use the data bars conditional formatting feature or for that matter, a chart? First, data bars are not *backwards compatible* — anyone who doesn't have Excel 2007 or Excel 2010 can't use them. Plus, conditional formatting adds overhead and a level of maintenance that may not be feasible with complex data. As for standard charts, they take up much more space than in-cell charting. In-cell charting gives you an easy-to-implement alternative that doesn't require a lot of real estate or setup.

To push this further, imagine that you had then number 30 in cell A1. You could, in cell B1, type **=REPT("|", A1)**. This would show 30 pipe characters in cell B1, giving you a visualization of the number in A1.

This works just fine until you get to really big numbers. For instance, you can imagine that repeating the pipe character 200 times isn't all that useful. In situations where you have large values, you can cut the number down to size by dividing it by 10, 100, 1000, or whatever makes sense.

So if Cell A1 contains 200, you can use =REPT("|",A1/10). This effectively returns 20 pipe characters instead of 200. Figure 10-15 demonstrates this concept; note the formula being used in the Formula bar.

B1		f_x =REPT("|",A1/10)	
	A	B	C	D	E
1	30					
2	50							
3	56							
4	75									
5	90											
6	100												
7	124													
8	200																						
9	143																
10			

Figure 10-15: When using the REPT function with large values, divide the values into smaller increments.

Another way to limit the number of times a character is repeated is to define a maximum for the formula. You can do this by getting a bit fancy and using Excel's MAX function. To understand this, take a look at Figure 10-16.

PMT		× ✓ f_x =REPT("|",A1/MAX($A$1:$A$8)*25)	
	A	B	C	D	E	F	G
1	700,000	$A$8)*25)	
2	555,555	|||||||||||||||||||||	
3	655,555	||||||||||||||||||||||||	
4	500,000	|||||||||||||||||	
5	221,345	|||||||	
6	556,677	|||||||||||||||||||||	
7	435,543	|||||||||||||||	
8	423,321	||||||||||||||	
9			

Figure 10-16: You can incorporate a MAX function into your formula to limit the number of characters repeated.

In Figure 10-16, note the formula in the Formula bar:

```
=REPT("|", A1/MAX($A$1:$A$8)*25)
```

Note

Be sure to make the range used in the MAX function an *absolute reference.* That is to say, be sure to include a dollar sign ($) in front of the column and row references, such as MAX($A$1:$A$8). With the $ character, you tell Excel to not increment the column and row references when you copy a range. This ensures that the range being referenced is locked when you copy the formula.

This formula basically tells Excel to take the value being referenced and divide it by the maximum value for entire range. Then take that answer and multiply it by 25. The value shown in A1, 700000, is indeed the maximum value in the entire range. So in the case of Cell A1 the formula essentially translates to =REPT("|",700000/700000*25). Mathematically, 700000/700000*25 gives you 25.

In the case of cell A2, the formula would translate to =REPT("|",555555/700000*25). Mathematically, 555555/700000*25 gives you 19.84.

Stand back and think about what this means. The maximum number of characters that can possibly be returned by this formula is 25. This formula essentially limits the number of pipe characters no matter how big your numbers are.

Because the value returned by the REPT function is nothing more than a text string, you can apply formatting to it just as you would any other text. You can change font, change pitch, add color, apply conditional formatting, and even change alignment. Figure 10-17 shows how you can get fancy with in-cell charting to achieve some nifty looking analysis just by adjusting various formatting options.

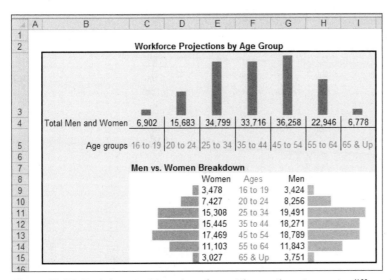

Figure 10-17: Experiment with various formatting options to create different visualizations.

Using fancy fonts

With the release of Excel 2007, Microsoft enhanced Excel's conditional formatting to offer users the ability to add icon sets to presentations. With icons, you can distinguish values from one another by using different shapes and colors. The problem is that Icon Sets aren't backwards compatible — anyone who doesn't have Excel 2010 or Excel 2007 can't use them.

A creative alternative to using the Icon Sets offered with conditional formatting is to use the various fancy fonts that come with Office. These are Wingdings, Wingdings2, Wingdings3, and Webdings. These fonts display icons for each character instead of the standard numbers and letters.

Take a look at Figure 10-18. Columns A–C list numbers and letters in the Arial font. The same numbers and letters are shown in the various fancy fonts. As you can see, a few of the icons (highlighted in Figure 10-18) look similar to the Icons Sets offered with conditional formatting.

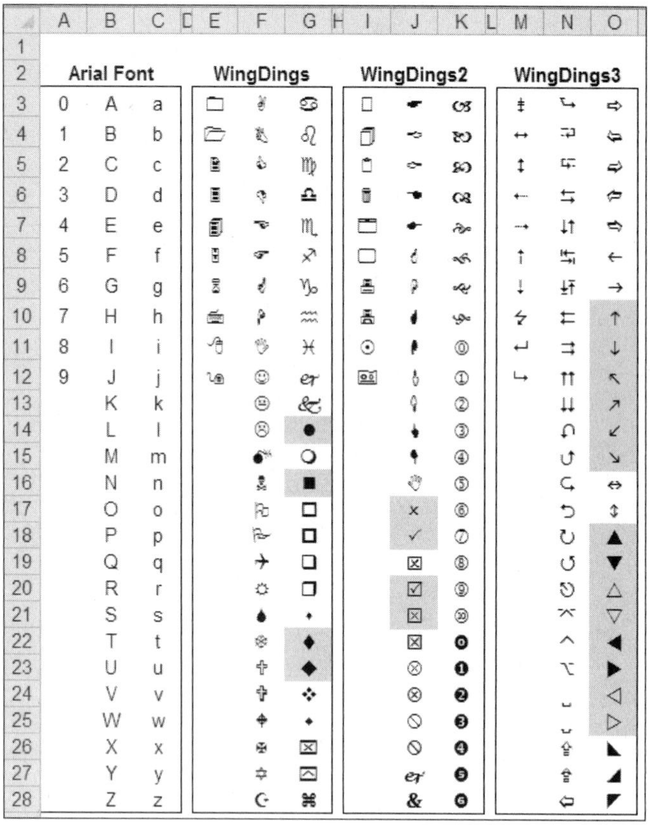

Figure 10-18: You can use the various fancy fonts to return icons instead of standard numbers and letters.

The simple implementation of this concept is demonstrated in Figure 10-19. Here, you have several formulas that evaluate the numbers in column Q. Each formula returns a character. For example, the formulas in column T will return either an O or a P depending on the value in column Q. In a standard font, this makes no sense. However, that same formula in varying fonts allows for some interesting graphics.

Figure 10-20 expands this concept to a real world scenario. Here, fancy fonts are being used to highlight the variances in each market.

⊿	Q	R	S	T	U
1		=IF(Q3>50,"True","False"	=IF(Q3>50,"J","L")	=IF(Q3>50,"O","P")	=IF(Q3>50,"p","q")
2		Arial	Windings	Windings2	Windings3
3	10	False	☹	×	▼
4	20	False	☹	×	▼
5	30	False	☹	×	▼
6	40	False	☹	×	▼
7	50	False	☹	×	▼
8	60	True	☺	✓	▲
9	70	True	☺	✓	▲
10	80	True	☺	✓	▲
11	90	True	☺	✓	▲
12	100	True	☺	✓	▲
13					

Figure 10-19: You can adjust your formulas to return characters that can be formatted into any one of the available fancy fonts.

⊿	A	B	C	D	E	F	G
					Wingdings 3 font		
			Previous	Current			
1	Region	Market	Month	Month	Variance		
2	North	Great Lakes	70,261	72,505	3.2%	▲	=IF(E2>0, "p", "q")
3	North	New England	217,858	283,324	30.0%	▲	
4	North	New York North	157,774	148,790	-5.7%	▼	
5	North	New York South	53,670	68,009	26.7%	▲	
6	North	Ohio	100,512	98,308	-2.2%	▼	
7	North	Shenandoah Valley	149,742	200,076	33.6%	▲	
8	South	South Carolina	249,535	229,473	-8.0%	▼	
9	South	Florida	111,606	136,104	22.0%	▲	
10	South	Gulf Coast	253,703	245,881	-3.1%	▼	
11	South	Illinois	129,148	131,538	1.9%	▲	
12	South	Indiana	152,471	151,699	-0.5%	▼	
13	South	Kentucky	224,524	225,461	0.4%	▲	
14	North	North Carolina	124,600	130,791	5.0%	▲	
15	South	Tennessee	307,490	268,010	-12.8%	▼	

Figure 10-20: An example where fancy fonts can come in handy.

Using symbols

Symbols are essentially tiny graphics, not unlike those you see when you use the Wingdings, Webdings, or the other fancy fonts. However, symbols are not really fonts. They're *Unicode* characters. Unicode characters are a set of industry standard text elements designed to provide a reliable character-set that remain viable on any platform regardless of international font differences.

One example of a commonly used symbol is the Copyright symbol (©). This symbol is a Unicode character. You can use this symbol on a Chinese, Turkish, French, and American PC and it will reliably be available with no international differences.

In terms of Excel presentations, Unicode characters (or symbols) can be used in places where fancy fonts cannot. For instance, in the chart labels that you see in Figure 10-21, you'll notice that the X-Axis shows some trending arrows that allow for an extra layer of analysis. This couldn't be done with fancy fonts because changing the font (to Wingdings let's say) will make the entire label look wacky.

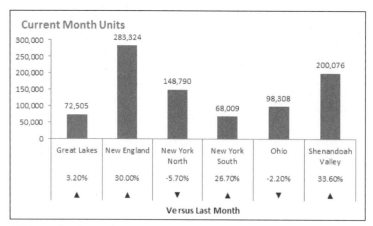

Figure 10-21: Use symbols to add an extra layer of analysis to charts.

Let's take some time to review the steps that led to the chart in Figure 10-22. We start with the data shown in Figure 10-22.

	vs. Prior Month	Market	Current Month
	3.20%	Great Lakes	72,505
	30.00%	New England	283,324
	-5.70%	New York North	148,790
	26.70%	New York South	68,009
	-2.20%	Ohio	98,308
	33.60%	Shenandoah Valley	200,076

Figure 10-22: Starting table.

1. To designate a holding cell to hold your *UP* symbol, click in B1 and then select the symbol on the Insert tab.

   In this case, the holding cell will be cell B1.

   This step opens the Symbol dialog box (see Figure 10-23).

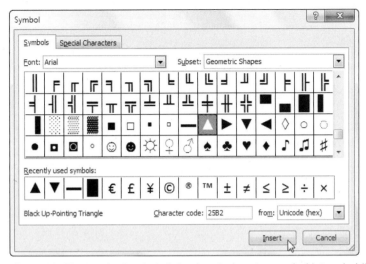

Figure 10-23: Use the Symbol dialog box to insert a symbol into a holding cell.

2. Select an appropriate UP symbol, and then click Insert. Click Close.

3. To designate a holding cell where your *DOWN* symbol will reside, click in C1 and then select the symbol on the Insert tab.

4. In the Symbol dialog box, select an appropriate DOWN symbol, click Insert, and then Close.

   Now you can use B1 and C1 in a simple formula that will assign an UP or DOWN symbol to each market based on the variance percent. You'll notice (see Figure 10-24), it's quite similar to the one you used in the previous fancy font exercise.

A4		f_x =IF(B4>0, $B$1, $C$1)

	A	B	C	D
1		▲	▼	
2				
3	Up/Down	vs. Prior Month	Market	Current Month
4	▲	3.20%	Great Lakes	72,505
5	▲	30.00%	New England	283,324
6	▼	-5.70%	New York North	148,790
7	▲	26.70%	New York South	68,009
8	▼	-2.20%	Ohio	98,308
9	▲	33.60%	Shenandoah Valley	200,076

Figure 10-24: Build a simple formula that assigns one of the symbols based on the variance.

5. Insert a new column chart using just the Market and Current Month columns, as seen in Figure 10-25.

   In order to get the effect we're looking for, the other fields will have to be added to the X-Axis after the chart is created.

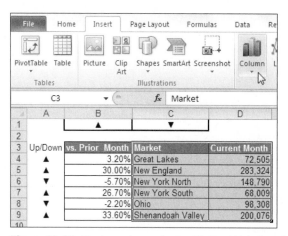

Figure 10-25: Start a column chart with the Market and Current Month columns.

6. Select the chart, click the Design tab, and select Select Data.

   This opens the Select Data Source dialog box.

7. Click the Edit button under Horizontal Category (Axis) Labels, and then select A4:C9 (see Figure 10-26).

8. Click OK.

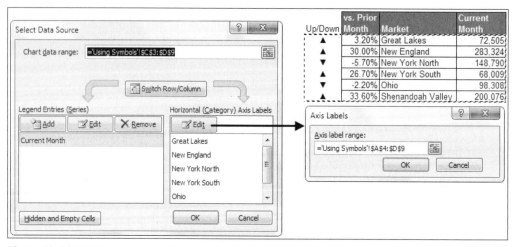

Figure 10-26: Point your X-Axis Category label to your symbols.

If all went well, you should have a chart that looks similar to one seen in Figure 10-21. Needless to say, this is just one of a countless ways you can leverage symbols to enhance your formulas, highlight problem areas, and add visual appeal to your presentations.

Creating Advanced Dashboard Components

Components that Show Trending

In This Chapter

- Understanding basic dashboard trending concepts

- Comparing trends across multiple series

- Emphasizing distinct periods of time in your trends

- Working past other anomalies in trending data

One of the most common concepts used in dashboards and reports is the concept of *trending.* A trend is a measure of variance over some defined interval — typically time periods, like days, months, or years.

The reason trending is so popular is that it provides a rational expectation of what might happen in the future. If we know this book has sold 5,000 copies a month over the last 12 months, we have reason to believe that sales next month will be around 5,000 copies. In short, trending tells you where you've been and where you might be going.

In this chapter, you explore basic trending concepts and some of the advanced dashboard techniques you can use to take your trending components beyond simple line charts.

Trending Dos and Don'ts

Building trending components for your dashboards has some dos and don'ts. This section helps you avoid some common trending *faux pas.*

Using chart types appropriate for trending

It would be nice if you could definitively say which chart type you should use when building trending components. But, the truth is, no chart type is the silver bullet for all situations. For effective trending, you'll want to understand which chart types are most effective in different trending scenarios.

We discuss Excel chart basics in Part II of this book.

Cross-Ref

Using line charts

Line charts are the kings of trending. In business presentations, a line chart almost always indicates movement across time. Even in areas not related to business, the concept of lines is used to indicate time — consider timelines, family lines, bloodlines, and so on. The benefit of using a line chart for trending is that it is instantly recognized as a trending component, avoiding any delay in information processing.

Line charts are especially effective in presenting trends with many data points — as the top chart in the Figure 11-1 shows. You can also use a line chart to present trends for more than one time period, as shown in the bottom chart in Figure 11-1.

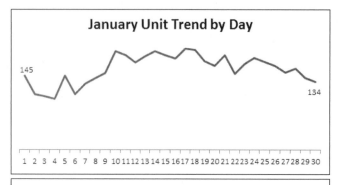

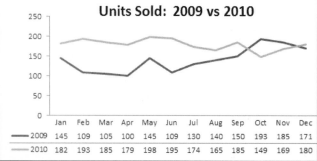

Figure 11-1: Line charts are the chart of choice when you need to show trending over time.

Using area charts

An *area chart* is essentially a line chart that's been filled in. So, technically, area charts are appropriate for trending. They're particularly good at highlighting trends over a large time span. For example, the chart in Figure 11-2 spans over 120 days of data.

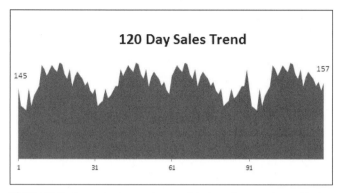

Figure 11-2: Area charts can be used to trend over a large time span.

Using column charts

If you're trending one series of time, a line chart is absolutely the way to go. However, if you're comparing two or more time periods on the same chart, columns may best bring out the comparisons.

Figure 11-3 demonstrates how a combination chart can instantly call attention to the exact months when 2010 sales fell below 2009. A combination of line and column charts is an extremely effective way to show the difference in units sold between two time periods. We show you how to create this type of chart later in this chapter .

Figure 11-3: Using columns and lines emphasize the trending differences between two time periods.

Starting the vertical scale at zero

The vertical axis on trending charts should almost always start at zero. The reason we say *almost* is because you may have trending data that contains negative values or fractions. In those situations, it's generally best to keep Excel's default scaling. However, in situations where there are only non-negative integers, ensure that your vertical axis starts at zero.

The reason is that the vertical scale of a chart can have a significant impact on the representation of a trend. For instance, the two charts shown in Figure 11-4 contain the same data. The only difference is that in the top chart, we did nothing to fix the vertical scale assigned by Excel (it starts at 96), but in the bottom chart, we fixed the scale to start at zero.

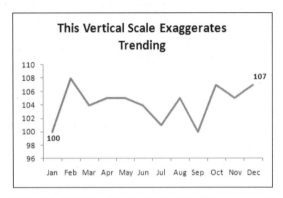

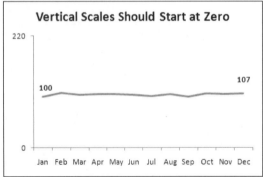

Figure 11-4: Vertical scales should always start at zero.

Now you may think the top chart is more accurate because it shows the ups and downs of the trend. However, if you look at the numbers closely, you see that the units represented went from 100 to 107 in 12 months. That's not exactly a material change, and it certainly doesn't warrant such a dramatic chart. In truth, the trend is relatively flat, yet the top chart makes it look as though the trend is way up.

The bottom chart more accurately reflects the true nature of the trend. I achieved this effect by locking the Minimum value on the vertical axis to zero.

To adjust the scale of your vertical axis, follow these simple steps:

1. Right-click the vertical axis and choose Format Axis.

   The Format Axis dialog box appears. (See Figure 11-5.)

2. In the Format Axis dialog box, select the Fixed radio button next to the Minimum property, and then set the Minimum value to 0.

3. (Optional) You can set the Major Unit value to twice the Maximum value in your data.

   This ensures that your trend line gets placed in the middle of your chart.

4. Click the Close button to apply your changes.

Figure 11-5: Always set the Minimum value of your vertical axis to zero.

Tip

Many would argue that the bottom chart shown in Figure 11-4 hides the small-scale trending that may be important. That is, a seven unit difference may be very significant in some businesses. Well, if that's true, why use a chart at all? If each unit has such an impact on the analysis, why use a broad-sweep representation like a chart? A table with conditional formatting would do a better job at highlighting small-scale changes than any chart ever could.

Leveraging Excel's logarithmic scale

In some situations your trending may start with very small numbers and ends with very large numbers. In these cases, you'll end up with charts that don't accurately represent the true trend. Take Figure 11-6, for instance. In this figure, you see the unit trending for both 2009 and 2010. As you can see in the source data, 2009 started with a modest 50 units. As the months progressed, the monthly unit count increased to 11,100 units through December 2010. Because the two years are on such different scales, it's difficult to discern a comparative trending for the two years together.

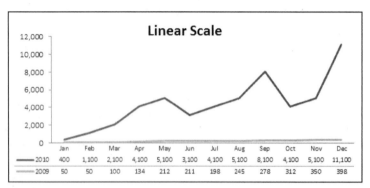

	Jan	Feb	Mar	Apr	May	Jun	Jul	Aug	Sep	Oct	Nov	Dec
2010	400	1,100	2,100	4,100	5,100	3,100	4,100	5,100	8,100	4,100	5,100	11,100
2009	50	50	100	134	212	211	198	245	278	312	350	398

Figure 11-6: A standard linear scale doesn't allow for accurate trending in this chart.

The solution is to use a logarithmic scale instead of a standard linear scale.

Without going into high school math, a logarithmic scale allows your axis to jump from 1 to 10, to 100 to 1000, and so on without changing the spacing between axis points. In other words, the distance between 1 and 10 is the same as the distance between 100 and 1000.

Figure 11-7 shows the same chart as that in Figure 11-6, but in a logarithmic scale. Notice that the trending for both years is now clear and accurately represented.

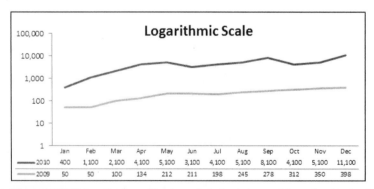

	Jan	Feb	Mar	Apr	May	Jun	Jul	Aug	Sep	Oct	Nov	Dec
2010	400	1,100	2,100	4,100	5,100	3,100	4,100	5,100	8,100	4,100	5,100	11,100
2009	50	50	100	134	212	211	198	245	278	312	350	398

Figure 11-7: Using the logarithmic scale helps bring out trending in charts that contain very small and very large values.

To change the vertical axis of a chart to logarithmic scaling, follow these steps:

1. Click anywhere in the chart.

   This opens the Chart Tools tab on the Ribbon.

2. Select the Layout tab found under the Chart Tools sub tab.

3. Click the Axis button and select Primary Vertical Axis.

4. Click the Show Axis with Log Scale option. (See Figure 11-8.)

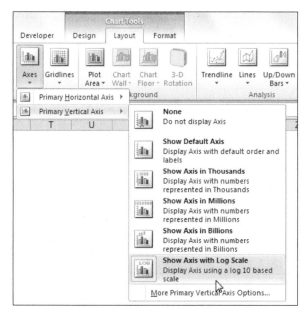

Figure 11-8: Setting the vertical axis to Log scale.

Logarithmic scales work only with positive numbers.

Note

Applying creative label management

As trivial as it may sound, labeling can be one of the sticking points to creating effective trending components. Trending charts tend to hold lots of data points, whose category axis labels take up lots of room. Inundating users with a gaggle of data labels can definitely distract from the main message of the chart. In this section, you find a few tips to help manage the labels in your trending components.

Abbreviating instead of changing alignment

Month names look and feel very long when you have to place them in a chart — especially when that chart has to fit on a dashboard. However, the solution isn't to change their alignment, as shown in Figure 11-9. Words that are placed on their sides inherently cause a reader to stop for a moment and read the labels. This isn't ideal when you want them to think about your data and not spend time reading with their heads tilted.

Although it's not always possible, the first option is always to keep your labels normally aligned. So instead of jumping right to the alignment option to squeeze them in, try abbreviating the month names. As you can see in Figure 11-9, even using the first letter of the month name is appropriate.

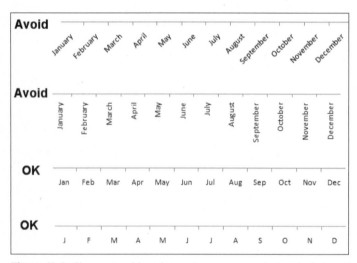

Figure 11-9: Choose to abbreviate category names instead of changing alignment.

Implying labels to reduce clutter

When you're listing the same months over the course of multiple years, you may be able to imply the labels for months instead of labeling each and every one of them.

Take Figure 11-10, for example. In this figure, you see a chart that shows trending through two years. There are so many data points that the labels are forced to be vertically aligned. To reduce clutter, as you can see, only certain months are explicitly labeled. The others are implied by a dot. To achieve this effect, you can simply replace the label in the original source data with a dot (or whatever character you like).

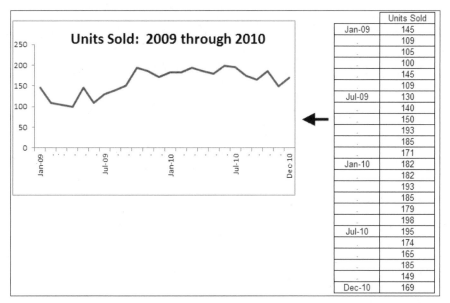

	Units Sold
Jan-09	145
	109
	105
	100
	145
	109
Jul-09	130
	140
	150
	193
	185
	171
Jan-10	182
	182
	193
	185
	179
	198
Jul-10	195
	174
	165
	185
	149
Dec-10	169

Figure 11-10: To save real estate on your dashboard, try labeling only certain data points.

Going vertical when you have too many data points for horizontal

Trending data by day is common, but it does prove to be painful if the trending extends to 30 days or more. In these scenarios, it becomes difficult to keep the chart to a reasonable size and even more difficult to effectively label it.

One solution is to show the trending vertically using a bar chart. (See Figure 11-11.) With a bar chart, you have room to label the data points and keep the chart to a reasonable size. This isn't something to aspire to, however. Trending vertically isn't as intuitive and may not convey your information in a very readable form. Nevertheless, this solution can prove to be just the work-around you need when the horizontal view proves to be impractical.

Nesting labels for clarity

Often times, the data you're trying to chart has multiple time dimensions. In these cases, you can call out these dimensions by nesting your labels. Figure 11-12 demonstrates how including a year column next to the month labels clearly partitions each year's data. You would simply include the year column when identifying the data source for your chart.

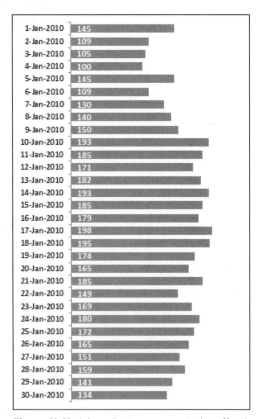

Figure 11-11: A bar chart can prove to be effective when trending days extending to 30 or more data points.

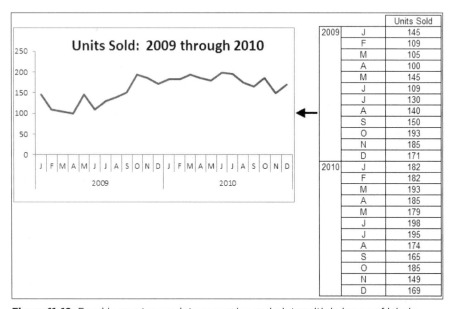

Figure 11-12: Excel is smart enough to recognize and plot multiple layers of labels.

Comparative Trending

Although the name is fancy, *comparative trending* is a simple concept. You chart two or more data series on the same chart so that the trends from those series can be visually compared. In this section, you walk through a few techniques that allow you to build components that present comparative trending.

Creating side-by-side time comparisons

Figure 11-13 shows a chart that presents a side-by-side time comparison of three time periods. With this technique, you can show different time periods in different colors without breaking the continuity of the overall trending.

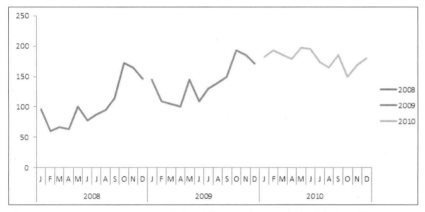

Figure 11-13: You can show trends for different time periods side-by-side.

1. To create this type of chart, structure your source data similar to the structure shown in Figure 11-14.

   Note that instead of placing the all the data into one column, you're staggering the data into respective years. This tells the chart to create three separate lines (allowing for the three colors).

2. Select the entire table and create a line chart.

   This creates the chart shown in Figure 11-13.

3. If you want to get a bit fancy, click the chart to select it, and then right-click. Select Change Chart Type from the context menu that opens.

4. When the Change Chart Type dialog box opens, select Stacked Column Chart.

   As you can in Figure 11-15, your chart now shows the trending for each year in columns.

		2008	2009	2010
2008	J	96		
	F	60		
	M	67		
	A	63		
	M	101		
	J	78		
	J	88		
	A	95		
	S	115		
	O	172		
	N	165		
	D	146		
2009	J		145	
	F		109	
	M		105	
	A		100	
	M		145	
	J		109	
	J		130	
	A		140	
	S		150	
	O		193	
	N		185	
	D		171	
2010	J			182
	F			193
	M			185
	A			179
	M			198
	J			195
	J			174
	A			165
	S			185
	O			149
	N			169
	D			180

Figure 11-14: The source data needed to display side-by-side trends.

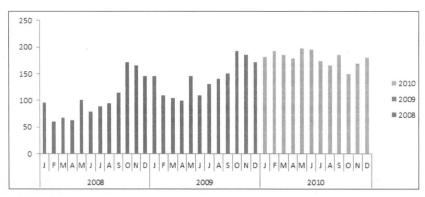

Figure 11-15: Change the chart type to Stacked Column Chart to present columns instead of lines.

Would you like a space in between the years? Adding a space in the source data (between each 12 month sequence) adds a space in the chart. (See Figure 11-16.)

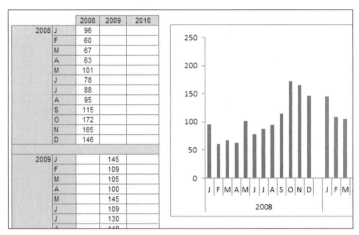

Figure 11-16: If you want to separate each year with a space, simply add a space into the source data.

Creating stacked time comparisons

The stacked time comparison places two series on top of each other instead of side-by-side. Although this removes the benefit of having an unbroken overall trending, it replaces it with the benefit of an at-a-glance comparison within a compact space. Figure 11-17 illustrates a common stacked time comparison.

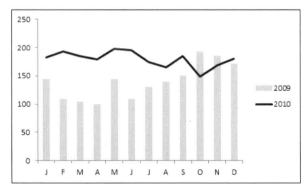

Figure 11-17: A stacked time comparison allows you to view and compare two years of data in a compact space.

1. Create a new structure and add data to it like the one shown in Figure 11-18.

2. Highlight the entire structure and create a column chart.

3. Select and right-click any of the bars for the 2010 data series and then choose Change Chart Type.

4. When the Change Chart Type dialog box opens, select the Line type.

	A	B	C
1		2009	2010
2	J	145	182
3	F	109	193
4	M	105	185
5	A	100	179
6	M	145	198
7	J	109	195
8	J	130	174
9	A	140	165
10	S	150	185
11	O	193	149
12	N	185	169
13	D	171	180

Figure 11-18: Start with a structure containing the data for two time periods.

Tip

This technique works well with two time series. You generally want to avoid stacking any more than that. Stacking more than two series often muddies the view and causes users to constantly reference the legend to keep track of the series they're evaluating.

Trending with a secondary axis

In some trending components, you'll have series that trends two very different units of measure. For instance, in Figure 11-19, you have a table that shows a trend for People Count and a trend for % of Labor Cost.

	A	B	C
1		People Count	% Labor Cost
2	J	145	20%
3	F	109	21%
4	M	105	23%
5	A	100	23%
6	M	145	24%
7	J	109	25%
8	J	130	24%
9	A	140	25%
10	S	150	24%
11	O	193	26%
12	N	185	28%
13	D	171	29%

Figure 11-19: You often need to trend two very different units of measure, such as counts and percentages.

These are two very different units of measure that, when charted, produce the unimpressive chart you see in Figure 11-20. Because Excel builds the vertical axis to accommodate the largest number, the percentage of labor cost trending gets lost at the bottom of the chart. Even a logarithmic scale doesn't help in this scenario.

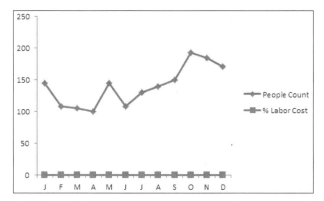

Figure 11-20: The trending for percentage of labor cost gets lost at the bottom of the chart.

Because the default vertical axis (or primary axis) doesn't work for both series, the solution is to create another axis to accommodate the series that doesn't fit into the primary axis. This other axis is the *secondary axis.*

To place a data series on the secondary axis, follow these steps:

1. Right-click the data series and select Format Data Series.

   The Format Data Series dialog box appears (see Figure 11-21).

2. In the Format Data Series dialog box, select the Series Options button in the left pane and then select the Secondary Axis radio button.

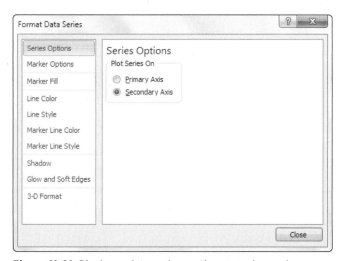

Figure 11-21: Placing a data series on the secondary axis.

Figure 11-22 illustrates the newly added axis to the right of the chart. Any data series on the secondary axis has its vertical axis labels shown on the right.

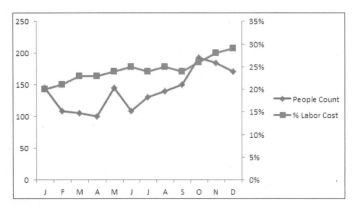

Figure 11-22: Thanks to the secondary axis, both trends are clearly defined.

Again, changing the chart type of any one of the data series can help in comparing the two trends. In Figure 11-23, the chart type for the People Count trend has been changed to a column. Now you can easily see that although the number of people has gone down in November and December, the percentage of labor cost continues to rise.

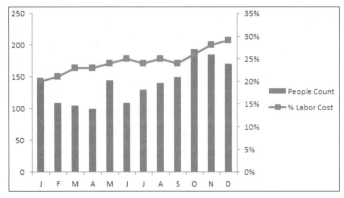

Figure 11-23: Changing the chart type of one data series can underscore comparisons.

Tip

Technically, it doesn't matter which data series you place on the secondary axis. A general rule is to place the problem data series on the secondary axis. In this scenario, because the data series for percentage of labor cost seems to be the problem, we place that series on the secondary axis.

Emphasizing Periods of Time

Some of your trending components may contain certain periods where a special event occurred, causing an anomaly in the trending pattern. For instance, you may have an unusually large spike or dip in the trend caused by some occurrence in your organization. Or maybe you need to mix actual data with forecasts in your charting component. In such cases, it could be helpful to emphasize specific periods in your trending with special formatting.

Formatting specific periods

Imagine you just created the chart component illustrated in Figure 11-24, and you want to explain the spike in October. You could, of course, use a footnote somewhere, but that would force your audience to look for an explanation elsewhere on your dashboard. Calling attention to an anomaly directly on the chart helps give your audience context without the need to look away from the chart.

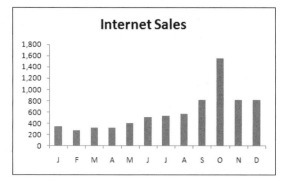

Figure 11-24: The spike in October warrants emphasis.

A simple solution is to format the data point for October to display in a different color and then add a simple text box that explains the spike.

To format a single data point:

1. Click the data point once.

   This places dots on all the data points in the series.

2. Click the data point again to ensure Excel knows you're formatting only that one data point.

   The dots disappear from all but the target data point.

3. Right-click and select Format Data Point.

   This opens the Format Data Point dialog box, as shown in Figure 11-25. The idea is to adjust the formatting properties of the data point as you see fit.

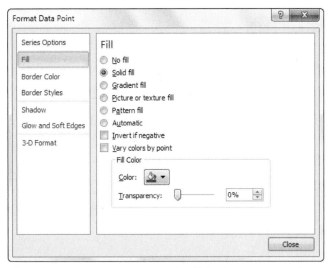

Figure 11-25: The Format Data Point dialog box gives you formatting options for a single data point.

Note

The dialog box shown in Figure 11-25 is for a column chart. Different chart types have different options in the Format Data Point dialog box. Nevertheless, the idea remains the same in that you can adjust the properties in the Format Data Point dialog box to change the formatting of a single data point.

After changing the fill color of the October data point and adding a text box with some context, the chart nicely explains the spike. (See Figure 11-26.)

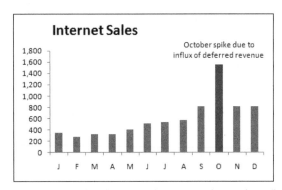

Figure 11-26: The chart now draws attention to the spike in October and provides instant context via a text box.

Note

To add a text box to a chart, click the Insert tab on the Ribbon and select the Text Box icon. Then click inside the chart to create an empty text box, which you can fill with your words.

Visit Chapter 10 for a detailed refresher on dynamic labeling.

Cross-Ref

Using dividers to mark significant events

Every now and then a particular event shifts the entire paradigm of your data permanently. A good example is a price increase. The trend shown in Figure 11-27 has permanently been affected by a price increase implemented in October. As you can see, a dividing line (along with some labeling) provides a distinct marker for the price increase, effectively separating the old trend from the new.

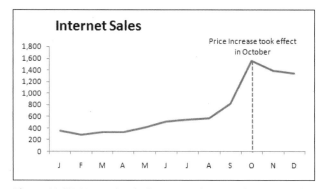

Figure 11-27: Use a simple line to mark particular events along a trend.

Although there are lots of fancy ways to create this effect, you will rarely need to get any fancier that manually drawing a line yourself. To draw a dividing line inside a chart, take the following steps:

1. Click the chart to select it.
2. Select the Insert tab on the Ribbon and click the Shapes button.
3. Select the line shape, go to your chart, and draw the line where you want it.
4. Right-click your newly drawn line and select Format Shape.
5. Use the Format Shape dialog box to format your line's color, thickness, and style.

Representing forecasts in your trending components

It's common to be asked to show both actual data and forecast as a single trending component. When you do show the two together, you want to ensure that your audience can clearly distinguish where actual data ends and where forecasting begins. To see what I mean, take a look at Figure 11-28.

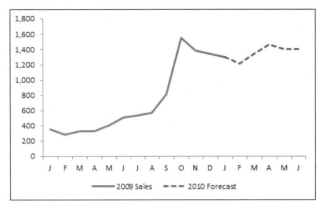

Figure 11-28: You can easily see where sales trending ends and forecast trending begins.

The best way to achieve this effect is to start with a data structure similar to the one shown in Figure 11-29. As you can see, sales and forecasts are in separate columns so that when charted, you get two distinct data series. Also note the value in cell B14 is actually a formula referencing C14. This value serves to ensure a continuous trend line (with no gaps) when the two data series are charted together.

	A	B 2009 Sales	C 2010 Forecast
1		2009 Sales	2010 Forecast
2	J	355	
3	F	284	
4	M	327	
5	A	326	
6	M	408	
7	J	514	
8	J	541	
9	A	571	
10	S	815	
11	O	1,553	
12	N	1,385	
13	D	1,341	
14	J	1,297	1,297
15	F		1,212
16	M		1,341
17	A		1,469
18	M		1,405
19	J		1,405
20			
21			
22		=C14	
23			

Figure 11-29: Start with a table that places your actual data and your forecasts in separate columns.

When you have the appropriately structured dataset, you can create a line chart. At this point, you can apply special formatting to the 2010 forecast data series. Follow these steps:

1. Click the data series that represents 2010 forecast.

   This places dots on all the data points in the series.

2. Right-click and select Format Data Series.

   This opens the Format Data Series dialog box. When the Format Data Series dialog box opens, you can adjust the properties to format the series color, thickness, and style.

Other Trending Techniques

In this section, you'll explore a few techniques that go beyond the basic concepts covered so far.

Avoiding overload with directional trending

Do you work with a manager that's crazy for data? Are you getting headaches from trying to squeeze three years of monthly data into a single chart? Although it's understandable to want to see a three-year trend, placing too much information on a single chart can make for a convoluted trending component that tells you almost nothing.

When you're faced with the need to display impossible amounts of data, step back and think about the true purpose of the analysis. When your manager asks for a three-year sales trend by month, what's he really looking for? It could be that he's really asking whether current monthly sales are declining versus history. Do you really need to show each and every month or can you show the directional trend?

A *directional trend* is one that uses simple analysis to imply a relative direction of performance. The key attribute of a directional trend is that the data used is often a set of calculated values as opposed to actual data values. For instance, instead of charting each month's sales for a single year, you could chart the average sales for Q1, Q2, Q3, and Q4. With such a chart, you'd get a directional idea of monthly sales, without the need to look into detailed data.

Take a look at Figure 11-30, which shows two charts. The top chart trends each year's monthly data in a single trending component. You can see how difficult it is to discern much from this chart. It looks like monthly sales are dropping in all three years. The bottom chart shows the same data in a directional trend, showing average sales for key time periods. The trend really jumps at you, showing that sales have flattened out after healthy growth in 2008 and 2009.

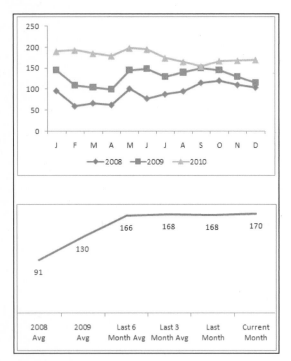

Figure 11-30: Directional trending (bottom) can help you reveal trends that may be hidden in more complex charts.

Smoothing data

Certain lines of business lend themselves to wide fluctuations in data from month to month. For instance, a consulting practice may go months without a steady revenue stream before a big contract comes along and spikes the sales figures for a few months. Some call these ups and downs *seasonality* or *business cycles.*

Whatever you call them, wild fluctuations in data can prevent you from effectively analyzing and presenting trends. Figure 11-31 demonstrates how highly volatile data can conceal underlying trends.

This is where the concept of *smoothing* comes in. Smoothing does just what it sounds like — it forces the range between the highest and lowest values in a dataset to smooth to a predictable range without disturbing the proportions of the dataset.

Now, you can use lots of different techniques to smooth a dataset. Take a moment to walk through two of the easier ways to apply smoothing.

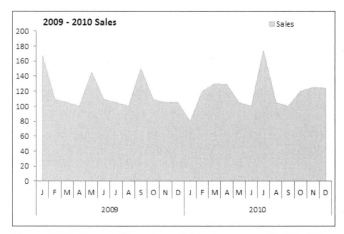

Figure 11-31: The volatile nature of this data makes it difficult to seek the underlying trend.

Smoothing with Excel's moving average functionality

Excel has a built-in smoothing mechanism in the form of a moving average trend line. That is, a trend line that calculates and plots the moving average at each data point. A moving average is a statistical operation that is used to track daily, weekly, or monthly patterns. A typical moving average starts calculating the average of a fixed number of data points, then with each new day's (or week's or month's) numbers, the oldest number is dropped, and the newest number is included in the average. This calculation is repeated over the entire data set, creating a trend that represents the average at specific points in time.

Figure 11-32 illustrates how Excel's moving average trend line can help smooth volatile data, highlighting a predictable range.

In this example, a four-month moving average has been applied.

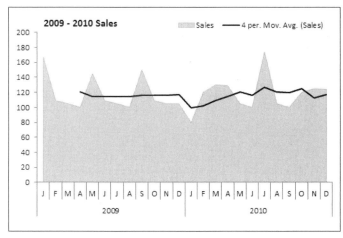

Figure 11-32: A four-month moving average trend line has been added to smooth the volatile nature of the original data.

To add a moving average trend line, follow these steps:

1. Right-click the data series that represents the volatile data, and then select Add Trendline.

2. In the Format Trendline dialog box that opens (see Figure 11-33), select Moving Average, and then specify the number of periods.

   In this case, Excel will average a four-month moving trend line.

3. Click the Close button to confirm the change.

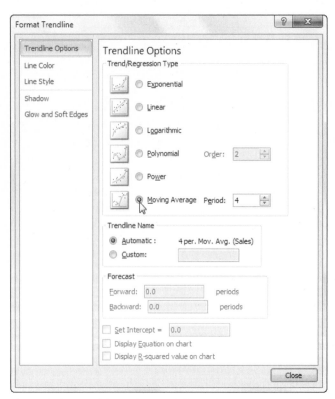

Figure 11-33: Applying a four-month moving average trend line.

Creating your own smoothing calculation

As an alternative to Excel's built in trend lines, you can create your own smoothing calculation and simply include it as a data series in your chart. In Figure 11-34, a calculated column (appropriately called smoothing) provides the data points needed to create a smoothed data series.

B	C	D	E
		Sales	Smoothing
2009	J	167	
	F	109	=AVERAGE($D$2:D3)
	M	105	127
	A	100	120
	M	145	125
	J	109	123
	J	105	120
	A	100	118
	S	150	121
	O	109	120
	N	105	119
	D	105	117
2010	J	80	115

Figure 11-34: A calculated smoothing column feeds a new series to your chart.

In this example, the second row of the smoothing column contains a simple average formula that averages the first data point and the second data point. Note that the reference to the first data point (cell D2) is locked as an absolute value with dollar ($) signs. This ensures that when this formula is copied down, the range grows to include all previous data points.

Once the formula is copied down to fill the entire smoothing column, it can simply be included in the data source for the chart. Figure 11-35 illustrates the smoothed data plotted as a line chart.

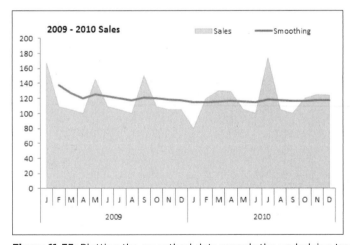

Figure 11-35: Plotting the smoothed data reveals the underlying trend.

12

Components that Group Data

In This Chapter

- Showing top and bottom views
- Tracking progress using histograms
- Emphasizing top values in charts

It's often helpful to organize your data into logical groups. Grouping allows you to focus on manageable sets of information that have key attributes. For example, instead of looking at all customers in one giant view, you can analyze customers who buy only one product. This allows you to focus attention and resources on those customers who have the potential to buy more products. The benefit is that you can more easily pick out groups that fall outside the norm for your business.

In this chapter, you'll focus on how you can organize groups of data using dashboard components.

Listing Top and Bottom Values

When you look at the list of Fortune 500 companies, you often look for the top 20 companies. Then perhaps you look at who eked out at the bottom 20 slots. It's unlikely that you would check to see which company came in at number 251. It's not necessarily because you don't care about number 251; it's just that you can't spend the time or energy to process all 500 companies. So you process the top and bottom of the list.

This is the same concept behind creating top and bottom displays. Your audience has only a certain amount of time and resources to dedicate to solving any issues you can emphasize in your dashboard. Showing them the top and bottom values in your data can help them pinpoint where and how they can have the most impact with the time and resources they do have.

Organizing source data

The top and bottom displays you create can be as simple as source data that you incorporate into your dashboard. Typically placed to the right of a dashboard, this data can emphasize details a manager may use to take action on a metric. For example, the simple dashboard shown in Figure 12-1 shows sales information with top and bottom sales reps.

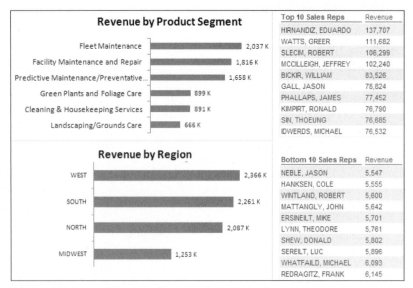

Figure 12-1: Top and bottom displays that emphasize certain metrics.

To get a little fancier, you can supplement your top and bottom displays with some ranking information, some in-cell bar charts, or some conditional formatting. (See Figure 12-2.)

You can create the in-cell bar charts with the REPT function, covered in Chapter 10. The arrows are simple conditional formatting rules that are evaluated against the variance in current and last months' ranks.

Cross-Ref

For more information about the REPT function, see Chapter 10. For more information about sparklines, see Chapter 9.

Using pivot tables for interactive views

If you read Chapter 7, you know that a pivot table is an amazing tool that can help create interactive reporting. Take a moment now to walk through an example of how pivot tables can help you build interactive top and bottom displays.

On the Web

You can open the `Chapter 12 Sample File.xlsx` file, found on this book's companion Web site at `www.wiley.com/go/exceldr` to follow along.

Top 10 Sales Reps	Sales		Rank	Last Month	vs Last Month
HIRNANDIZ, EDUARDO	$137,707		1	1	⇨ 0
WATTS, GREER	$111,682		2	3	⇧ 1
SLECIM, ROBERT	$106,299		3	5	⇧ 2
MCCILLEIGH, JEFFREY	$102,240		4	2	⇩ -2
BICKIR, WILLIAM	$83,526		5	3	⇩ -2
GALL, JASON	$78,824		6	12	⇧ 6
PHALLAPS, JAMES	$77,452		7	7	⇨ 0
KIMPIRT, RONALD	$76,790		8	9	⇧ 1
SIN, THOEUNG	$76,685		9	8	⇩ -1
IDWERDS, MICHAEL	$76,532		10	4	⇩ -6

Bottom 10 Sales Reps	Sales		Rank	Last Month	vs Last Month
NEBLE, JASON	$5,547		244	244	⇨ 0
CELIMAN, WILLIAM	$9,779		243	241	⇩ -2
KRIZILL, ADAM	$11,454		242	235	⇩ -7
MIDANA, FRANK	$15,044		241	221	⇩ -20
GRANGIR, DAVID	$16,129		240	240	⇨ 0
DALLEARE, ANDRE	$16,265		239	239	⇨ 0
HICKLIBIRRY, JERRY	$16,670		238	225	⇩ -13
VAN HUILE, KENNETH	$18,821		237	242	⇧ 5
RACHERDSEN, KENNETH	$19,675		236	237	⇧ 1
STIGALL, DAVID	$20,092		235	243	⇧ 8

Figure 12-2: You can use the REPT function and some conditional formatting to add visual components to your top and bottom displays.

Follow these steps to display data with a pivot table:

1. Start with a pivot table that shows the data you want to display with your top and bottom views.

   In this case, the pivot table shows Sales Rep and Sales_Amount (see Figure 12-3).

	A	B
1	Region	(All)
2	Market	(All)
3		
4	**Sales Rep**	**Sales_Amount**
5	ABERRA, CHRISTOPHER	$28,370
6	ADEMO, DANIEL	$20,259
7	ADEMS, KYLE	$21,500
8	ADEMS, TAIWAN	$27,593
9	ALCERO, ROBERT	$42,697
10	ANDIRSEN, DORAN	$47,857
11	ASHEM, CHRIS	$23,283
12	ATKANS, TERRY	$24,297
13	BEALIY, CHRISTOPHER	$38,132
14	BECHMAN, JOHN	$20,310
15	BECKMAN, ADRIAN	$9,236
16	BEKKA, KENNETH	$12,901

Figure 12-3: Start with a pivot table that contains the data you want to filter.

2. Right-click any Sales Rep name in the pivot table, and choose Filter ➜ Top 10 (see Figure 12-4).

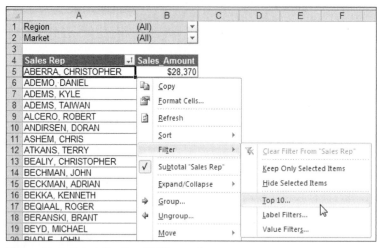

Figure 12-4: Select the Top 10 filter option.

The Top 10 Filter (Sales Rep) dialog box appears. (See Figure 12-5.)

Figure 12-5: Specify the filter you want to apply.

3. In the Top 10 Filter (Sales Rep) dialog box, define the view you're looking for. In this example, you want the Top 10 Items (Sales Reps) as defined by the Sales_Amount field.

4. Click OK to apply the filter.

At this point, your pivot table is filtered to show you the top ten sales reps for the selected Region and Market. You can change the Market filter to Charlotte and get the top ten sales reps for Charlotte only (see Figure 12-6).

5. To view the bottom ten Sales Rep list, copy the entire pivot table and paste it next to the existing one.

6. Repeat Steps 2–4 in the newly copied pivot table except this time choose to filter on the *bottom* ten items as defined by the Sales_Amount field.

If all went well, you now have two pivot tables similar to Figure 12-7: one that shows the top ten sales reps, and one that shows the bottom ten. You can link back to these two pivot tables in the analysis layer of your data model using formulas. This way, when you update the data, your top and bottom values display the new information.

	A	B
1	Region	(All)
2	Market	CHARLOTTE
3		
4	**Sales Rep**	**Sales_Amount**
5	MCCILLEIGH, JEFFREY	$98,090
6	CERDWILL, TIMOTHY	$54,883
7	BRADFERD, JAMES	$49,435
8	DIDLIY, CHARLES	$47,220
9	SWANGIR, ADAM	$46,608
10	SKILTEN, JAMES	$43,569
11	PIORSEN, HEYWARD	$41,005
12	CRIOMIR, TIMOTHY	$34,169
13	PERSENS, GREGORY	$33,026
14	BIOCH, RONALD	$30,168
15	**Grand Total**	**$478,172**

Figure 12-6: You can interactively filter your pivot table report to instantly show the top ten sales reps for any Region and Market.

	A	B	C	D	E
1	**Top Sales Reps**			**Bottom Sales Reps**	
2	Region	(All)		Region	(All)
3	Market	CHARLOTTE		Market	CHARLOTTE
4					
5	**Sales Rep**	**Sales_Amount**		**Sales Rep**	**Sales_Amount**
6	MCCILLEIGH, JEFFREY	$98,090		MEERE, TERRY	$27,149
7	CERDWILL, TIMOTHY	$54,883		BRAGHT, THOMAS	$25,005
8	BRADFERD, JAMES	$49,435		CRAVIY, ANTHONY	$22,761
9	DIDLIY, CHARLES	$47,220		WALLAEMS, SHAUN	$15,477
10	SWANGIR, ADAM	$46,608		HERVIY, CHRISTOPHER	$15,260
11	SKILTEN, JAMES	$43,569		HELT, CHRISTOPHER	$15,147
12	PIORSEN, HEYWARD	$41,005		REBIRTS, ADAMS	$13,237
13	CRIOMIR, TIMOTHY	$34,169		BECKMAN, ADRIAN	$9,236
14	PERSENS, GREGORY	$33,026		GERRUIS, ROBERT	$7,786
15	BIOCH, RONALD	$30,168		MEERE, RUSSELL	$6,635
16	**Grand Total**	**$478,172**		**Grand Total**	**$157,693**

Figure 12-7: You now have two pivot tables that show top and bottom displays.

Note

If there's a tie for any rank in the top or bottom values, Excel shows you all the tied records. This means, you may get more than the number you filtered for. If you filtered for the top 10 sales reps and there's a tie for the number 5 rank, Excel shows you 11 sales reps (both reps ranked at number 5 will be shown).

Using Histograms to Track Relationships and Frequency

A *histogram* is essentially a graph that plots *frequency distribution*. A frequency distribution shows how often an event or category of data occurs. With a histogram, you can visually see the general distribution of a certain attribute.

Take a look at the histogram shown in Figure 12-8. This histogram represents the distribution of units sold in one month among your sales reps. As you can see, most reps sell somewhere between 5 and 25 units a month. As a manager, you want the hump in the chart to move to the right — more people selling a higher number of units per month. So you set a goal to have a majority of your sales reps to sell between 15 and 25 units within the next three months. With this histogram, you can visually track the progress toward that goal.

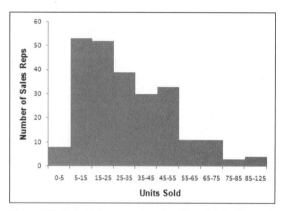

Figure 12-8: A histogram showing the distribution of units sold per month among your sales force.

This chapter discusses how to create a histogram using formulas and pivot tables. The techniques covered here fit nicely in data models where we separate data, analysis, and presentation information. In addition, these techniques allow for a level of automation and interactivity that come in handy when updating dashboards each month.

 We discuss how to develop a data model in Chapter 2.

Cross-Ref

Adding formulas to group data

First, you need a table that contains your raw data. The raw data should ideally consist of records that represent unique counts for the data you want to group. For instance, the raw data table in Figure 12-9 contains unique sales reps and the number of units each has sold. Follow these steps to create a formula-driven histogram:

1. Before you create your histogram, you need to create a bin table (see Figure 12-9).

   The bin table dictates the grouping parameters that are used to break your raw data into the frequency groups. The bin table tells Excel to cluster all sales reps selling fewer than 5 units into the first frequency group, any sales reps selling 5 to 14 units in the second frequency group, and so on.

	A	B	C	D
1	Raw Data			
2	Sales Rep	Units Sold		Bins
3	ERSINEILT, MIKE	5		0
4	HANKSEN, COLE	5		5
5	LYNN, THEODORE	5		15
6	MATTANGLY, JOHN	5		25
7	NEBLE, JASON	5		35
8	SEREILT, LUC	5		45
9	SHEW, DONALD	5		55
10	WINTLAND, ROBERT	5		65
11	BLANCHIT, DANNY	6		75
12	BLEKE JR, SAMUEL	6		85
13	ETEVAC, ROBERT	6		125
14	KNEIR, ANTHONY	6		
15	MEEDE, RUSSELL	6		

Figure 12-9: Start with your raw data table and a bin table.

Tip

You can freely set your own grouping parameters when you build your bin table. However, it's generally a good idea to keep your parameters as equally spaced as possible. We typically end our bin tables with the largest number in my dataset. This allows us to have clean groupings that end in a finite number — not in an open-ended *greater than* designation.

2. Create a new column that holds the FREQUENCY formulas. Name the new column Frequency Formulas as seen in Figure 12-10.

   Excel's FREQUENCY function counts how often values occur within the ranges you specify in a bin table.

3. Select a number of cells equal to the cells in your bin table.

4. Type the FREQUENCY formula you see in Figure 12-10 and then press Ctrl+Shift+Enter on your keyboard.

Note

The FREQUENCY function does have a quirk that often confuses first-time users. The FREQUENCY function is an *array formula* — that is, it's a formula that returns many values at one time. In order for this formula to work properly, you have to press Ctrl+Shift+Enter on your keyboard after typing the formula. If you just press the Enter key, you won't get the results you need.

	A	B	C	D	E
1	Raw Data				
2	Sales Rep	Units Sold		Bins	Frequency Formulas
3	ERSINEILT, MIKE	5		0	=FREQUENCY(B3:B246,D3:D13)
4	HANKSEN, COLE	5		5	
5	LYNN, THEODORE	5		15	
6	MATTANGLY, JOHN	5		25	
7	NEBLE, JASON	5		35	
8	SEREILT, LUC	5		45	
9	SHEW, DONALD	5		55	
10	WINTLAND, ROBERT	5		65	
11	BLANCHIT, DANNY	6		75	
12	BLEKE JR, SAMUEL	6		85	
13	ETEVAC, ROBERT	6		125	
14	KNEIP, ANTHONY	6			

Figure 12-10: Type the FREQUENCY formula you see here; be sure to hold down the Ctrl+Shift+Enter keys on your keyboard.

At this point, you should have a table that shows the number of sales reps that fall into each of your Bins. You could chart this table, but the data labels would come out wonky. For the best results, build a simple chart feeder table that creates appropriate labels for each bin. You do this in the next step.

5. Create a new table that feeds the charts a bit more cleanly (see Figure 12-11). Use a simple formula that concatenates Bins into appropriate labels. Use another formula to bring in the results of your FREQUENCY calculations.

   In Figure 12-11, we made the formulas in the first record of the chart feeder table visible. These formulas are essentially copied down to create a table appropriate for charting.

6. Use your newly-created chart feeder table to plot the data into a column chart.

   Figure 12-12 illustrates the resulting chart. You can very well use the initial column chart as your histogram.

   If you like your histograms to have spaces between the data points, you're done. If you like the continuous blocked look you get with no gaps between the data points, follow the next few steps.

7. Right-click any of the columns in the chart and choose Format Data Series.

   The Format Data Series dialog box appears.

8. In the dialog box, select the Series Options button and adjust the Gap Width property to 0% (see Figure 12-13).

D	E	F	G	H
Frequency Formulas			**Chart Feeder**	
Bins	Frequency Formulas		Units Sold	Count of Sales Reps
0	0		=D3& "-" &D4	=E4
5	8		5-15	53
15	53		15-25	52
25	52		25-35	39
35	39		35-45	30
45	30		45-55	33
55	33		55-65	11
65	11		65-75	11
75	11		75-85	3
85	3		85-125	4
125	4			

Figure 12-11: Build a simple chart feeder table that creates appropriate labels for each bin.

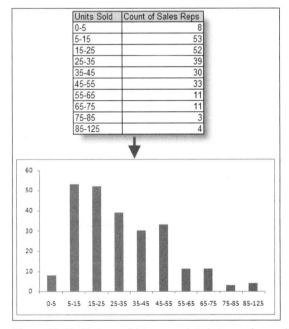

Figure 12-12: Plot your histogram data into a column chart.

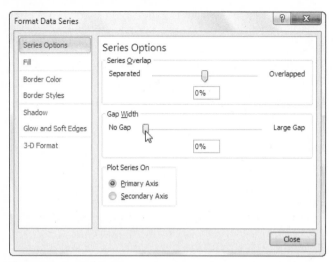

Figure 12-13: To eliminate the spaces between columns, set the Gap Width to 0%.

Adding a cumulative percent

A nice feature to add to your histograms is a cumulative percent series. With a cumulative percent series, you can show the percent distribution of the data points to the left of the point of interest.

Figure 12-14 shows an example of a cumulative percent series. At each data point in the histogram, the cumulative percent series tells you the percent of the population that fills all the Bins up to that point. For instance, you can see that 25% of the sales reps represented sold 15 units or less. In other words, 75% of the sales reps sold more than 15 units.

Take another look at the chart in Figure 12-14 and find the point where you see 75% on the cumulative series. At 75%, look at the label for that Bin range (you see 35–45). The 75% mark tells you that 75% of sales reps sold between 0 and 45 units. This means that only 25% of sales reps sold more than 45 units.

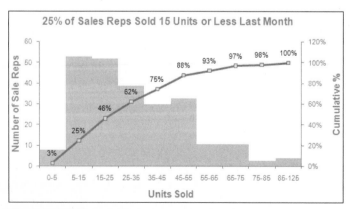

Figure 12-14: The cumulative percent series shows the percent of the population that fills all the bins up to each point in the histogram.

To create a cumulative percent series for your histogram, follow these steps:

1. After you perform Steps 1 through 5 of creating a histogram (which I outline in the earlier in this chapter), add a column to your chart feeder that calculates the percent of total sales reps for the first bin (see Figure 12-15).

   Note the dollar symbols ($) used in the formula to lock the references while you copy the formula down.

2. Copy the formula down for all the bins in the table.

3. Use the chart feeder table to plot the data into a line chart.

   As you can see in Figure 12-16, the resulting chart needs some additional formatting.

4. Right-click the series that makes up your histogram (Count of Sales Rep), select Change Chart Type, and then change the chart type to a column chart.

5. Right-click any of the columns in the chart and choose Format Data Series.

6. Select the Series Options button and adjust the Gap Width property to 0%, as shown in Figure 12-13.

7. Right-click Cumulative Percent series and choose Format Data Series.

8. In the Format Data Series dialog box, select the Series Options button. Change the Plot Series On option to Secondary Axis.

9. Right-click Cumulative Percent series and choose Add Data Labels.

At this point, your base chart is complete. It should look similar to the one shown at the beginning of this section in Figure 12-14. When you get to this point, you can adjust the colors, labels, and other formatting.

F	G	H	I
	Chart Feeder		
	Units Sold	Count of Sales Reps	Cumulative %
	0-5	8	=SUM($H$3:H3)/SUM($H$3:$H$12)
	5-15	53	
	15-25	52	
	25-35	39	
	35-45	30	
	45-55	33	
	55-65	11	
	65-75	11	
	75-85	3	
	85-125	4	

Figure 12-15: In a new column, create a formula that calculates the percent of total sales reps for the first bin.

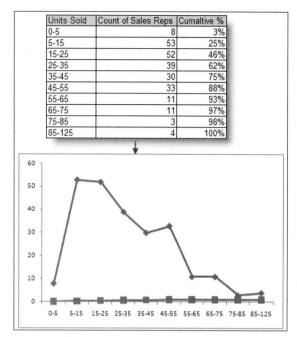

Units Sold	Count of Sales Reps	Cumaltive %
0-5	8	3%
5-15	53	25%
15-25	52	46%
25-35	39	62%
35-45	30	75%
45-55	33	88%
55-65	11	93%
65-75	11	97%
75-85	3	98%
85-125	4	100%

Figure 12-16: You initial chart will need some formatting to make it look like a histogram.

Using a pivot table

Did you know you can use a pivot table as the source for a histogram? That's right. With a little-known trick, you can create a histogram that is as interactive as a pivot chart!

As in the formula-driven histogram, the first step in creating a histogram with a pivot table is to create a frequency distribution. Here's how you do it:

1. Create a pivot table and plot the data values in the row area (not the data area). As you can see in Figure 12-17, the SumOfSales Amount field is placed in the Row Labels area. Place the Sales Rep field in the Values area as a Count.

2. Right-click any value in the Row Labels area and choose Group.

   The Grouping dialog box appears. (See Figure 12-18.)

3. In the dialog box, set the start and end values and then set the intervals.

   This essentially creates your frequency distribution. In Figure 12-18, the distribution is set to start at 5,000 and to create groups in increments of 1,000 until it ends at 100,000.

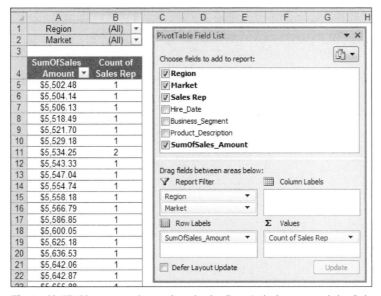

Figure 12-17: Place your data values in the Row Labels area and the Sales Rep field in the Values area as a Count.

Figure 12-18: The Grouping dialog box.

4. Click OK to confirm your settings.

The pivot table calculates the number of sales reps for each defined increment, just as in a frequency distribution. (See Figure 12-19.) You can now leverage this result to create a histogram!

	A	B
1	Region	(All) ▾
2	Market	(All) ▾
3		
4	SumOfSales Amount ▾	Count of Sales Rep
5	5000-6000	69
6	6000-7000	78
7	7000-8000	58
8	8000-9000	66
9	9000-10000	41
10	10000-11000	45
11	11000-12000	39
12	12000-13000	33
13	13000-14000	25
14	14000-15000	25
15	15000-16000	22
16	16000-17000	18

Figure 12-19: The resulting of grouping the values in the Row area is a frequency distribution that can be charted into a histogram.

The obvious benefit to this technique is that after you have a frequency distribution and a histogram, you can interactively filter the data based on other dimensions, like Region and Market. For instance, you can see the histogram for the Canada market and then quickly switch to see the histogram for the California market.

Tip

Note that you can't add cumulative percentages to a histogram based on a pivot table.

Emphasizing Top Values in Charts

Sometimes a chart is indeed the best way to display a set of data, but you still would like to call attention to the top values in that chart. In these cases, you can use a technique that *actually* highlights the top values in your charts. That is to say, you can use Excel to figure out which values in your data series are in the top *n*th value and then apply special formatting to them. Figure 12-20 illustrates an example where the top five quarters are highlighted and given a label.

The secret to this technique lies in Excel's obscure LARGE function. The large function returns the *n*th largest number from a dataset. In other words, you tell it where to look and the number rank you want.

To find the largest number in the dataset, you'd enter the formula LARGE(Data_Range, 1). To find the fifth largest number in the dataset, you'd use LARGE(Data_Range, 5). Figure 12-21 illustrates how the LARGE function works.

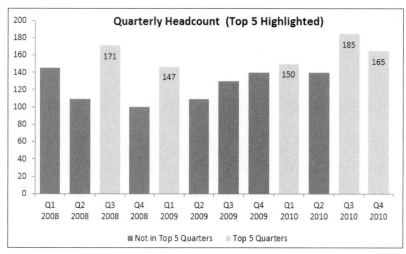

Figure 12-20: This chart highlights the top five quarters with different font and labeling.

	A	B	C	D	E
1			People Count		
2		J	145		
3		F	109		
4		M	171		
5		A	100		
6		M	147		
7		J	109		
8		J	130		
9		A	140		
10		S	150		
11		O	140		
12		N	185		
13		D	165		
14					
15		Largest Value	185	←	=LARGE(C2:C13,1)
16					
17		5th Largest Value	147	←	=LARGE(C2:C13,5)
18					

Figure 12-21: Using the LARGE function returns the *n*th largest number from a dataset.

The idea is fairly simple. In order to identify the top five values in a dataset, you first need to identify the fifth largest number (LARGE function to the rescue) and then test each value in the dataset to see if it's bigger than the fifth largest number. Here's what you do:

1. Build a chart feeder that consists of formulas that link back to your raw data. The feeder should have two columns: one to hold data that isn't in the top five, and one to hold data that is in the top five. (See Figure 12-22.)

2. In the first row of the chart feeder, enter the formulas shown in Figure 12-22.

   The formula for the first column (F4) checks to see if the value in cell C4 is less than the number returned by the LARGE formula (the fifth largest value). If it is, the value in Cell C4 is returned. Otherwise, NA is used. The formula for the second column works in the same way except the if statement is reversed: If the value in cell C4 is greater than or equal to the number returned by the LARGE formula, then the value is returned; other-wise NA is used.

3. Copy the formulas down to fill the table.

4. Use the chart feeder table to plot the data into a stacked column chart.

   You immediately see a chart that displays two data series: one for data points not in the top five, and one for data points in the top five. (See Figure 12-23.)

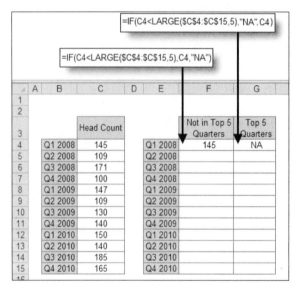

Figure 12-22: Build a new chart feeder that consists of formulas that plots values into one of two columns.

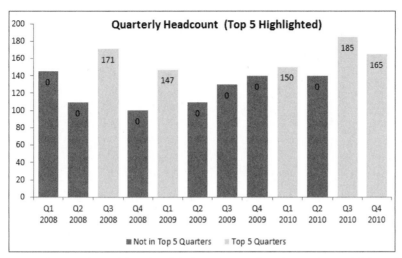

Figure 12-23: After adding data labels to the top five data series and doing a bit of formatting, your chart should look similar to the one shown here.

Notice in Figure 12-23 that the chart shows some rogue zeros. You can fix the chart so that the zeros don't display by performing the next few steps.

5. Right-click any of the data labels for the top five series and choose Format Data Labels.

6. In the Format Data Labels dialog box, select the Numbers button and select Custom in the Category list.

7. Enter #,##0;; as the custom number format, as shown in Figure 12-24.

8. Click the Add button and then click Close.

When you go back to your chart, you see that the rogue zeros are now hidden and your chart is ready for colors, labels, and other formatting you want to apply.

You can apply the same technique to highlight the bottom five values in your data set. The only difference is that instead of using the LARGE function, you use the SMALL function. Whereas the LARGE function returns the largest nth value from a range, the SMALL function returns the smallest nth value.

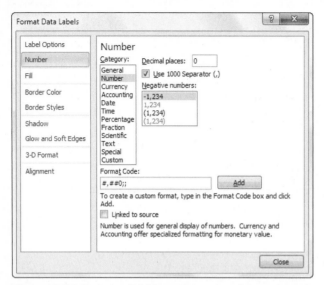

Figure 12-24: Entering #,##0;; as the custom format for a data label renders all zeros in that data series hidden.

Figure 12-25 illustrates the formulas you'd use to apply the same technique outlined here for the bottom five values.

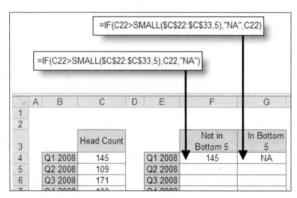

Figure 12-25: Use the SMALL function to highlight the bottom values in a chart.

The formula for the first column (F4) checks to see if the value in cell C22is greater than the number returned by the SMALL formula (the fifth smallest value). If it is, the value in Cell C22 is returned. Otherwise, NA is used. The formula for the second column works in the same way except the IF statement is reversed: If the value in cell C22 is greater than the number returned by the SMALL formula, then NA is used; otherwise the value is returned.

13

Components that Show Performance against a Target

In This Chapter

- Using variance to compare performance with a target
- Displaying performance against organizational trends
- Creating a Thermometer-style chart
- Creating a bullet graph
- Showing performance against a target range

No matter what business or industry you talk about, you can always point to some sort of target to measure data against. That target could be anything from a certain amount of revenue to the number of boxes shipped or phone calls made. The business world is full of targets and goals. Your job is to find effective ways to represent performance against those targets.

What is performance against a target? Imagine your goal is to break the land speed record (currently 763 miles per hour). Your target speed is 764 miles per hour. After you jump into your car and go as fast as you can, you will have a final speed of some number. That number is considered to be your performance against the target.

In this chapter, we discuss some new and interesting ways to create components that show performance against a target.

Showing Performance with Variances

The standard way of displaying performance against a target is to plot the target and then plot the performance. This is usually done with a line chart or a combination chart, such as the one shown in Figure 13-1.

Figure 13-1: A typical chart showing performance against a target.

Although this chart allows you to visually pick the points where performance exceeded or fell below targets, it gives you a rather one-dimensional view and provides minimal information. Even if this chart offered labels that showed the actual percent of sales revenue versus target, you'd still get only a mildly informative view.

A more impactful and informative way of displaying performance against a target is to plot the variances between the target and the performance. Figure 13-2 shows the same performance data you see in Figure 13-1, but includes the variances (sales revenue minus target). This way, you not only see where performance exceeded or fell below targets, but you get an extra layer of information showing the dollar impact of each rise and fall.

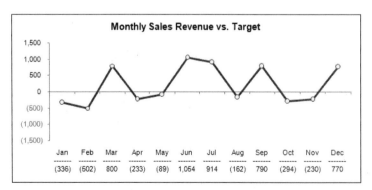

Figure 13-2: Consider using variances to plot performance against a target.

Showing Performance against Organizational Trends

The target you use to measure performance doesn't necessarily have to be set by management or organizational policy. In fact, some of the things you measure may never have a target or goal set for them. In situations where you don't have a target to measure against, it's often helpful to measure performance against some organizational statistic.

For example, the component in Figure 13-3 measures the sales performance for each division against the median sales for all the divisions. You can see that divisions 1, 3, and 6 fall well below the median for the group.

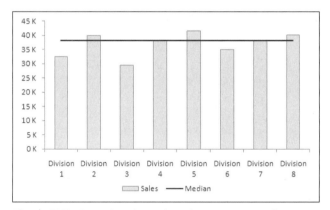

Figure 13-3: Measuring data when there's no target for a measure.

Here's how you'd create a median line similar to the one you see in Figure 13-3:

1. Start a new column next to your data and type the simple MEDIAN formula, as shown in Figure 13-4.

   Note that this formula can be any mathematical or statistical operation that works for the data you are representing. Just ensure that the values returned are the same for the entire column. This gives you a straight line.

2. Copy the formula down to fill the table.

   Again, all the numbers in the newly created column should be the same.

3. Plot the table into a column chart.

4. Right-click the Median data series and choose Change Chart Type.

5. Change the chart type to a line chart.

	A	B	C
1		Sales	Median
2	Division 1	32,526	=MEDIAN($B$2:$B$9)
3	Division 2	39,939	
4	Division 3	29,542	
5	Division 4	38,312	
6	Division 5	41,595	
7	Division 6	35,089	
8	Division 7	38,270	
9	Division 8	40,022	
10			

Figure 13-4: Start a new column and enter a formula.

Using a Thermometer-Style Chart

A *thermometer-style chart* offers a unique way to view performance against a goal. As the name implies, the data points shown in this type of chart resemble a thermometer. Each performance value and its corresponding target are stacked on top of one another, giving an appearance similar to that of mercury rising in a thermometer. In Figure 13-5, you see an example of a thermometer-style chart.

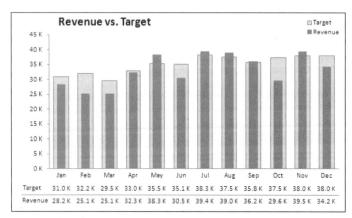

Figure 13-5: Thermometer-style charts offer a unique way to show performance against a goal.

To create this type of chart, follow these steps:

1. Starting with a table that contains revenue and target data, plot the data into a new column chart.

2. Right-click the Revenue data series and choose Format Data Series.

   The Format Data Series dialog box appears.

3. In the Format Data Series dialog box, select the Series Options button and then select Secondary Axis.

4. Go back to your chart and delete the new axis that was added; it's the vertical axis to the right of the chart.

5. Right-click the Target series and choose Format Data Series.

   The Format Data Series dialog box appears again.

6. In the dialog box, select the Series Options button and adjust the Gap Width property so that the Target series is slightly wider than the Revenue series — between 45% and 55% is typically fine.

Using a Bullet Graph

A *bullet graph* is a type of column/bar graph developed by visualization expert Stephen Few to serve as a replacement for dashboard gauges and meters. He developed bullet graphs to allow for the clear display of multiple layers of information without occupying a lot of space on a dashboard. A bullet graph, as seen in Figure 13-6, contains a single performance measure (such as YTD [year-to-date] revenue), compares that measure to a target, and displays it in the context of qualitative ranges, such as Poor, Fair, Good, and Very Good.

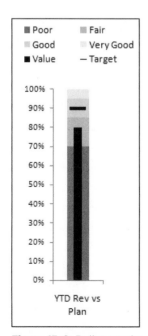

Figure 13-6: Bullet graphs display multiple perspectives in an incredibly compact space.

Figure 13-7 breaks down the three main parts of a bullet graph. The *performance bar* represents the performance measure. The *target marker* represents the comparative measure. And the *background fills* represent the qualitative range.

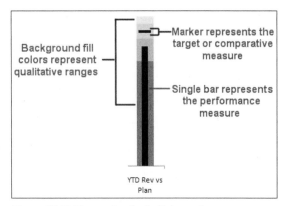

Figure 13-7: The parts of a bullet graph.

Creating a bullet graph

Creating a bullet graph in Excel isn't necessarily difficult. Follow these steps to create your first bullet graph:

1. Start with a data table that gives you all the data points you need to create the three main parts of the bullet graph.

    Figure 13-8 illustrates what that data table looks like. The first four values in the data set (Poor, Fair, Good, and Very Good) make up the qualitative range. You don't have to have four values — you can have as many or as few as you need. In this scenario, we want our qualitative range to span from 0 to 100%. Therefore, the percentages (75%, 15%, 10%, and 5%) must add up to 100%. Again, this can be adjusted to suit your needs. The fifth value in Figure 13-8 (Value) creates the performance bar. The sixth value (Target) makes the target marker.

	A	B
1		YTD Rev vs Plan
2	Poor	70%
3	Fair	15%
4	Good	10%
5	VeryGood	5%
6	Value	80%
7	Target	90%

Figure 13-8: Start with data that contains the main data points of the bullet graph.

2. Select the entire table and plot the data on a stacked column chart.

   The chart that's created is initially plotted in the wrong direction.

3. To fix the direction, click the chart and select the Switch Row/Column button, as shown in Figure 13-9.

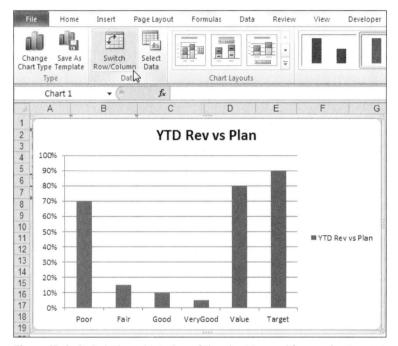

Figure 13-9: Switch the orientation of the chart to read from columns.

4. Right-click the Target series and choose Change Chart Type. Change the chart type to a line chart (with markers).

5. Right-click the Target series again and choose Format Data Series.

   The Format Data Series dialog box appears.

6. In the Format Data Series dialog box, click the Series Options button and click Secondary Axis.

7. Still in the Format Data Series dialog box, click the Marker Options button and adjust the marker to look like a dash, as shown in Figure 13-10.

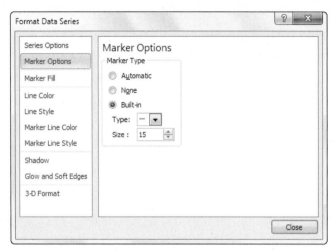

Figure 13-10: Adjust the marker to a dash.

8. Still in the Format Data Series dialog box, click the Marker Fill button and select the Solid Fill property to set the color of the marker to black.

9. Still in the Format Data Series dialog box, click the Line Color button and select the No Line option, then set the Marker Line Color to None.

10. Go back to your chart and delete the new secondary axis that was added to the right of your chart (see Figure 13-11).

This is an important step to ensure the scale of the chart is correct for all data points.

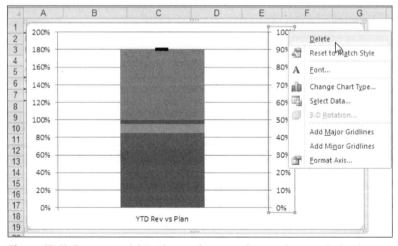

Figure 13-11: Be sure to delete the newly created secondary vertical axis.

11. Right-click the Value series and choose Format Data Series. The Format Data Series dialog box appears again.

12. In the Format Data Series dialog box, click the Series Options button and click Secondary Axis.

13. Still in the Format Data Series dialog box under Series Options, adjust the Gap Width property so that the Value series is slightly narrower than the other columns in the chart — between 205% and 225% is typically okay.

14. Still in the Format Data Series dialog box, click the Fill button and select the Solid Fill property to set the color of the Value series to black.

All that's left to do is change the color for each qualitative range to incrementally lighter hues.

At this point, your bullet graph is essentially done! You can apply whatever minor formatting adjustments to size and shape of the chart to make it look the way you want.

Adding data to your bullet graph

After you've built your chart for the first performance measure, you can use the same chart for any additional measures. Take a look at Figure 13-12.

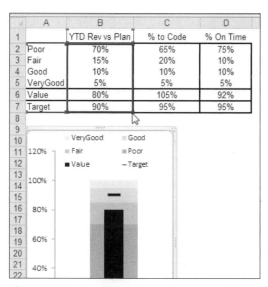

Figure 13-12: To add more data to your chart, manually expand the chart's data source range.

As you can see in Figure 13-12, you've already created this bullet graph with the first performance measure. Imagine that you add two more measures and want to graph those. Here's how to do it:

1. Click the chart so that the blue outline appears around the original source data.

2. Hover your mouse over the blue dot in the lower-right corner of the blue box.

   Your cursor turns into an arrow, as seen in Figure 13-12.

3. Click and drag the blue dot to the last column in your expanded data set.

   Figure 13-13 illustrates how the new data points are added without one ounce of extra work!

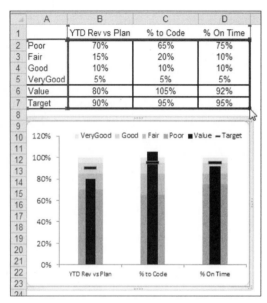

Figure 13-13: Expanding the data source automatically creates new bullet graphs.

Final thoughts on formatting bullet graphs

Before wrapping up this introduction to bullet graphs, we discuss two final thoughts on formatting:

➤ Creating qualitative bands

➤ Creating horizontal bullet graphs

Creating qualitative bands

First, if the qualitative ranges are the same for all the performance measures in your bullet graphs, you can format the qualitative range series to have no gaps between them. For instance, Figure 13-14 shows a set of bullet graphs where the qualitative ranges have been set to 0 Gap Width. This creates the clever effect of qualitative bands.

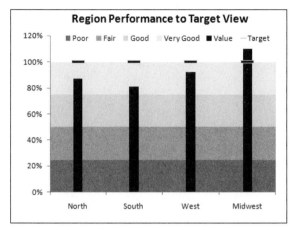

Figure 13-14: Try setting gap widths to zero to create clean-looking qualitative bands.

1. Right-click any one of the qualitative series and choose Format Data Series.

   The Format Data Series dialog box appears.

2. In the dialog box, select Series Options and adjust the Gap Width property to 0%.

Creating horizontal bullet graphs

For those of you who are waiting on the section about horizontal bullet graphs, there's good and bad news. The bad news is that creating a horizontal bullet graph from scratch in Excel is a much more complex endeavor than creating a vertical bullet graph — one that doesn't warrant the time and effort it takes to create them.

The good news is that your clever authors have come up with a way get a horizontal bullet graph from a vertical one — and in three steps, no less. Here's how you do it:

1. Create a vertical bullet graph.

   For more on creating bullet graphs, see the section earlier in this chapter.

2. Change the alignment for the axis and other labels on the bullet graph so that they're rotated 270 degrees (see Figure 13-15).

3. Use Excel's Camera tool to take a picture of the bullet graph.

    After you have a picture, you can rotate it to be horizontal. Figure 13-16 illustrates a horizontal bullet graph.

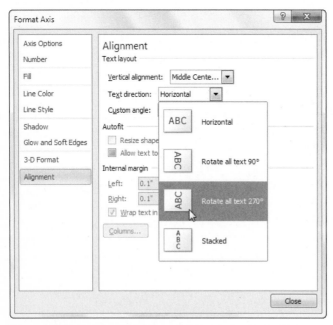

Figure 13-15: Rotate all labels so that they're on their sides.

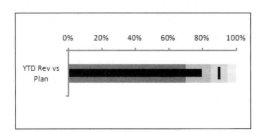

Figure 13-16: A horizontal bullet graph.

The nifty thing about this trick is that because the picture is taken with the Camera tool, the picture automatically updates when the source table changes.

Tip

Never heard of the Camera tool? Check out Chapter 6 for a detailed look at Camera tool.

Showing Performance against a Target Range

In some businesses, a target isn't one value — it's a range of values. That is to say, the goal is to stay within a defined target range. Imagine you manage a small business selling boxes of meat. Part of your job is to keep your inventory stocked between 25 and 35 boxes in a month. If you have too many boxes of meat, the meat will go bad. If you have too few boxes, you'll lose money.

To track how well you do at keeping your inventory of meat between 25 and 35 boxes, you need a performance component that displays on-hand boxes against a target range. Figure 13-17 illustrates a component you can build to track performance against a target range. The gray band represents the target range you must stay within each month. The line represents the trend of on-hand meat.

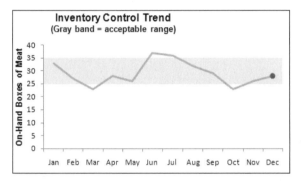

Figure 13-17: You can create a component that plots performance against a target range.

Obviously, the trick to this type of component is to set up the band that represents the target range. Here's how you do it:

1. Set up a *limit table* where you can define and adjust the upper and lower limits of your target range.

   Cells B2 and B3 in Figure 13-18 serve as the place to define the limits for the range.

2. Build a chart feeder that's used to plot the data points for the target range.

   This feeder consists of the formulas revealed in cells B8 and B9 in Figure 13-18.

   The idea is to copy these formulas across all the data.

   The values you see for Feb, Mar, and Apr are the results of these formulas.

3. Add a row for the actual performance values (see Figure 13-19).

   These data points create the performance trend line.

◢	A	B	C	D
1	**Limit Table**			
2	Lower Limit	25		
3	Upper Limit	35		
4				
5				
6				
7		Jan	Feb	Mar
8	Lower Limit	=$B$2	25	25
9	Upper Limit	=$B$3-$B$2	10	10

Figure 13-18: Create a chart feeder that contains formulas that define the data points for the target range.

◢	A	B	C	D	E	F	G
1	**Limit Table**						
2	Lower Limit	25					
3	Upper Limit	35					
4							
5							
6							
7		Jan	Feb	Mar	Apr	May	Ju
8	Lower Limit	25	25	25	25	25	2
9	Upper Limit	10	10	10	10	10	1
10	Values	33	27	23	28	26	3

Figure 13-19: Add a row for the performance values.

4. Select the entire chart feeder table and plot the data on a stacked area chart.

5. Right-click the Values series and choose Change Chart Type. Change the chart type to a line chart (no markers).

6. Right-click the Values data series again and choose Format Data Series.

   The Format Data Series dialog box appears.

7. In the dialog box, click the Series Options button and select Secondary Axis.

8. Go back to your chart and delete the new axis that was added; it's the vertical axis to the right of the chart.

9. Right-click the Lower Limit data series and choose Format Data Series.

   The Format Data Series dialog box appears again.

10. In the dialog box, click the Fill button and select the No Fill option.

That's it. All that's left to do is apply the minor adjustments to colors, labels, and other formatting.

PART V

Automating Your Dashboards and Reports

14

Macro-Charged Reporting

In This Chapter

- Introducing macros
- Recording macros
- Setting up trusted locations for your macros
- Adding macros to your dashboards and reports

A *macro* is essentially a set of instructions or code that you create to tell Excel to execute any number of actions. In Excel, macros can be written or recorded. The key word here is *recorded*.

Recording a macro is like programming a phone number into your cell phone. You first manually dial and save a number. Then when you want, you can redial those numbers with the touch of a button. Just as on a cell phone, you can record your actions in Excel while you perform them. While you record, Excel gets busy in the background, translating your keystrokes and mouse clicks to written code (also known as *Visual Basic for Applications* (VBA)). After a macro is recorded, you can play back those actions anytime you want.

In this chapter, you'll explore macros and learn how you can use macros to automate your recurring processes to simplify your life.

Why Use a Macro?

The first step in using macros is admitting you have a problem. Actually, you may have several problems:

> ➤ **Problem 1: Repetitive tasks.** As each new month rolls around, you have to *make the donuts* (that is, crank out those reports). You have to import that data. You have to

update those pivot tables. You have to delete those columns, and so on. Wouldn't it be nice if you could fire up a macro and have those more redundant parts of your dashboard processes done automatically?

➤ **Problem 2: You're making mistakes.** When you go hand-to-hand combat with Excel, you're bound to make mistakes. When you're repeatedly applying formulas, sorting, and moving things around manually, there's always that risk of catastrophe. Add to that the looming deadlines and constant change request, and your error rate goes up. Why not calmly record a macro, ensure that everything is running correctly, and then forget it? The macro is sure to perform every action the same way every time you run it; reducing the chance of errors.

➤ **Problem 3: Awkward navigation.** Remember that you're creating these dashboards and reports for an audience that probably has a limited knowledge of Excel. If your reports are a bit too difficult to use and navigate, you'll find that you'll slowly lose support for your cause. It's always helpful to make your dashboard more user friendly. Here are some ideas for macros that make things easier for everyone:

- A macro to format and print a worksheet or range of worksheets at the touch of a button.

- Macros that navigate a multi-sheet worksheet with a navigation page or with a *go to* button for each sheet in your workbook.

- A macro that saves the open document in a specified location and then closes the application at the touch of a button.

Obviously, you can perform each of the preceding examples in Excel without the aid of a macro. However, your audience will appreciate these little touches that help make perusal of your dashboard a bit more pleasant.

Introducing the Macro Recorder

If you're coming straight from Excel 2003 with its familiar menu bars, you may have found it difficult to pinpoint the *macro recorder* (the mechanism that lets you record macros). This is because the macro functionality in Excel 2007 and 2010 is on the Developer tab, which is initially hidden. By hidden, I mean you won't see a tab called Developer when you first open Excel 2010. You have to explicitly tell Excel to make it visible.

To enable the Developer tab, follow these steps:

1. Go to the Ribbon and select the File tab.

2. To open the Excel Options dialog box, click the Options button.

3. Click the Customize Ribbon button.

   In the list box on the right, you'll see all the available tabs.

4. Select the Developer tab (see Figure 14-1).

5. Click OK.

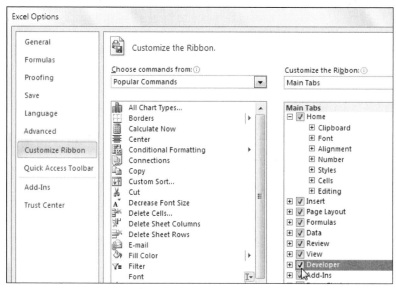

Figure 14-1: Enabling the Developer tab.

The Record Macro dialog box

Now that you have the Developer tab showing in the Excel Ribbon, you can fire up the macro recorder and examine other critical macro options. Start up the macro recorder by selecting Record Macro from the Developer tab. This opens the Record Macro dialog box, as shown in Figure 14-2.

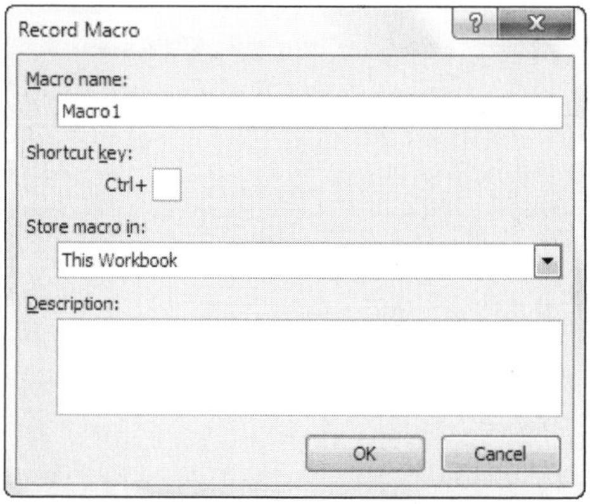

Figure 14-2: The Record Macro dialog box.

Here are the four fields in the Record Macro dialog box:

➤ **Macro Name:** Excel gives a default name to your macro, such as Macro1, but it's best practice to give your macro a name more descriptive of what it actually does. For example, you might name a macro that formats a generic table as FormatTable.

➤ **Shortcut Key:** Optional. Every macro needs an *event,* or something to happen, for it to run. This event can be a button press, a workbook opening, or in this case, a keystroke combination. When you assign a shortcut key to your macro, entering that combination of keys triggers your macro to run. You need not enter a shortcut key to run your macro.

➤ **Store Macro In:** This Workbook is the default option. Storing your macro in This Workbook simply means that the macro is stored along with the active Excel file. The next time you open that particular workbook, the macro will be available to run. Similarly, if you send the workbook to another user, that user can run the macro as well (provided the macro security is properly set by your user — but more on that later).

➤ **Description:** Optional. Useful if you have numerous macros in a spreadsheet or if you need to give a user a more detailed description about what the macro does.

Recording macros with absolute references

The first thing you need to understand before you begin recording macros is that Excel has two modes for recording — absolute reference and relative reference.

Excel's default recording mode is in absolute reference. As you may know, the term *absolute reference* is often used in the context of cell references found in formulas. When a cell reference in a formula is an absolute reference, it does not automatically adjust when the formula is pasted to a new location.

Let's look at an example of a recorded macro. Open the `Chapter 14 Sample File.xlsx` file and record a macro that counts the rows in the branch list worksheet (see Figure 14-3).

On the Web

The example file `Chapter 14 Sample File.xlsx` **is on the companion Web site for this book at** `www.wiley.com/go/exceldr`.

Follow these steps to record the macro:

1. Select cell A1.

2. From the Developer tab, select Record Macro.

3. Name the macro **AddTotals**.

4. Select This Workbook for the save location.

	A	B	C	D	E	F	G	H	I
1		Region	Market	Branch			Region	Market	Branch
2		NORTH	BUFFALO	601419			SOUTH	CHARLOTTE	173901
3		NORTH	BUFFALO	701407			SOUTH	CHARLOTTE	301301
4		NORTH	BUFFALO	802202			SOUTH	CHARLOTTE	302301
5		NORTH	CANADA	910181			SOUTH	CHARLOTTE	601306
6		NORTH	CANADA	920681			SOUTH	DALLAS	202600
7		NORTH	MICHIGAN	101419			SOUTH	DALLAS	490260
8		NORTH	MICHIGAN	501405			SOUTH	DALLAS	490360
9		NORTH	MICHIGAN	503405			SOUTH	DALLAS	490460
10		NORTH	MICHIGAN	590140			SOUTH	FLORIDA	301316
11		NORTH	NEWYORK	801211			SOUTH	FLORIDA	701309
12		NORTH	NEWYORK	802211			SOUTH	FLORIDA	702309
13		NORTH	NEWYORK	804211			SOUTH	NEWORLEANS	601310
14		NORTH	NEWYORK	805211			SOUTH	NEWORLEANS	602310
15		NORTH	NEWYORK	806211			SOUTH	NEWORLEANS	801607

Figure 14-3: Your pre-totaled worksheet containing two tables.

5. To start recording, click OK.

   Excel is now recording your actions. While Excel is recording, perform the following steps.

6. Click in cell A16 and type **Total** in the cell.

7. Click in the first empty cell in Column D (D16) and type **= COUNTA(D2:D15)**.

   This gives a count of branch numbers at the bottom of column D. You need to use the COUNTA function because the branch numbers are stored as text.

8. To end recording the macro, select Stop Recording from the Developer tab.

The formatted worksheet should look like something like the one in Figure 14-4.

	A	B	C	D	E	F	G	H	I
1		Region	Market	Branch			Region	Market	Branch
2		NORTH	BUFFALO	601419			SOUTH	CHARLOTTE	173901
3		NORTH	BUFFALO	701407			SOUTH	CHARLOTTE	301301
4		NORTH	BUFFALO	802202			SOUTH	CHARLOTTE	302301
5		NORTH	CANADA	910181			SOUTH	CHARLOTTE	601306
6		NORTH	CANADA	920681			SOUTH	DALLAS	202600
7		NORTH	MICHIGAN	101419			SOUTH	DALLAS	490260
8		NORTH	MICHIGAN	501405			SOUTH	DALLAS	490360
9		NORTH	MICHIGAN	503405			SOUTH	DALLAS	490460
10		NORTH	MICHIGAN	590140			SOUTH	FLORIDA	301316
11		NORTH	NEWYORK	801211			SOUTH	FLORIDA	701309
12		NORTH	NEWYORK	802211			SOUTH	FLORIDA	702309
13		NORTH	NEWYORK	804211			SOUTH	NEWORLEANS	601310
14		NORTH	NEWYORK	805211			SOUTH	NEWORLEANS	602310
15		NORTH	NEWYORK	806211			SOUTH	NEWORLEANS	801607
16	Total			14					

Figure 14-4: Your post-totaled worksheet.

To see your macro in action, delete the Total row that you just added and play back your macro by following these steps:

1. Select Macros from the Developer tab.

2. Find and select the AddTotals macro that you just recorded.

3. Click the Run button.

If all goes well, the macro plays back your actions to a T and gives your table a total. Now here's the thing. No matter how hard you try, you can't make the AddTotals macro work on the second table. Why? Because you recorded it as an absolute macro.

To understand what this means, examine the underlying code. To examine the code, select Macros from the Developer tab to get the Macro dialog box you see in Figure 14-5.

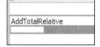

Figure 14-5: The Macro dialog box.

Select the AddTotals macro and click the Edit button. This opens the Visual Basic Editor to show you the code that was written when you recorded your macro:

```
Sub AddTotals()
    Range("A16").Select
    ActiveCell.FormulaR1C1 = "Total"
    Range("D16").Select
    ActiveCell.FormulaR1C1 = "=COUNTA(R[-14]C:R[-1]C)"
End Sub
```

Pay particular attention to lines two and four of the macro. When you asked Excel to select cell range A16 and then D16, those cells are exactly what it selected. Because the macro was recorded in absolute reference mode, Excel interpreted your range selection as absolute. In other words, if you select cell A16, that cell is what Excel gives you.

Recording macros with relative references

In the context of Excel macros, *relative* means relative to the currently active cell. So you should use caution with your active cell choice — both when you record the relative reference macro and when you run it.

First, make sure the `Chapter 14 Sample File.xlsx` file is open (this file is available on this book's companion Web site). Then, use the following steps to record a relative reference macro:

1. From the Developer tab, select the Use Relative References option, as it appears in Figure 14-6.

2. Before recording, select cell A1.

3. From the Developer tab, select Record Macro.

4. Name the macro **AddTotalRelative**.

5. Select This Workbook for the save location.

6. Click OK to start recording.

7. Click in cell A16 and type **Total** in the cell.

8. Select the first empty cell in Column D (D16) and type **=COUNTA(D2:D15)**.

9. To end recording the macro, select Stop Recording from the Developer tab.

Figure 14-6: Select relative reference macro recording.

At this point, you have two macros recorded. Take a moment to examine the code for your newly created macro.

Select Macros from the Developer tab to open the Macro dialog box. Here, choose the AddTotalRelative macro and click Edit.

Again, this opens the Visual Basic Editor to show you the code that was written when you recorded your macro. This time, your code looks something like the following:

```
Sub AddTotalRelative()
    ActiveCell.Offset(15, 0).Range("A1").Select
    ActiveCell.FormulaR1C1 = "Total"
    ActiveCell.Offset(0, 3).Range("A1").Select
    ActiveCell.FormulaR1C1 = "=COUNTA(R[-14]C:R[-1]C)"
End Sub
```

Notice that there are no references to any specific cell ranges at all (other than the starting point in cell A1). Let's take a moment to take a quick look at what the relevant parts of this VBA code really mean.

Notice that in line 2, Excel uses the Offset property of the active cell. This property tells the cursor to move a certain number of cells up or down and a certain number of cells left or right.

The Offset property code tells Excel to move 15 rows down and 0 columns across from the active cell (in this case, A1). So there's no need for Excel to explicitly select a cell as it did when recording an absolute reference macro.

To see this macro in action, delete the Total row for both tables and do the following.

1. Click in cell Al.

2. From the Developer tab, select Macros.

3. Find and select the AddTotalRelative macro.

4. Click the Run button.

5. Click in cell F1.

6. Select Macros from the Developer tab.

7. Find and select the AddTotalRelative macro.

8. Click the Run button.

Notice that this macro, unlike your previous macro, works on both sets of data. Because the macro applies the totals *relative* to the currently active cell, the totals are applied correctly.

For this macro to work, you simply need to ensure that

➤ You've selected the correct starting cell before running the macro.

➤ The block of data has the same number of rows and columns as the data on which you recorded the macro.

Hopefully this simple example has given you a firm grasp of macro recording with both absolute and relative references.

Assigning a macro to a button

When you create macros, you want to give your audience a clear and easy way to run each macro. A button, used directly in the dashboard or report, can provide a simple but effective UI.

Excel Form controls (see Chapter 15 for more information) enable you to create UI directly on your worksheets that simplifies work for your users. Form controls range from buttons (the most-commonly used control) to scrollbars and check boxes.

For a macro, you can place a Form control in a worksheet and then assign that macro to it — that is, a macro you've already recorded. When a macro is assigned to the control, that macro is executed, or *played,* each time the control is clicked.

Take a moment to create a button for the AddTotalRelative macro you created earlier. Here's how:

1. Click the Insert drop-down list under the Developer tab (see Figure 14-7).

2. Select the Button Form control.

3. Click the location you want to place your button. When you drop the button control into your worksheet, the Assign Macro dialog box, as shown in Figure 14-8, opens and asks you to assign a macro to this button.

4. Select the macro that you want to assign to the button and then click OK.

Figure 14-7: You can find the Form Controls in the Developer tab.

 # Form controls versus ActiveX controls

Notice the Form controls and ActiveX controls in Figure 14-7. Although they look similar, they're quite different. Form controls are designed specifically for use on a worksheet, and ActiveX controls are typically used on Excel UserForms. As a general rule, you always want to use Form controls when working on a worksheet. Why? Form controls need less overhead, so they perform better, and configuring Form controls is far easier than configuring their ActiveX counterparts.

Figure 14-8: Assign a macro to the newly added button.

At this point, you have a button that runs your macro when you click it. Keep in mind that all the controls in the Forms toolbar work in the same way as the command button, in that you assign a macro to run when the control is selected.

Tip

The buttons you create come with a default name, such as Button3. To rename your button, right-click the button and then click the existing name. Then you can delete the existing name and replace it with a name of your choosing.

Enabling Macros in Excel 2010

With the Release of Office 2010, Microsoft introduced significant changes to its Office security model. One of the most significant changes is the concept of *Trusted Documents*. Without getting into the technical minutia, a Trusted Document is essentially a workbook you have deemed safe by enabling macros.

Viewing the new Excel security message

If you open a workbook that contains macros in Excel 2010, you'll get a small message under the Ribbon stating that Macros (active content) has in effect, been disabled. The message looks like Figure 14-9.

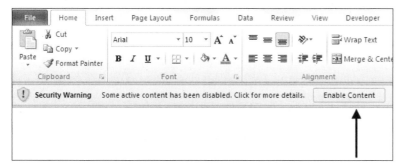

Figure 14-9: Security warning when macros are present.

If you click Enable, it automatically becomes a Trusted Document. This means you will no longer be prompted to enable the content as long as you open that file on your computer. The idea is that if you told Excel that you trust a particular workbook by enabling macros, it is highly likely that you will enable macros each time you open it. Thus, Excel remembers that you've enabled macros before and inhibits any further messages about macros (for that workbook).

This is great news for you and your clients. After enabling your macros just one time, they won't be annoyed at the constant messages about macros, and you won't have to worry that your macro-enabled dashboard will fall flat because macros have been disabled.

Setting up trusted locations

If the thought of any macro message coming up (even one time) unnerves you, you can set up a trusted location for your files. A *trusted location* is a directory that is deemed a safe zone where only trusted workbooks are placed. A trusted location allows you and your clients to run a macro-enabled workbook with no security restrictions as long as the workbook is in that location.

To set up a trusted location, follow these steps:

1. Select the Macro Security button on the Developer tab.

   This opens the Trust Center dialog box.

2. Click the Trusted Locations button.

   This opens the Trusted Locations menu (see Figure 14-10).

   You see all the directories that Excel considers trusted.

3. Click the Add New Location button.

4. Click Browse to find and specify the directory that will be considered a trusted location.

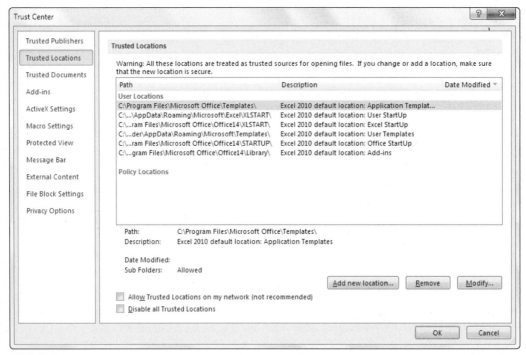

Figure 14-10: The Trusted Locations menu allows you to add directories that are considered trusted.

After you specify a trusted location, any Excel file that's opened from this location will have macros automatically enabled. The idea is to have your clients specify a trusted location and use your Excel files from there.

Macro-enabled file extensions

If you've skipped Excel 2007 and came straight from Excel 2003, you'll be interested to know that Microsoft has created a separate file extension for workbooks that contain macros.

You see, Excel 2010 workbooks have the standard file extension `.xlsx`. Files with the xlsx extension cannot contain macros. If your workbook contains macros and you then save that workbook as an `.xlsx` file, your macros are removed automatically. Of course, Excel warns you that macro content will be disabled when saving a workbook with macros as an `.xlsx` file.

If you want to retain the macros, you must save your file as an *Excel Macro-Enabled Workbook*. This gives your file an `.xlsm` extension. The idea is that all workbooks with an `.xlsx` file extension are automatically known to be safe whereas you can recognize `.xlsm` files as a potential threat.

Excel Macro Examples

Covering the fundamentals of building and using macros is one thing. Coming up with good ways to incorporate them into your reporting processes is another. Take a moment to review a few examples of how you can implement macros in your dashboards and reports.

On the Web

Open the `Chapter 14 Sample File.xlsm` **file that you can find at** `www.wiley.com/go/exceldr` **to follow along in the next section.**

Building navigation buttons

The most common use of macros is navigation. Workbooks that have many worksheets or tabs can be frustrating to navigate. To help your audience, you can create some sort of a switchboard, like the one shown in Figure 14-11. When a user clicks the Example 1 button, he's taken to the Example 1 sheet.

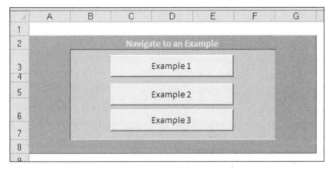

Figure 14-11: Use macros to build buttons that help users navigate your reports.

Creating a macro to navigate to a sheet is quite simple.

1. Start at the sheet that will become your switchboard or starting point.

2. Start recording a macro.

3. While recording, click the destination sheet (the sheet this macro will navigate to).

4. After you click in the destination sheet, stop recording the macro.

5. Assign the macro to a button.

Tip

It's useful to know that Excel has a built-in hyperlink feature, allowing you to convert the contents of a cell into a hyperlink that links to another location. That location can be a separate Excel workbook, a Web site, or even another tab in the current workbook. Although using a hyperlink may be easier than setting up a macro, you can't apply a hyperlink to Form controls (like buttons). Instead of a button, you'd use text to let users know where they'll go when they click the link.

Dynamically rearranging pivot table data

In the example illustrated in Figure 14-12, macros allow a user to change the perspective of the chart simply by selecting any one of the buttons shown.

Cross-Ref

For more information about pivot tables, refer to Chapter 7. For more information about pivot charts, refer to Chapter 8.

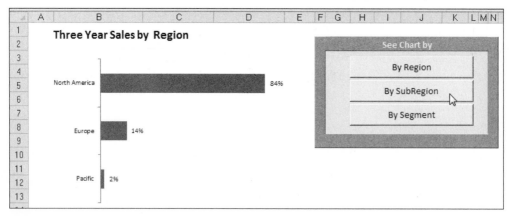

Figure 14-12: This report allows users to choose their perspective

Figure 14-13 reveals that the chart is actually a pivot chart tied to a pivot table. The recorded macros assigned to each button are doing nothing more than rearranging the pivot table to slice the data using various pivot fields.

Here are the high-level steps needed to create this type of setup:

1. Create your pivot table and a pivot chart.

2. Start recording a macro.

3. While recording, move a pivot field from one area of the pivot table to the other. When you're done, stop recording the macro.

4. Record another macro to move the data field back to its original position.

5. After both macros are set up, assign each one to a separate button.

You can fire your new macros in turn to see your pivot field dynamically move back and forth.

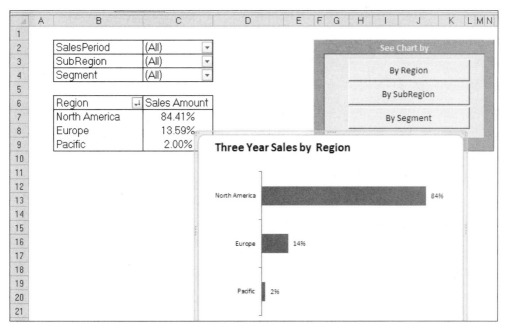

Figure 14-13: The macros behind these buttons rearrange the data fields in a pivot table.

Offering one-touch reporting options

The last two examples demonstrate that you can record any action that you find of value. That is, if you think users would appreciate a certain feature being automated for them, why not record a macro to do so?

In Figure 14-14, notice that you can filter the pivot table for top or bottom 20 customers. Because the steps to filter a pivot table for the top and bottom 20 have been recorded, anyone can get the benefit of this functionality without knowing how to do it themselves. Also, recording specific action allows you to manage risk a bit. That is to say, you'll know that your users will interact with your reports in a method that has been developed and tested by you.

This not only saves them time and effort, but it also allows users that don't know how to take these actions to benefit from them.

Tip

Feel free to visit Chapter 7 for a refresher on how create the top and bottom reports you see in Figure 14-14.

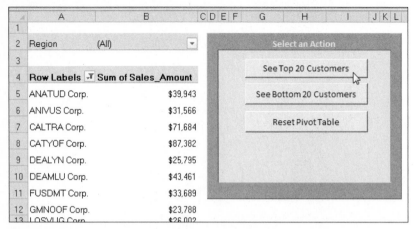

Figure 14-14: Offering pre-recorded views not only saves time and effort, but it also allows users that don't know how to use advanced features benefit from them.

Figure 14-15 demonstrates how you can give your audience a quick and easy way to see the same data on different charts. Don't laugh too quickly at the uselessness of this example. It's not uncommon to be asked to see the same data different ways. Instead of taking up real estate, just recorded a macro that changes the Chart Type of the chart. Your clients will be able to switch views to their heart's content.

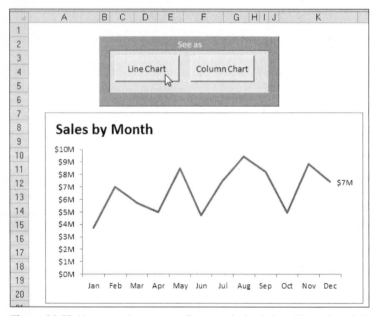

Figure 14-15: You can give your audience a choice in how they view data.

Adding Interactive Controls to Your Dashboard

In This Chapter

- Introducing Form controls
- Using a button control
- Using a check box control to toggle a chart series
- Using an option button to filter your views
- Using a combo box to control multiple pivot tables
- Using a list box to control multiple charts

Today, business professionals increasingly want to be *empowered* to switch from one view of data to another with a simple list of choices. For those of us who build dashboards and reports, this empowerment comes with a whole new set of issues. The overarching question — how do you handle a user who wants to see multiple views for multiple regions or markets?

Fortunately, Excel offers a handful of tools that enable you to add interactivity into your presentations. With these tools and a bit of creative data modeling, you can accomplish these goals with relative ease. In this chapter, we discuss how to incorporate various controls (such as buttons, check boxes, and scroll bars) into your dashboards and reports and present you with several solutions that you can implement.

Getting Started with Form Controls

Excel offers a set of controls called *Form controls,* designed specifically for adding UI elements directly onto a worksheet. After you place a Form control on a worksheet, you can then configure it to perform a specific task. Later in the chapter, we demonstrate how to apply the most useful controls to a presentation.

Finding Form controls

You can find Excel's Form controls on the Developer tab, which is initially hidden in Excel 2010. To enable the Developer tab, follow these steps:

1. Go to the Ribbon and select the File tab.

2. To open the Excel Options dialog box, click the Options button.

3. Click the Customize Ribbon button.

   In the list box on the right, you'll see all the available tabs.

4. Select the check box next to the Developer tab (see Figure 15-1).

5. Click OK.

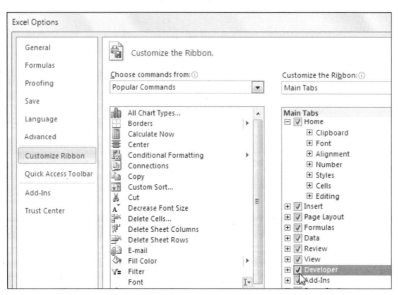

Figure 15-1: Enabling the Developer tab.

Now, select the Developer tab and choose the Insert command, as shown in Figure 15-2. Here you find two sets of controls: Form controls and ActiveX controls. Form controls are designed specifically for use on a spreadsheet whereas ActiveX Controls are typically used on Excel UserForms. Because Form controls need less overhead and can be configured far easier than their ActiveX counterparts, you generally want to use Form controls.

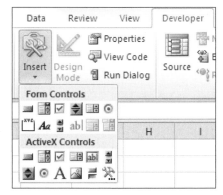

Figure 15-2: Form controls and ActiveX controls.

Here are the nine Form controls that you can add directly to a worksheet (see Figure 15-3). They are as follows:

> **Button:** Executes an assigned macro when a user clicks the button.

> **Combo Box:** Gives a user an expandable list of options from which to choose.

> **Check Box:** Provides a mechanism for a select/deselect scenario. When selected, it returns a value of True. Otherwise, it returns False.

> **Spin Button:** Enables a user to easily increment or decrement a value by clicking the up and down arrows.

> **List Box:** Gives a user a list of options from which to choose.

> **Option Button:** Enables a user to toggle through two or more options one at a time. Selecting one option automatically deselects the others.

> **Scroll Bar:** Enables a user to scroll to a value or position using a sliding scale that can be moved by clicking and dragging the mouse.

> **Label:** Allows you to add text labels to your worksheet. You can also assign a macro to the label, effectively using it as a button of sorts.

> **Group Box:** Typically used for cosmetic purposes, this control serves as a container for groups of other controls.

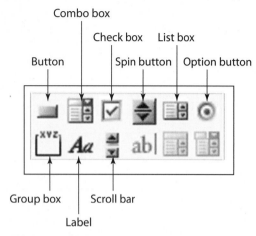

Figure 15-3: Nine Form controls labeled that you can add to your worksheet.

Adding a control to a worksheet

To add a control to a worksheet, simply click the control that you require and click the approximate location that you want to place the control. You can easily move and resize the control later just as you would a chart or shape.

After you add a control, you want to configure it to define its look, behavior, and utility. Each control has its own set of configuration options that allow you to customize it for your purposes. To get to these options, right-click the control and select Format Control, as demonstrated in Figure 15-4. This opens the Format Control dialog box with all the configuration options for that control.

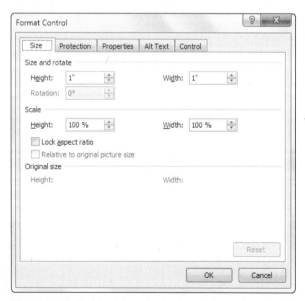

Figure 15-4: Right-click and select Format Control to open a dialog box with the configuration options.

Each control has its own set of tabs that allows you to customize everything from formatting, to security, to configuration arguments. You'll see different tabs based on which control you're using, but most Form controls have the Control tab. The Control tab is where the meat of the configuration lies. Here, you find the variables and settings that need to be defined in order for the control to function.

Note

The button and label controls don't have the Control tab. They have no need for one. The button simply fires whichever macro you assign it. As for the Label, it's not designed to run macro events.

Throughout the rest of the chapter, you will walk through a few exercises that demonstrate how to use the most useful controls in a reporting environment. At the end of this chapter, you'll have a solid understanding of Form controls and how they can enhance your dashboards and reports.

Using the Button Control

The button control gives your audience a clear and easy way to execute the macros you've recorded. To insert and configure a button control, follow these steps:

1. Select Insert drop-down list under the Developer tab.

2. Select the button Form control.

3. Click the location in your spreadsheet where you want to place your button.

   The Assign Macro dialog box appears and asks you to assign a macro to this button (see Figure 15-5).

4. Edit the text shown on the button by right-clicking the button, highlighting the existing text, and then overwriting it with your own.

Figure 15-5: Assign a macro to the newly added button.

Tip

To assign a different macro to the button, simply right-click and select Assign Macro to reactivate the Assign Macro dialog box, as shown in Figure 15-5.

Using the Check Box Control

The check box control provides a mechanism for selecting/deselecting options. When a check box is selected, it returns a value of True. When it isn't selected, False is returned. To add and configure a check box control, follow these steps:

1. Select the Insert drop-down list under the Developer tab.

2. Select the check box Form control.

3. Click the location in your spreadsheet where you want to place your check box.

4. After you drop the check box control onto your spreadsheet, right-click the control and select Format Control.

5. Click the Control tab to see the configuration options, as shown in Figure 15-6.

6. Select the state in which the check box should open.

   The default selection (Unchecked) typically works for most scenarios, so it's rare you have to update this selection.

7. In the Cell Link box, enter the cell to which you want the check box to output its value.

   By default, a check box control outputs either True or False, depending on whether it's checked. Notice in Figure 15-6 that this particular check box outputs to cell A5.

8. (Optional) You can check the 3D property if you want the control to have a 3-D appearance.

9. Click OK to apply your changes.

Tip

To rename the check box control, right-click the control, select Edit Text, and then overwrite the existing text with your own.

As Figure 15-7 illustrates, the check box outputs its value to the specified cell. If the check box is selected, a value of True is output. If the check box isn't selected, a value of False is output.

Figure 15-6: Formatting the check box control.

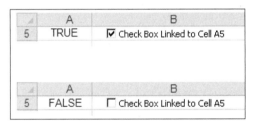

Figure 15-7: The two states of the check box.

If you're having a hard time figuring out how this could be useful, take a stab at this next exercise which illustrates how a check box can be used to toggle a chart series on and off.

Check box example: Toggling a chart series on and off

Figure 15-8 shows the same chart twice. Notice that the top chart contains only one series, with a check box offering to Show 2009 Trend data. The bottom chart shows the same chart with the check box selected. The on/off nature of the check box control is ideal for interactivity that calls for a visible/not visible state.

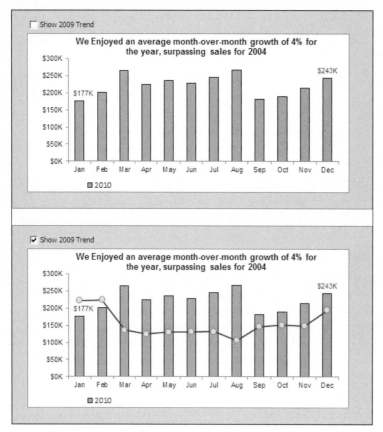

Figure 15-8: A check box can help create the disappearing data series effect.

On the Web

To download the `Chapter 15 Sample File.xlsx` **file, go to the companion Web site for the book at** `www.wiley.com/go/exceldr`.

We start with the raw data (in `Chapter 15 Sample File.xlsx`) that contains both 2009 and 2010 data (see Figure 15-9). In the first column is a cell where the check box control will output its value (cell A12 in this example). This cell will either contain True or False.

	A	B	C	D	E	F	G
10			Raw Data				
11	Toggle for 2009 Data		Jan	Feb	Mar	Apr	May
12	TRUE	2009	$222,389	$224,524	$136,104	$125,260	$130,791
13		2010	$176,648	$201,000	$265,720	$225,461	$235,494
14							

Figure 15-9: Start with raw data and a cell where a check box control can output its value.

Next, we create our analysis layer (staging table) that consists of all formulas, as shown in Figure 15-10. The idea is that the chart actually reads from this data, not the raw data. This way, we can control what the chart sees.

	A	B	C	D	E	
4						
5			Jan	Feb	Mar	
6		2009	=IF($A12=TRUE,C12,NA())	=IF($A12=TRUE,D12,NA())	=IF($A12=TRUE,E12,NA())	=IF($
7		2010	=C13	=D13	=E13	=F1;
8						
9						
10			Raw Data			
11	Toggle for 2004 Data		Jan	Feb	Mar	
12	TRUE	2009	222389	224524	136104	125;
13		2010	176648	201000	265720	225
14						

Figure 15-10: Create a staging table that will feed the chart. The values of this data are all formulas.

As you can see in Figure 15-10, the formulas for the 2010 row simply reference the cells in the raw data for each respective month. We do that because we want the 2010 data to show at all times.

For the 2009 row, we test the value of cell A12 (the cell that contains the output from the check box). If A12 reads True, we reference the respective 2009 cell in the raw data. If A12 doesn't read True, the formula uses Excel's NA() function to return an #N/A error. Excel charts can't read any cell with the #N/A error. Therefore, they simply don't show the data series for any cell that contains #N/A. This is ideal when you don't want a data series to be shown at all.

Tip

Notice that the formula shown in Figure 15-10 uses an absolute reference with cell A12. That is, the reference to cell A12 in the formula is prefixed with a $ sign ($A12). This ensures that the column references in the formulas don't shift when they're copied across.

Figure 15-11 illustrates the two scenarios in action in the staging tables. In the scenario shown at the top of Figure 15-11, cell A12 is True, so our staging table actually brings in 2009 data. In the scenario shown at the bottom of Figure 15-11, cell A12 is False, so the staging table returns #N/A for 2009.

Finally, we create the chart that you saw earlier in this section (in Figure 15-8) using the staging table. Keep in mind that you can scale this to as many series as you'd like. It's easy to imagine a chart with ten or more series that are all controlled by check boxes. This way, you can make all but two series invisible so you can compare those two series unhindered. Then you can make another two visible, comparing those.

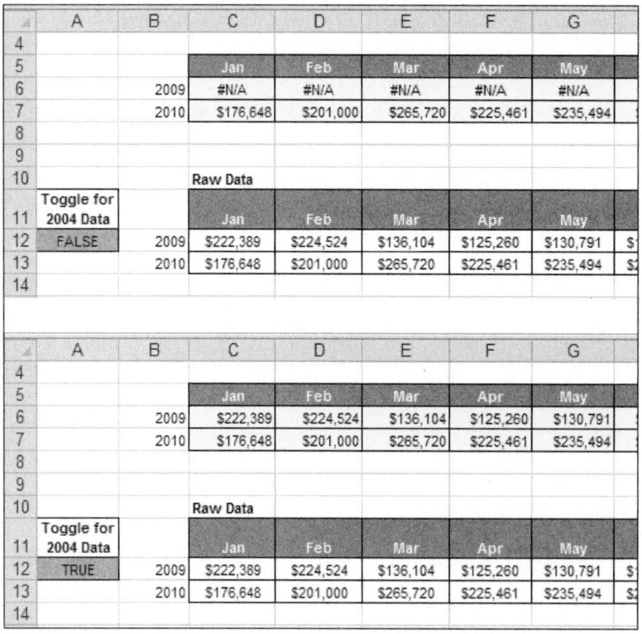

Figure 15-11: When cell A12 reads True, 2009 data is displayed; when it reads False, the 2009 row shows only #N/A errors.

Using the Option Button Control

Option buttons allow users to toggle through several options one at a time. The idea is to have two or more option buttons in a group. Then selecting one option button automatically deselects the others. To add option buttons to your worksheet, follow these steps:

1. Click the Insert drop-down list under the Developer tab.

2. Select the option button Form control.

3. Click the location in your spreadsheet where you want to place your option button.

4. After you drop the control onto your spreadsheet, right-click the control and select Format Control.

5. Click the Control tab to see the configuration options, as shown in Figure 15-12.

6. First, select the state in which the option button should open.

    The default selection (Unchecked) typically works for most scenarios, so it's rare you have to update this selection.

7. In the Cell Link box, enter the cell to which you want the option button to output its value. By default, an option button control outputs a number that corresponds to the order it was put onto the worksheet. For instance, the first option button you place on your worksheet outputs a number 1; the second outputs a number 2; the third outputs a number 3; and so on. Notice in Figure 15-12 that this particular control outputs to cell A1.

8. (Optional) You can check the 3D property if you want the control to have a three-dimensional appearance.

9. Click OK to apply your changes.

10. To add another option button, simply copy the button you created and paste as many option buttons as you need. The nice thing about copying and pasting is that all the configurations you made to the original persist in all the copies.

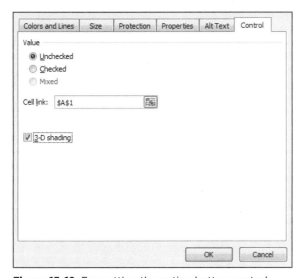

Figure 15-12: Formatting the option button control.

 Tip

To give your option button a meaningful label, right-click the control, select Edit Text, and then overwrite the existing text with your own.

Option button example: Showing many views through one chart

One of the ways you can use option buttons is to feed a single chart with different data, based on the option selected. Figure 15-13 illustrates an example of this. When each category is selected, the single chart is updated to show the data for that selection.

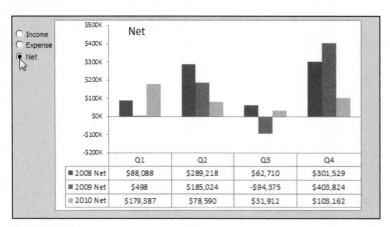

Figure 15-13: This chart is dynamically fed different data based on the selected option button.

Now, you could create three separate charts and show them all on your dashboard at the same time. However, using this technique as an alternative saves on valuable real estate by not having to show three separate charts. Plus, it's much easier to troubleshoot, format, and maintain one chart than it is three.

To create this example, we start with three raw datasets (as shown in Figure 15-14) that contain three categories of data; Income, Expense, and Net. Near the raw data, we reserve a cell where the option buttons output their values (Cell A8 in this example). This cell contains the ID of the option selected: 1, 2, or 3.

	A	B	C	D	E	F
7	Option Button Trigger					
8	1		Q1	Q2	Q3	Q4
9		2010 Income	$399,354	$573,662	$244,661	$790,906
10		2009 Income	$219,967	$495,072	$212,749	$687,744
11		2008 Income	$159,832	$289,825	$181,961	$456,016
12						
13		2010 Expense	$219,967	$495,072	$212,749	$687,744
14		2009 Expense	$219,468	$310,048	$307,124	$283,920
15		2008 Expense	$71,744	$607	$119,251	$154,487
16						
17		2010 Net	$179,387	$78,590	$31,912	$103,162
18		2009 Net	$498	$185,024	-$94,375	$403,824
19		2008 Net	$88,088	$289,218	$62,710	$301,529

Figure 15-14: Start with the raw datasets and a cell where the option buttons can output their values.

We then create our analysis layer (our staging table) that consists of all formulas, as shown in Figure 15-15. The idea is that the chart reads from this staging table, allowing you to control what the chart sees. The first cell of the staging table contains the following formula:

```
=IF($A$8=1,B9,IF($A$8=2,B13,B17))
```

This formula tells Excel to check the value of cell A8 (the cell where the option buttons output their values). If the value of cell A8 is 1, which represents the value of the Income option, the formula returns the value in the Income dataset (cell B9). If the value of cell A8 is 2, which represents the value of the Expense option, the formula returns the value in the Expense dataset (cell B13). If the value of cell B1 is not 1 or 2, the value in cell B17 is returned.

◢	A	B
1		
2		
3		=IF($A$8=1,B9,IF($A$8=2,B13,B17))
4		
5		
6		
7	Option Button Trigger	
8	1	
9		2010 Income
10		2009 Income
11		2008 Income
12		
13		2010 Expense
14		2009 Expense
15		2008 Expense
16		
17		2010 Net

Figure 15-15: Create a staging table and enter this formula in the first cell.

Tip

Notice that the formula shown in Figure 15-15 uses absolute references with cell A8. That is, the reference to cell A8 in the formula is prefixed with $ signs ($A$8). This ensures that the cell references in the formulas don't shift when they're copied down and across.

To test that the formula is working fine, you could change the value of cell A8 manually, from 1 to 3. When the formula works, you'd simply copy the formula across and down to fill the rest of the staging table.

When the setup is created, all that's left to do is create the chart using the staging table. Again, the major benefits you get from this type of setup is that any formatting changes can be made to one chart, and it's easy add another dataset by adding another option button and editing your formulas.

Using the Combo Box Control

The combo box control allows users to select from a list of predefined options from a drop-down list. The idea is that when an item from the combo box control is selected, some action is taken with that selection. To add a combo box to your worksheet, follow these steps:

1. Click the Insert drop-down list under the Developer tab.

2. Select the combo box Form control.

3. Click the location in your spreadsheet where you want to place your combo box.

4. After you drop the control onto your spreadsheet, right-click the control and select Format Control.

5. Click the Control tab to see the configuration options, as shown in Figure 15-16.

6. In the Input Range setting, identify the range that holds the predefined items you want to present as choices in the combo box.

   As you can see in Figure 15-16, this combo box is filled with months.

7. Next, in the Cell Link box, enter the cell to which you want the combo box to output its value. By default, a combo box control outputs the index number of the selected item. This means if the second item on the list was selected, the number 2 would be output. If the fifth item on the list was selected, the number 5 would be output. Notice in Figure 15-16 that this particular control outputs to cell E15.

8. In the Drop Down Lines box, enter the number of items you want shown at one time. You see in Figure 15-6, this control is formatted to show 12 items at one time. This means when the combo box is expanded, the user sees 12 items.

9. (Optional) You can check the 3D property if you want the control to have a three-dimensional appearance.

10. Click OK to apply your changes.

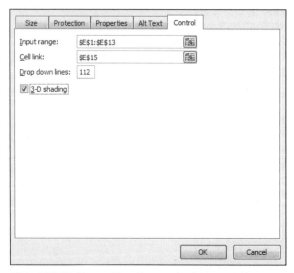

Figure 15-16: Formatting the combo box control.

Combo box example: Controlling multiple pivot tables with one combo box

The report in Figure 15-17 contains two pivot tables — one showing revenue for the selected market and one showing volume. Note that each pivot table has its own Filter field, allowing for the selection of a market. The problem is that each time a market is selected from the Filter field in one pivot table, the same market from the Filter field in the other pivot table must be selected to ensure the correct volume versus revenue.

	A	B	C	D	E	
3						
4		Market	Northeast		**Revenue Trend**	
5						
6		Sales Amount				
7			▣ 2009			
8		Segment	Qtr1	Qtr2	Qtr3	Q
9		Accessories	$1,545	$3,254	$12,426	$8,
10		Bikes	$604,274	$690,286	$540,421	$467
11		Clothing	$11,793	$18,882	$26,538	$23
12		Components	$52,285	$141,635	$180,818	$92
13		Grand Total	$669,898	$854,056	$760,202	$59:
14						
15						
16		Market	Northeast		**Volume Trend**	
17						
18		Sum of OrderQt				
19			▣			
20		Segment	Qtr1	Qtr2	Qtr3	Q
21		Accessories	84	181	557	3
22		Bikes	753	859	666	5
23		Clothing	403	629	1,077	8
24		Components	231	569	754	4
25		Grand Total	1,471	2,238	3,054	2,:

Figure 15-17: You must synchronize multiple pivot table reports to get the correct analysis.

Not only is it annoying to have to synchronize both pivot tables each time you want to analyze a new market's data, but there's a chance you, or your audience, may forget to do so.

A combo box control can help in this situation. The idea is to record a macro that automatically selects a market from the Market field of both tables. Then alter the macro to filter both pivot tables, using the value selected from a combo box control.

Tip

Feel free to review Chapter 14 for a refresher on how to record macros.

On the Web

Using the `Chapter 14 Sample File.slxs` **file located at** `www.wiley.com/go/` `exceldr`**, take a moment to walk through this example.**

For this example, use the pivot tables found in the Using Combo Box Controls tab of the sample file.

1. Create a new macro and call it SwitchMarkets. When recording starts, select the Southwest market from the Market field in both pivot tables and then stop recording.

2. Place a combo box onto your worksheet.

3. Right-click your combo box and select Format Control.

   The Format Control dialog box opens.

4. Specify an Input Range for the list you're using to fill your combo box. In this case, reference the list of markets already created in column Q.

5. Specify a Cell Link.

   This is the cell that shows the index number of the item you select (cell O2 is the cell link in this example). When you've configured your combo box, your dialog box should look similar to Figure 15-18.

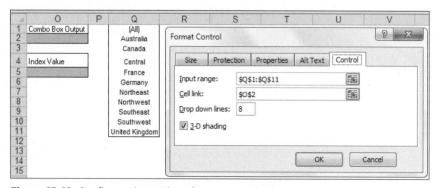

Figure 15-18: Configure the settings for your combo box.

At this point, you can now select a market from your combo box and see the associated index number in cell O2. In order to make use of this index number, you have to pass it through the INDEX function. The INDEX function converts an index number to a value that can be recognized.

An INDEX function requires two arguments in order to work properly. The first argument is the range of the list you're working with. In most cases, use the same range that's feeding your combo box. The second argument is the index number. If the index number is in a cell (like in cell O2), you can simply reference the cell.

6. In cell O5, enter an INDEX function that converts the index number in cell O2 to a value. As you can see in Figure 15-19, the formula used is =INDEX(Q1:Q11,O2).

   The trick now is to edit the SwitchMarkets macro you recorded earlier to use the value in cell O5, instead of a hard-coded value. This calls for editing the macro-generated code via the Visual Basic Editor.

7. Click the Macros button on the Developer tab. This opens the Macro dialog box, as shown in Figure 15-20. From here, you can select the SwitchMarkets macro and then click the Edit button.

Remember that when you recorded your macro, you selected the Southwest market from the Market field in both pivot tables. As you can see in Figure 15-21, the text "Southwest" is indeed hard-coded in the macro-generated code.

8. Replace "Southwest" with ActiveSheet.Range("O5").Valueas shown in Figure 15-22. This tells the macro to get the market name from cell O5. After you've edited the macro, close the Visual Basic Editor to get back to the worksheet.

The final step is to ensure the macro plays each time you select a market from the combo box.

9. Right-click the combo box and select Assign Macro. Select the SwitchMarkets macro and then click OK.

10. (Optional) You can clean up the formatting on your newly created report by hiding the rows and columns that hold the Filter fields in your pivot tables, plus any lists or formulas you don't want your audience to see.

	O	P	Q
1	Combo Box Output		(All)
2	3		Australia
3			Canada
4	Index Value		Central
5	=INDEX(Q1:Q11,O2)		France
6			Germany
7			Northeast
8			Northwest
9			Southeast
10			Southwest
11			United Kingdom

Figure 15-19: Use an INDEX formula to convert the index number output by the combo box to a textual value.

Figure 15-20: Select the SwitchMarkets macro and click the Edit button.

```
(General)                                              ▼   SwitchMarkets

    Sub SwitchMarkets()
    '
    '  SwitchMarkets Macro
    '


    '
        ActiveSheet.PivotTables("PivotTable1").PivotFields("Market").ClearAllFilters
        ActiveSheet.PivotTables("PivotTable1").PivotFields("Market").CurrentPage = _
            "Southwest"
        ActiveSheet.PivotTables("PivotTable2").PivotFields("Market").ClearAllFilters
        ActiveSheet.PivotTables("PivotTable2").PivotFields("Market").CurrentPage = _
            "Southwest"
    End Sub
```

Figure 15-21: The Southwest market is hard-coded in the macro code.

```
(General)                                              ▼   SwitchMarkets

    Sub SwitchMarkets()
    '
    '  SwitchMarkets Macro
    '


    '
        ActiveSheet.PivotTables("PivotTable1").PivotFields("Market").ClearAllFilters
        ActiveSheet.PivotTables("PivotTable1").PivotFields("Market").CurrentPage = _
            ActiveSheet.Range("O5").Value
        ActiveSheet.PivotTables("PivotTable2").PivotFields("Market").ClearAllFilters
        ActiveSheet.PivotTables("PivotTable2").PivotFields("Market").CurrentPage = _
            ActiveSheet.Range("O5").Value
    End Sub
```

Figure 15-22: Replace "Southwest" with ActiveSheet.Range("O5").Value.

As you can see in Figure 15-23, this setup provides an easy and reliable way to navigate pivot tables using one control.

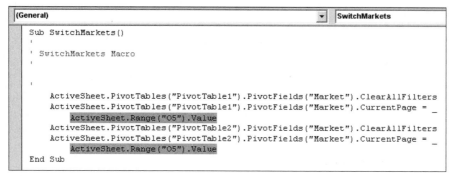

	A	B	C	D	E	F
1		**Select Market**				
2		Northeast				
3					Revenue Trend	
6		**Sales Amount**				
7			⊟ 2009			
8		**Segment**	Qtr1	Qtr2	Qtr3	Qt
9		Accessories	$1,545	$3,254	$12,426	$8,
10		Bikes	$604,274	$690,286	$540,421	$467
11		Clothing	$11,793	$18,882	$26,538	$23,
12		Components	$52,285	$141,635	$180,818	$92,
13		**Grand Total**	$669,898	$854,056	$760,202	$592
14						
15					Volume Trend	
18		**Sum of OrderQty**				
19			⊟			
20		**Segment**	Qtr1	Qtr2	Qtr3	Qt
21		Accessories	84	181	557	38
22		Bikes	753	859	666	57
23		Clothing	403	629	1,077	86
24		Components	231	569	754	44
25		**Grand Total**	1,471	2,238	3,054	2,2

Figure 15-23: You can now navigate two pivot tables with just one combo box.

Tip

You may notice your pivot table automatically adjusts the columns to fit the data each time you select a new market. This default behavior can be bothersome to someone using your pivot table reports. You can suppress this behavior by right-clicking each pivot table and selecting Table Options. This activates the PivotTable Options dialog box, where you can deselect the Autofit Column Widths On Update selection. Remember, you have to do this for each pivot table individually.

Using the List Box Control

The list box control allows users to select from a list of predefined choices. The idea is that when an item from the list box control is selected, some action is taken with that selection. To add a list box to your worksheet, follow these steps:

1. Select the Insert drop-down list under the Developer tab.

2. Select the list box Form control.

3. Click the location in your spreadsheet where you want to place your list box.

4. After you drop the control onto your worksheet, right-click the control and select Format Control.

5. Click the Control tab to see the configuration options, as shown in Figure 15-24.

6. In the Input Range setting, identify the range that holds the predefined items you want to present as choices in the combo box.

   As you can see in Figure 15-24, this list box is filled with region selections.

7. In the Cell Link box, enter the cell where you want the list box to output its value.

   By default, a list box control outputs the index number of the selected item. This means if the second item on the list was selected, the number 2 would be output. If the fifth item on the list was selected, the number 5 would be output. Notice in Figure 15-24 that this particular control outputs to cell P2. The Selection Type setting allows users to choose more than one selection in the list box. The choices here are Single, Multi, and Extended. Always leave this setting on Single, as Multi and Extended work only in the VBA environment.

8. (Optional) You can check the 3D property if you want the control to have a 3-D appearance.

9. Click OK to apply your changes.

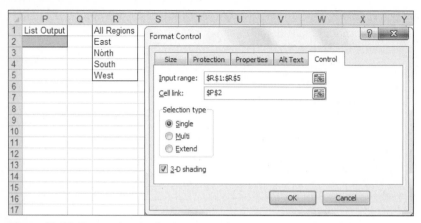

Figure 15-24: Formatting the list box control.

List box example: Controlling multiple charts with one selector

One of the more useful ways to use a list box is to control multiple charts with one selector. Figure 15-25 illustrates an example of this. As a region selection is made in the list box, all three charts are fed the data for that region, adjusting the charts to correspond with the selection made. Happily, all this is done without VBA code, just a handful of formulas and a list box.

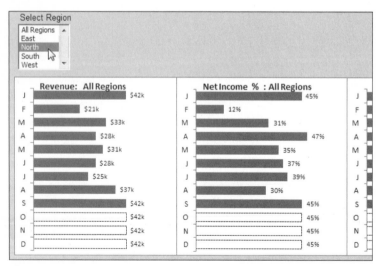

Figure 15-25: This list box feeds the region selection to multiple charts, changing each chart to correspond with the selection made.

To create this example, we start with three raw datasets (as shown in Figure 15-26) that contain three categories of data; Revenues, Net Income %, and Gross Margin. Each dataset contains a separate line for each region.

	A	B	C	D	E	F	
5							
6	Revenues	Jan	Feb	Mar	Apr	May	J
7	All Regions	98,741	54,621	96,555	109,625	87,936	84
8	East	27,474	22,674	35,472	36,292	31,491	27
9	North	41,767	20,806	32,633	28,023	31,090	27
10	South	18,911	1,125	17,020	34,196	12,989	18
11	West	10,590	10,016	11,430	11,115	12,367	10
12							
13	Net Income %	Jan	Feb	Mar	Apr	May	J
14	All Regions	49.9%	50.6%	48.7%	47.8%	41.4%	
15	East	63.1%	53.6%	55.8%	47.4%	41.5%	
16	North	45.3%	11.8%	31.0%	47.5%	35.2%	
17	South	31.2%	61.7%	41.8%	30.9%	9.0%	
18	West	60.1%	75.4%	66.1%	65.2%	79.8%	
19							
20	Gross Margin	Jan	Feb	Mar	Apr	May	J
21	All Regions	48,508	22,850	44,586	48,340	35,056	37
22	East	17,326	12,154	19,799	17,206	13,079	11
23	North	18,914	2,455	10,115	13,299	10,938	10
24	South	5,904	694	7,115	10,582	1,171	7
25	West	6,364	7,547	7,557	7,253	9,867	8

Figure 15-26: Start with the raw datasets that contain one line per region.

We then add a list box that outputs the index number of the selected item to cell P2 (see Figure 15-27).

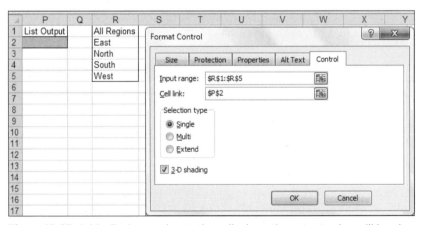

Figure 15-27: Add a list box and note the cell where the output value will be placed.

Next, we create a staging table that will consist of all formulas. In this staging table, we use the Excel's CHOOSE function to select the correct value from the raw data tables based on the selected region.

Tip

In Excel, the Choose function returns a value from a specified list of values based on a specified position number. For instance, the formula CHOOSE(3,"Red", "Yellow", "Green", "Blue") returns Green because Green is the third item in the list of values. The formula CHOOSE(1, "Red", "Yellow", "Green", "Blue") returns Red. See Chapter 2 to get a detailed look at the CHOOSE function.

As you can see in Figure 15-28, the CHOOSE formula retrieves the target position number from Cell P2 (the cell where the list box outputs the index number of the selected item) and then matches that position number to the list of cell references given. The cell references come directly from the raw data table.

In the example shown in Figure 15-28, the data that would be returned with this CHOOSE formula would be 98741. Why? Because cell P2 contains the number 1, and the first cell reference within the CHOOSE formula is cell B7.

	A	B	C	P	Q
1		Jan	Feb	List Output	
2	Revenues	=CHOOSE($P$2,B7,B8,B9,B10,B11)		1	
3	Net Income %				
4	Gross Margin				
5					
6	Revenues	Jan	Feb		
7	All Regions		98,741	54,621	
8	East		27,474	22,674	
9	North		41,767	20,806	
10	South		18,911	1,125	
11	West		10,590	10,016	

Figure 15-28: Use the CHOOSE function to capture the correct data corresponding to the selected region.

We entered the same type of CHOOSE formula into the Jan column and then copied it across. (See Figure 15-29.)

	A	B	C
1		Jan	Feb
2	Revenues	=CHOOSE($P$2,B7,B8,B9,B10,B11)	=CHOOSE($P$2,C7,C8,C9,C10,C11)
3	Net Income %	=CHOOSE($P$2,B14,B15,B16,B17,B18)	=CHOOSE($P$2,C14,C15,C16,C17,C18)
4	Gross Margin	=CHOOSE($P$2,B21,B22,B23,B24,B25)	=CHOOSE($P$2,C21,C22,C23,C24,C25)

Figure 15-29: Create similar CHOOSE formulas for each row/category of data and then copy the choose formulas across months.

To test that your formulas are working, change the value of cell P2 manually, entering **1**, **2**, **3**, **4**, or **5**. When the formulas work, all that's left to do is create the charts using the staging table.

PART VI

Working with the Outside World

Importing Microsoft Access Data into Excel

16

In This Chapter

- Importing data from a Microsoft Access database
- Using the drag-and-drop method
- Using the Access Export Wizard
- Using the Get External Data group
- Using Microsoft Query

Wouldn't it be wonderful if all data that you came across were neatly packed in one easy-to-use Excel table? The reality is that you will encounter situations when the data you need comes from external data sources. External data is exactly what it sounds like; data that is not located in the Excel workbook in which you are operating. Some examples of external data sources are text files, Access tables, SQL Server tables, and even other Excel workbooks

This chapter explores the most efficient ways to get Access data into Excel. Since it's also important to know when a particular method is more efficient than another, in this chapter, we introduce you to several methods and examine what circumstances make one method better suited than another.

Before jumping in, however, there are a couple of disclaimers your humble authors would like to throw out there. First, we focus on getting data from Access, mainly because the external data for the typical Excel user basically means Access. Second, there are numerous ways to get data into Excel. In fact, between the functionality found in the UI and the VBA/code techniques, there are too many to focus on in one chapter. So for this endeavor, you'll focus on a handful of techniques that can be implemented in most situations, and don't come with a lot of pitfalls and gotchas.

The Drag-and-Drop Method

For simplicity and ease, you just can't beat the drag-and-drop method. Try this — simultaneously open an empty Excel workbook, and an Access database from which you want to import a table or query. In this case, you can use the Zalex Corporation example database that you can down-loaded from the Web site for this book. Now resize each application's window such that they are both fully visible on your screen.

Hover on the Access table or query you want to copy into Excel. Now click and drag the mouse over to the blank worksheet in Excel (see Figure 16-1).

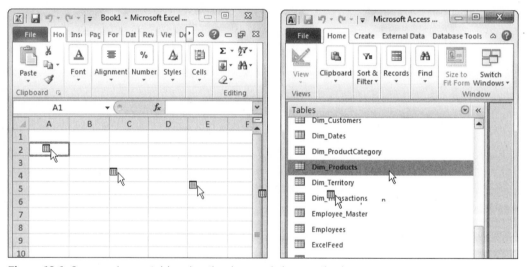

Figure 16-1: Copy an Access table using the drag-and-drop method.

The drag-and-drop method comes in handy when you are doing a quick one-time analysis where you need a specific set of data in Excel. It is not so useful if:

> ➤ You expect this step to occur routinely, as a part of a repeated analysis or report.

> ➤ You expect the users of your Excel presentation to get or update the data via this method.

> ➤ It's not possible or convenient for you to simply open up Access every time you need the information.

Under the preceding scenarios, it is much better to use another technique.

The Microsoft Access Export Wizard

Access has an Export Wizard and it's relatively simple to use.

1. With the Zalex Corporation example database open, click the Dim_Products table to select it.

2. On the External Data tab on the Ribbon, select the Excel icon under the Export group.

   This activates the wizard that you see in Figure 16-2.

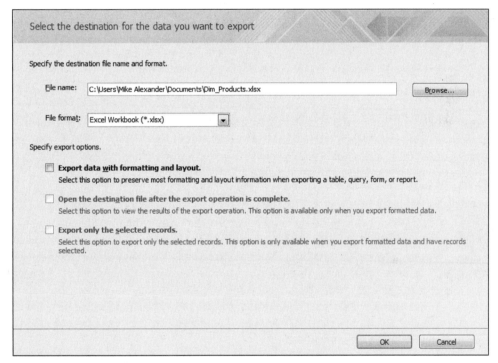

Figure 16-2: Export data to Excel using the Access Export Wizard.

As you can see in Figure 16-2, you have a few options that you can specify in the Excel Export Wizard. You can specify the file location, the file type, and some format preservation options.

3. Select the "Export data with formatting and layout" option.

4. Select the second menu option that asks if you want to open the destination file after the export operation is complete, and then click OK.

   Excel opens to show you the exported data.

In Access, the last page in the Export Wizard (Figure 16-3) asks if you want to save your export steps. Saving your export steps can be useful if you expect to frequently send that particular query or table to Excel.

Save Export Steps

Finished exporting 'Dim_Products' to file 'C:\Users\Mike Alexander\Documents\Dim_Products.xlsx' successfully.

Do you want to save these export steps? This will allow you to quickly repeat the operation without using the wizard.

☐ Save export steps

Close

Figure 16-3: Be sure to use the Save Export Steps option if you are going to export your data frequently.

The benefit to this method is that, unlike dragging and dropping, the ability to save export steps allows you to automate your exports by using macros.

The limitation of this export method is that it is done within Access. If you are creating an Excel dashboard or report where updated data must be under the Excel user's control, this method is not viable. In this circumstance, importing data from the Excel menu and/or using Microsoft Query (MS Query) in Excel is the more viable option (we discuss MS Query later in this chapter).

Caution

You may export your Access table or query to an existing Excel file instead of creating a new file. But note the following: by default, the name of the exported object is the name of the table or query in Access. Be careful if you have an Excel object with that same name in your workbook as it may be overwritten. For example, exporting the PriceMaster table to an Excel worksheet that already has a worksheet named PriceMaster will cause the worksheet to be overwritten. Also, make sure the workbook to which you are exporting is closed. If you try to export to an open workbook, you will likely an error in Access.

The Get External Data Icon

The option to pull data from Access has been available in Excel for many versions; it was just buried several layers deep in somewhat cryptic menu titles. This made getting Access data into Excel seem like a mysterious and tenuous proposition for many Excel analysts. With the introduction of the Ribbon in Excel 2007, Microsoft made importing Access data from Excel a little less nebulous including the option right on the Ribbon under the Data tab.

Using the Get External Data group in Excel allows you to establish a updatable data connection between Excel and Access. To see the power of this method, walk through these steps:

1. Open a new Excel workbook and select the Data tab on the Ribbon.

2. In the Get External Data group, select the From Access icon.

    This opens the Select Data Source dialog box that you see in Figure 16-4. If the database from which you want to import data is local, browse to the file location and select it. If you have an Access database on a network drive at another location, you may also select that database as well — provided that you have the proper authorization and access.

3. Navigate to the sample database found under `c:\ExcelDashboardsAndReports` (see Figure 16-4), and then click the Open button.

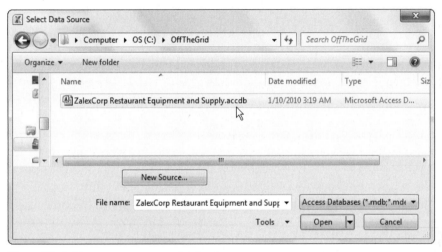

Figure 16-4: Choose your source database.

In some environments, a series of Data Link Properties dialog boxes open asking for credentials (that is, username and password). Most Access databases do not require login credentials, but if your database does require a username and password, type them in the Data Link Properties.

4. Click OK.

    The Select Table dialog box (see Figure 16-5) opens.

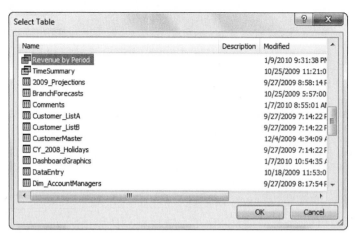

Figure 16-5: Select the Access Object you want to import.

5. Select Revenue by Period query and click OK.

   The Import Data dialog box opens (see Figure 16-6), which allows you to define where and how to import the table. You have the option of importing the data into a Table, a PivotTable Report, or a PivotChart and PivotTable Report.

   Note that if you choose PivotChart and PivotTable Report, the data is saved to a pivot cache without writing the actual data to the worksheet. This allows your pivot table to function as normal without having to import potentially hundreds of thousands of data rows twice (once for the pivot cache and once for the spreadsheet).

6. Select Table as the output view and define cell A1 as the output location (see Figure 16-6).

7. Click OK.

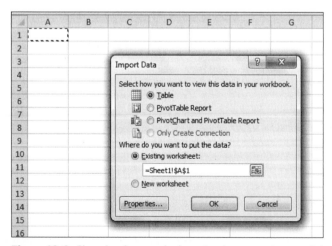

Figure 16-6: Choosing how and where to view your Access data.

Your reward for all the work will be a table similar to that shown in Figure 16-7, which contains the imported data from your Access database.

Region	Market	Business_Segment	SumofSales_Amount
CANADA	CANADA	Bar Equipment	35975.25
CANADA	CANADA	Commercial Appliances	71272.1
CANADA	CANADA	Concession Equipment	205874.6
CANADA	CANADA	Fryers	129636.2
CANADA	CANADA	Ovens and Ranges	1183772.75
CANADA	CANADA	Refrigerators and Coolers	1728600.95
CANADA	CANADA	Warmers	392969.3
Midwest	Chicago	Bar Equipment	3168
Midwest	Chicago	Commercial Appliances	9081
Midwest	Chicago	Concession Equipment	18218
Midwest	Chicago	Fryers	9846.8

Figure 16-7: Your imported Access data.

The incredibly powerful thing about importing data this way is that it's refreshable. That's right. If you import data from Access using this technique, Excel creates a table that you can update by right-clicking and selecting the Refresh option, as shown in Figure 16-8. When you update your imported data, Excel reconnects to your Access database and imports the data again. As long as a connection to your database is available, you will be able to refresh with a mere click of the mouse.

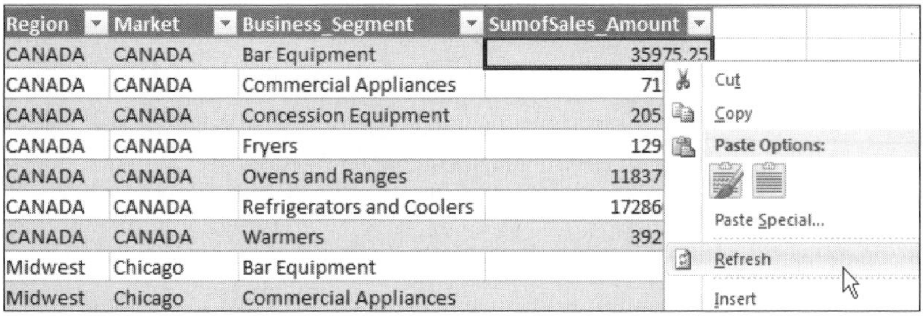

Region	Market	Business_Segment	SumofSales_Amount		
CANADA	CANADA	Bar Equipment	35975.25		
CANADA	CANADA	Commercial Appliances	71	Cut	
CANADA	CANADA	Concession Equipment	205	Copy	
CANADA	CANADA	Fryers	129	Paste Options:	
CANADA	CANADA	Ovens and Ranges	11837		
CANADA	CANADA	Refrigerators and Coolers	17286		
CANADA	CANADA	Warmers	392	Paste Special...	
Midwest	Chicago	Bar Equipment		Refresh	
Midwest	Chicago	Commercial Appliances		Insert	

Figure 16-8: As long as a connection to your database is available, you can update your table with the latest data.

Again, a major advantage to using the Get External Data group is that it allows you to establish a refreshable data connection between Excel and Access. In most cases, you can set up the connection one time, and then just update the data connection when needed. You can even record an Excel macro to update the data on some trigger or event, which is ideal for automating the transfer of data from Access.

The disadvantage to this method is that you have to take the data as it is in Access. So you give up the ability to use sorts, filters, and table joins to customize the data that you import into Excel.

Microsoft Query

MS Query is a stand-alone program, installed with the Office suite, that you can use to connect to external data sources from Excel. MS Query has one distinct advantage over the other methods of importing Access data into Excel — flexibility.

When transferring data using any of the previously mentioned methods, you can only import an existing table or query as is. You have no opportunity to parse, filter, or sort the data on the fly before importing it.

Not so with MS Query. With MS Query, you don't have to rely on the original tables or queries to be filtered or configured in a particular way. You can apply your own filters and sorts to your data pulls (through MS Query), essentially creating custom views that don't necessarily exist in the source database.

Note

MS Query may or may not be installed on your system, based on how you performed your Office installation. Keep in mind that if you do not have the MS Query program installed on your system, you will not be able to link to external data sources in Excel. To install MS Query, you will need your Microsoft Office installation disk. Start the Microsoft Office Setup and choose to customize your installation. While you are customizing your installation, look for Office Tools. You will find an entry called Microsoft Query under Office Tools. Make sure you set it to "Run from My Computer", and then complete the installation.

Start MS Query

Go to the Get External Data menu under the Data tab of the Excel Ribbon. To start MS Query, select the From Other Sources option and then select From Microsoft Query from the drop-down list. Figure 16-9 displays your options.

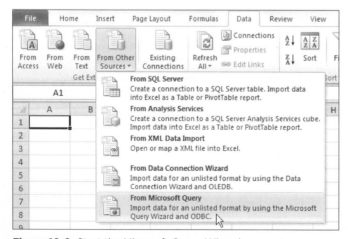

Figure 16-9: Start the Microsoft Query Wizard.

After MS Query opens, you see the Choose Data Source dialog box (see Figure 16-10). This is where you will start building your MS Query import.

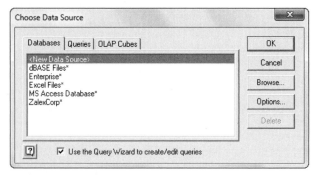

Figure 16-10: The Choose Data Source dialog box is your starting point.

Set up your data source connection

For this exercise, you will use the source data from the Zalexcorp example database that you downloaded. To set this database as an available data source, follow these steps:

1. From the Choose Data Source dialog, choose <New Data Source> from the Databases tab.

   This opens the Create New Data Source dialog box.

2. Type a name for your data source at the top of the dialog box: **ZalexCorp** (see Figure 16-11).

Figure 16-11: Name your new data source.

3. In the drop-down list, choose a type of driver for the database to which you want to connect. From this drop-down list, make sure you select Microsoft Access Driver (*.mdb, *.accdb), as shown in Figure 16-12.

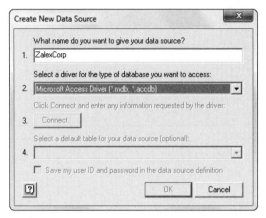

Figure 16-12: Choose the Access driver designed for .mdb and .accdb files.

4. Click Connect.

   This opens the ODBC Microsoft Access Setup dialog box shown in Figure 16-13.

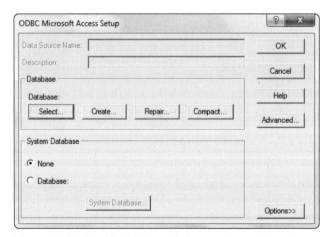

Figure 16-13: The ODBC Microsoft Access Setup dialog box.

5. In the Database section, click the Select button to find your database in the Select Database dialog box (see Figure 16-14).

   In this example, you will select the ZalexCorp database found in the c:\OffTheGrid directory.

6. Continue to click OK until you return to the Choose Data Source dialog box. ZalexCorp now shows up in the list of databases (see Figure 16-15).

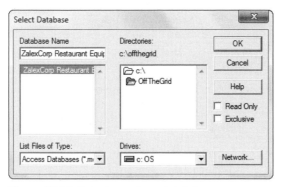

Figure 16-14: Select your target database.

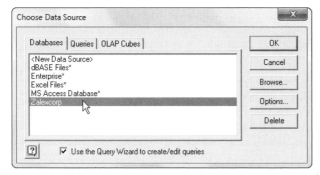

Figure 16-15: ZalexCorp is now in the list of available data sources.

Now that your ZalexCorp data source is set up, MS Query will remember its location, allowing you to use it repeatedly without the need to point to it each time you need to use it.

Tip

MS Query works equally well for non-local databases (those that reside on a net-worked drive or even on the Web). In the Select Database dialog box, you'll find a drop-down menu with a list of computer drives available to you.

If your target database is on a network drive that is already mapped to your computer, choose the drive from the drop-down menu, and browse the file hierarchy until you find the database that you are looking for.

If your database in on a network that isn't mapped to your computer, click the Network button (shown in the lower right of the dialog box in Figure 16-14). This will fire up a wizard to help you connect to a network drive or folder to which you are not currently mapped.

Build your custom data pull

Now that you have your ZalexCorp database set as an available data source, you can build your own custom data pull. If you've closed the MS Query Wizard, start it back up by going to the

Data tab of the Excel Ribbon, selecting the From Other Sources option, and then selecting From Microsoft Query.

1. Select your ZalexCorp data source, as shown in Figure 16-16, and click OK.

   In Figure 16-17, you see a dialog box that display tables and queries within the Zalexcorp database.

2. Select the Revenue by Period object and click the button with the right pointing arrow. Click the Next button.

3. You can change the order of the data fields by clicking the up and down arrows to the right of the Columns in Your Query list box. Arrange the columns so that Region and Market come before Period as shown in Figure 16-18. Click the Next button.

4. You can apply your own criteria to filter your data before importing (see Figure 16-19). Select the Period field to enable the filter options on the right. After filtering is enabled, select Is Greater Than from the condition drop-down control. Then select 200812 for criteria. Click the Next button.

5. Sort your query results by Period in ascending order, and then by SumofSalesAmount in descending order.

   Figure 16-20 illustrates what this step looks like after the needed sorts have been applied. Click the Next button.

6. Select the option to view our data in Excel and click the Finish button.

7. At this point, you should see the Import dialog box shown in Figure 16-21. Select the option to return the data to a Table in cell A1, and then click OK.

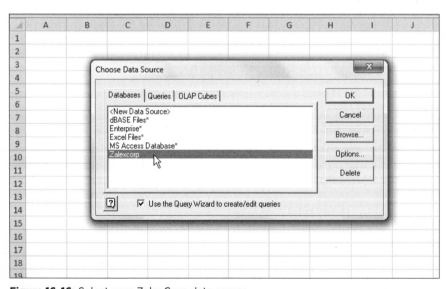

Figure 16-16: Select your ZalexCorp data source.

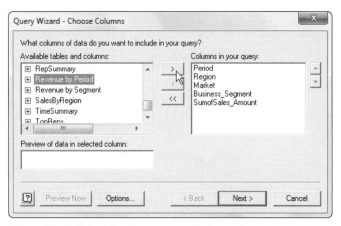

Figure 16-17: Select the Revenue by Period object.

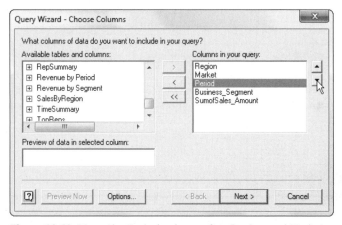

Figure 16-18: Move the Period column after Region and Market.

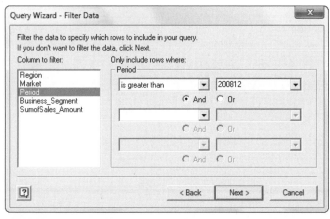

Figure 16-19: Set a filter telling MS Query to return only those records where the Period is greater than 200812.

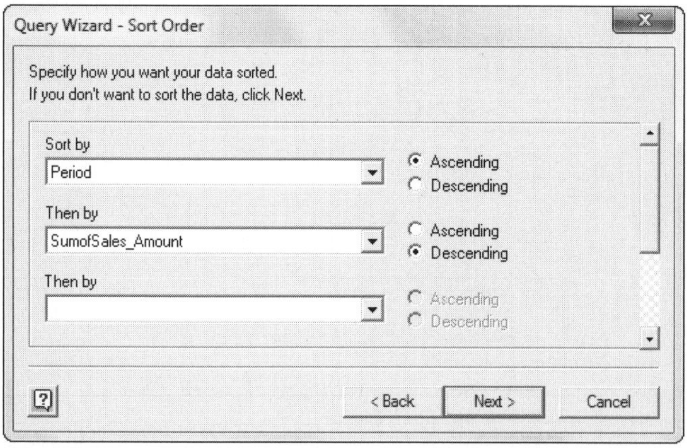

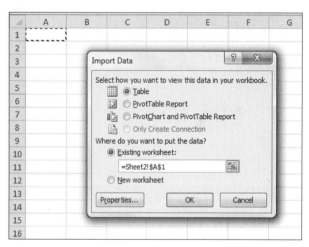

Figure 16-20: You can apply your own sorting to your query results.

Figure 16-21: Return your results to a Table on your spreadsheet.

If all went well, you should have a table similar to that shown in Figure 16-22. Note that as designed, your query results contain only records where the Period is greater than 200812. Also note that the columns have the correct order and sorting.

You can update the data by right-clicking anywhere inside your query table and selecting the Refresh button. You can also click the Refresh button found in the Design tab, which activates when you cursor is inside the query table.

Again, while setting up an MS Query seems like a lot of work, the ability to parse, filter, and sort data on the fly gives MS Query a distinct advantage over the previously mentioned methods for transferring data.

	A	B	C	D	E
1	Period ▾	Region ▾	Market ▾	Business_Segment ▾	SumofSales_Amount ▾
2	200901	South	Florida	Warmers	1216003.3
3	200901	South	Florida	Refrigerators and Coolers	724743
4	200901	South	Florida	Ovens and Ranges	526507.5
5	200901	West	California	Refrigerators and Coolers	240063
6	200901	Southeast	Charlotte	Warmers	210336.4
7	200901	South	Florida	Commercial Appliances	173578.4
8	200901	South	Florida	Concession Equipment	139441.25
9	200901	West	California	Ovens and Ranges	100405.6
10	200901	Southwest	Denver	Refrigerators and Coolers	96733
11	200901	West	California	Warmers	85768.5
12	200901	South	Dallas	Refrigerators and Coolers	81530
13	200901	South	Florida	Fryers	79506.95
14	200901	Southeast	Charlotte	Refrigerators and Coolers	65190.8

Figure 16-22: You've successfully created your first MS Query.

Managing external data properties

Your query tables have a few adjustable properties which are exposed via the Properties dialog box. You can get to the properties of a particular External data table by clicking the target table and selecting the Properties icon under the Data tab (see Figure 16-23).

Figure 16-23: Getting to the properties of an external data table dialog box.

Activating the properties of an query table calls up the dialog box shown in Figure 16-24. Adjusting these properties allows you to further customize your query tables to suit your needs. Take a moment to familiarize yourself with some the useful options on this dialog box.

continued

continued

External Data Properties

Connection

Name: Query from Zalexcorp

Data formatting and layout

☐ Include row numbers   ☑ Preserve column sort/filter/layout
☑ Adjust column width   ☑ Preserve cell formatting

If the number of rows in the data range changes upon refresh:
◉ Insert cells for new data, delete unused cells
○ Insert entire rows for new data, clear unused cells
○ Overwrite existing cells with new data, clear unused cells

[OK] [Cancel]

Figure 16-24: The External Data Properties dialog box.

- **Include Row Numbers:** This property is deselected by default. Selecting this property creates a dummy column that contains row numbers. The first column of your dataset will be this row number column upon refresh.

- **Adjust Column Width:** This property is selected by default, telling Excel to adjust the column widths each time the data is refreshed. Deselecting this option will cause the column widths to remain the same.

- **Preserve Column/Sort/Filter/Layout:** If this is selected, the order of the columns and rows of the Excel range remains unchanged. This way, you can rearrange and sort the columns and rows of the external data in your worksheet without worrying about blowing away your formatting each time you refresh. Deselecting this property will make the Excel range look like the query.

- **Preserve Cell Formatting:** This is selected by default, telling Excel to keep the applied cell formatting when you refresh.

- **Insert Cells For New Data, Delete Unused Cells:** This is the default setting for data range changes. When data rows decrease, you may have errors in adjacent cells that reference your external range. The cells these formulas referenced are deleted, so you will get an #VALUE error in your formula cells.

- **Insert Entire Rows for New Data, Clear Unused Cells:** When the unused cells are cleared instead of deleted, the formula may no longer return an error. Instead, it continues to reference cells from the original range — even though some of them are blank now. This could still give you erroneous results.

- **Overwrite Cells For New Data, Clear Unused Cells:** The third option should be the same as option two when rows decrease as unused cells are cleared.

Sharing Your Work with the Outside World

In This Chapter

- Controlling access to your dashboards and reports
- Displaying your Excel dashboards in PowerPoint
- Saving your dashboards and reports to a PDF file

The focus of this chapter is preparing your dashboard for life outside your PC. Here, we discuss the various methods of protecting your work from accidental and purposeful meddling and discover how you can distribute your dashboards via PowerPoint and PDF files.

Securing Your Dashboards and Reports

Before distributing any Excel-based work, you should always consider protecting your file by using the security capabilities native to Excel. Although none of Excel's protection methods are hacker-proof, they do serve to protect the formulas, data structures, and other objects that make your dashboard tick.

Securing access to the entire workbook

Perhaps the best way to protect your Excel file is to use Excel's file sharing protection options. These options enable you to apply security at the workbook level, requiring a password to view or make changes to the file. This method is by far the easiest to apply and manage since there's no need to protect each worksheet one at a time. You can apply a blanket protection to guard against unauthorized access and edits. Take a moment to review the file sharing options, which are as follows:

> ➤ Forcing read-only access to a file until a password is given

➤ Requiring a password to open an Excel file

➤ Removing workbook-level protection

The next few sections discuss these options in detail.

Permitting read-only access unless a password is given

You can force your workbook to go into read-only mode until the user types in the password. This way you can keep your file safe from unauthorized changes, yet still allow authorized users to edit the file.

Here are the steps to force read-only mode:

1. With your file open, click the File tab.

2. To open the Save As dialog box, select Save As.

3. In the Save As dialog box, click the Tools button and select General Options (see Figure 17-1).

   The General Options dialog box appears.

4. Type an appropriate password in the Password to Modify input box (see Figure 17-2) and click OK.

5. Excel asks you to reenter your password, so reenter your chosen password.

6. Save your file to a new name.

   At this point, your file is password protected from unauthorized changes. If you were to open your file, you'd see something similar to Figure 17-3. Failing to type the correct password causes the file to go into read-only mode.

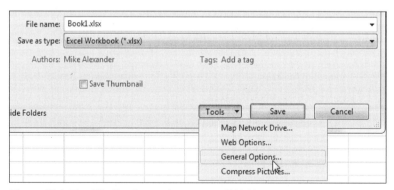

Figure 17-1: The File Sharing options are well hidden away in the Save As dialog box under General Options.

Figure 17-2: Type the password needed to modify the file.

Figure 17-3: A password is now needed to make changes to the file.

Note that Excel passwords are case-sensitive, so make sure Caps Lock on your keyboard is in the off position when entering your password.

Tip

Requiring a password to open an Excel file

You may have instances where your Excel dashboards are so sensitive only certain users are authorized to see them. In these cases, you can require your workbook to receive a password to open it. Here are the steps to set up a password for the file.

1. With your file open, click the File tab.

2. To open the Save As dialog box, select Save As.

3. In the Save As dialog box, click the Tools button and select General Options (see Figure 17-1).

   The General Options dialog box opens.

4. Type an appropriate password in the Password to Open text box (as shown in Figure 17-4) and click OK.

5. Excel asks you to reenter your password.

6. Save your file to a new name.

   At this point, your file is password protected from unauthorized viewing.

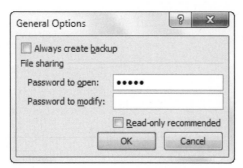

Figure 17-4: Type the password needed to modify the file.

Removing workbook-level protection

Removing workbook-level protection is as easy as clearing the passwords from the General Options dialog box. Here's how you do it:

1. With your file open, click the File tab.

2. To open the Save As dialog box, select Save As.

3. In the Save As dialog box, click the Tools button and select General Options (see Figure 17-1).

   The General Options dialog box opens.

4. Clear the Password to Open input box as well as the Password to Modify input box and click OK.

5. Save your file.

Tip

When you select the Read-Only Recommended check box in the General Options dialog box (refer to Figure 17-4), you get a cute but useless message recommending read-only access upon opening the file. This message is only a recommendation and does not prevent anyone from opening the file as read/write.

Limiting access to specific worksheet ranges

You may find that you need to lock specific worksheet ranges, preventing users from taking certain actions. For example, you may not want users to break your data model by inserting or deleting columns and rows. You can prevent this by locking those columns and rows.

Unlocking editable ranges

By default, all cells in a worksheet are set to be locked when you apply worksheet-level protection. The cells on that worksheet can't be altered in any way. That being said, you may find you need certain cells or ranges to be editable even in a locked state, like the example shown in Figure 17-5.

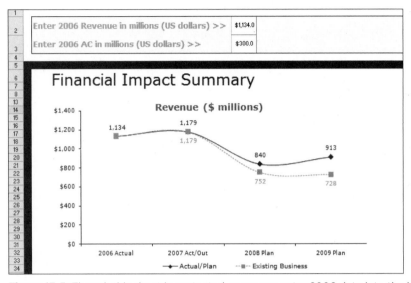

Figure 17-5: Though this sheet is protected, users can enter 2006 data into the input cells provided.

Before you protect your worksheet, you can unlock the cell or range of cells that you want users to be able to edit. (The next section shows you how to protect your entire worksheet.) Here's how to do it:

1. Select the cells you need to unlock.

2. Right-click and select Format Cells.

3. On the Protection tab, as shown in Figure 17-6, deselect the Locked check box.

4. Click OK to apply the change.

Figure 17-6: To ensure a cell remains unlocked when the worksheet is protected, deselect the Locked check box.

Applying worksheet protection

After you've selectively unlocked the necessary cells, you can begin to apply worksheet protection. Just follow these steps:

1. To open the Protect Sheet dialog box, click the Protect Sheet button on the Review tab of the Ribbon (see Figure 17-7).

2. Type a password in the text box (see Figure 17-8), and then click OK.

   This is the password that removes worksheet protection. Note that specifying a password is optional, as you can apply and remove worksheet protection without one.

3. In the list box (see Figure 17-8), select which elements users can change after you protect the worksheet.

   When a check box is cleared for a particular action, Excel prevents users from taking that action.

4. If you provided a password, reenter the password.

5. Click OK to apply the worksheet protection.

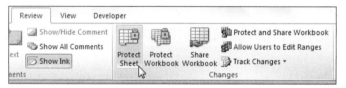

Figure 17-7: Select Protect Sheet in the Review tab.

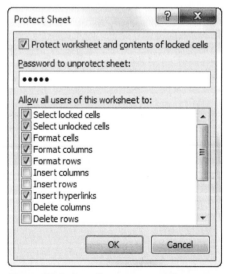

Figure 17-8: Specify a password that removes worksheet protection.

Protect sheet elements and actions

Take a moment to familiarize yourself with the some of the other actions you can limit when protecting a worksheet (see Figure 17-8). They are as follows:

- **Select Locked Cells:** Allows or prevents the selection of locked cells.
- **Select Unlocked Cells:** Allows or prevents the selection of unlocked cells.
- **Format Cells:** Allows or prevents the formatting of cells.
- **Format Columns:** Allows or prevents the use of column formatting commands, including changing column width or hiding columns.
- **Format Rows:** Allows or prevents the use of row formatting commands, including changing row height or hiding rows.
- **Insert Columns:** Allows or prevents the inserting of columns.
- **Insert Rows:** Allows or prevents the inserting of rows.
- **Insert Hyperlinks:** Allows or prevents the inserting of hyperlinks.
- **Delete Columns:** Allows or prevents the deleting of columns. Note that if Delete Columns is protected and Insert Columns is not protected, you can technically insert columns you can't delete.
- **Delete Rows:** Allows or prevents the deleting of rows. Note that if Delete Rows is protected and Insert Rows is not protected, you can technically insert columns you can't delete.
- **Sort:** Allows or prevents the use of Sort commands. Note that this doesn't apply to locked ranges. Users can't sort ranges that contain locked cells on a protected worksheet, regardless of this setting.
- **Use AutoFilter:** Allows or prevents use of Excel's AutoFilter functionality. Users can't create or remove AutoFiltered ranges on a protected worksheet, regardless of this setting.
- **Use PivotTable Reports:** Allows or prevents the modifying, refreshing, or formatting pivot tables found on the protected sheet.
- **Edit Objects:** Allows or prevents the formatting and altering of shapes, charts, text boxes, controls, or other graphics objects.
- **Edit Scenarios:** Allows or prevents the viewing of scenarios.

Removing worksheet protection

Just follow these steps to remove any worksheet protection you may have applied:

1. Click the Unprotect Sheet button on the Review tab.

2. If you specified a password while protecting the worksheet, Excel asks you for that password (see Figure 17-9). Type the password and click OK to immediately remove protection.

Figure 17-9: The Unprotect Sheet button removes worksheet protection.

Protecting the workbook structure

If you look under the Review tab in the Ribbon, you see the Protect Workbook button next to the Protect Sheet button. Protecting the workbook enables you to prevent users from taking any action that affects the structure of your workbook, such as adding/deleting worksheets, hiding/unhiding worksheets, and naming or moving worksheets. Just follow these steps to protect a workbook:

1. To open the Protect Structure and Windows dialog box, click the Protect Workbook button on the Review tab of the Ribbon, as shown in Figure 17-10.

2. Choose which elements you want to protect: workbook structure, windows, or both. When a check box is cleared for a particular action, Excel prevents users from taking that action.

3. If you provided a password, reenter the password.

4. Click OK to apply the worksheet protection.

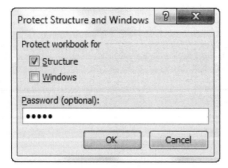

Figure 17-10: The Protect Structure and Windows dialog box.

Selecting Structure prevents users from

- ➤ Viewing worksheets that you've hidden
- ➤ Moving, deleting, hiding, or changing the names of worksheets
- ➤ Inserting new worksheets or chart sheets
- ➤ Moving or copying worksheets to another workbook
- ➤ Displaying the source data for a cell in a pivot table Values area or displaying pivot table Filter pages on separate worksheets
- ➤ Creating a scenario summary report
- ➤ Using any Analysis ToolPak utility that requires results to be placed on a new worksheet
- ➤ Recording new macros

Choosing Windows prevents users from changing, moving, or sizing the workbook windows while the workbook is opened.

Linking Your Excel Dashboards to PowerPoint

Several methods exist for linking Excel data to a PowerPoint presentation. For our purposes, we focus on the method that is most conducive to presenting frequently updated dashboards and reports in PowerPoint — creating a *dynamic link*. A dynamic link allows your PowerPoint presentation to automatically pick up changes that you make to data in your Excel worksheet.

Tip

This technique of linking Excel charts to PowerPoint is ideal if you aren't proficient at building charts in PowerPoint. Build the chart in Excel and then create a link for the chart in PowerPoint.

Creating the link between Excel and PowerPoint

When you copy and paste a range of data, you're simply creating a picture of the range. However, when you create a link to a range, PowerPoint stores the location information to your source field and then displays a representation of the linked data. The net effect is that when the data in your source file changes, PowerPoint updates its representation of the data to reflect the changes.

On the Web

You can find the example Chapter 17 Sample Data.xlsx **file for this chapter on this book's companion Web site at** www.wiley.com/go/exceldr.

To test this concept of linking to an Excel range, follow these steps:

1. Open the `Chapter 17 Sample File.xlsx` file.

2. Click the chart to select it and press Ctrl+C on your keyboard to copy the chart.

3. Open a new PowerPoint presentation and place your cursor at the location that you want to display the linked table.

4. On the Home tab in PowerPoint, choose Paste ➜ Paste Special, as shown in Figure 17-11.

Figure 17-11: Select Paste Special from the Home tab in PowerPoint.

The Paste Special dialog box appears (see Figure 17-12).

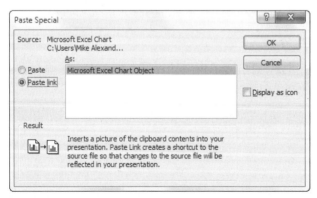

Figure 17-12: Be sure to select Paste Link and set the link as an Excel Chart Object.

5. Select the Paste Link radio button and choose Microsoft Excel Chart Object from the list of document types.

6. Click OK to apply the link.

Your chart on your PowerPoint presentation now links back to your Excel worksheet (see Figure 17-13).

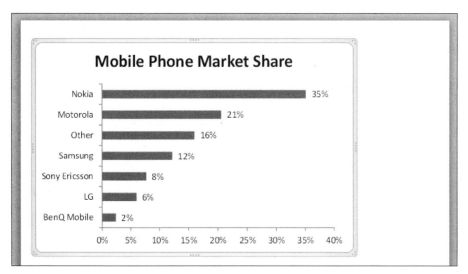

Figure 17-13: Your Excel chart is now linked into your new PowerPoint presentation.

Tip

If you're copying multiple charts, select the range of cells that contain the charts and press Ctrl+C to copy. This way, you're copying everything in that range of cells — charts and all.

Manually updating links to capture updates

The nifty thing about dynamic links is they can be updated, enabling you to capture any new data in your Excel worksheets without recreating the links. To see how this works, follow these steps:

1. Go back to your Excel file (from the example in the previous section) and change the values for Samsung and Nokia, as shown in Figure 17-14.

   Note the chart has changed.

2. Return to PowerPoint, right-click the chart link in your presentation and choose Update Link, as demonstrated in Figure 17-15.

   You see that your linked chart automatically captures the changes.

3. Save and close both your Excel file and your PowerPoint presentation, and then open only your newly created PowerPoint presentation.

Now you see the message shown in Figure 17-16. Clicking the Update Links button updates all links in the PowerPoint presentation. Each time you open any PowerPoint presentation with links, it asks you whether you want to update the links.

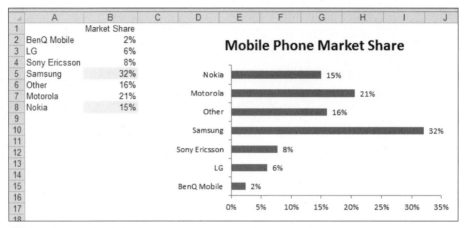

Figure 17-14: With a linked chart, you can make changes to the raw data without worrying about re-exporting the data into PowerPoint.

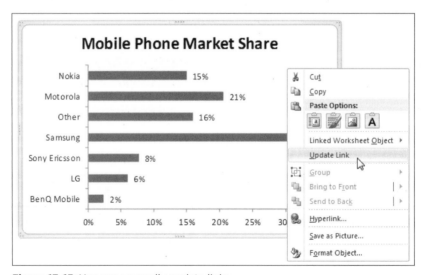

Figure 17-15: You can manually update links.

Figure 17-16: PowerPoint, by default, asks if you want to update all links in the presentation.

Automatically updating links

Having PowerPoint ask you whether you want to update the links each and every time you open your presentation quickly gets annoying. You can avoid this message by specifying that PowerPoint automatically updates your dynamic links upon opening the presentation file. Here's how:

1. In PowerPoint, click the File tab to get to the Backstage View.

2. In the Info Pane, select Edit Links to Files, as shown in Figure 17-17.

   The Links dialog box opens (see Figure 17-18).

3. Click each of your links and select the Automatic radio button.

When your links are set to update automatically, PowerPoint automatically synchronizes with your Excel worksheet file and ensures that all your updates are displayed.

Tip

To select multiple links in the Links dialog box, press the Ctrl key on your keyboard while you select your links.

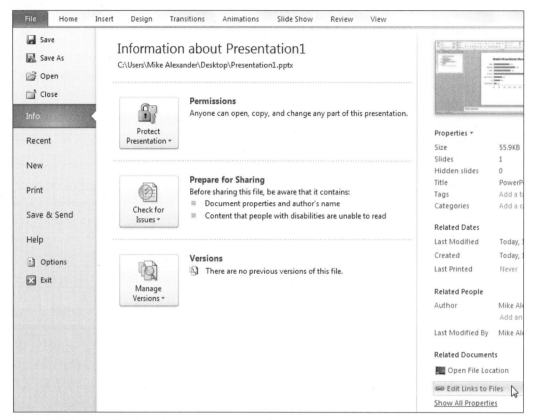

Figure 17-17: Open the dialog box to manage your links.

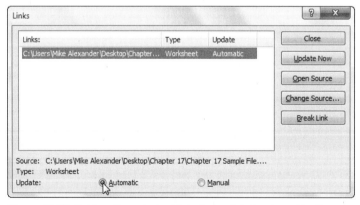

Figure 17-18: Setting the selected links to updated automatically.

Distributing Your Dashboards Via a PDF

In Excel 2010, Microsoft has made it possible to convert your Excel worksheets to a PDF document. A PDF is the standard document sharing format developed by Adobe. Distributing your reports and dashboards as a PDF file allows you to share your final product without sharing all the formulas and backend plumbing that comes the workbook.

To convert your workbook to a PDF, follow these simple steps:

1. Click File tab, and then choose the Save As command.

2. In the Save As dialog box, select PDF as the Save As type (see Figure 17-19).

3. To open the Options dialog box, click the Options button box as shown in Figure 17-20.

   Here, you can specify what you would like to print. You have the option of printing the entire workbook, specific pages, or a range that you've selected.

4. Click OK to confirm your selections.

5. Click Save.

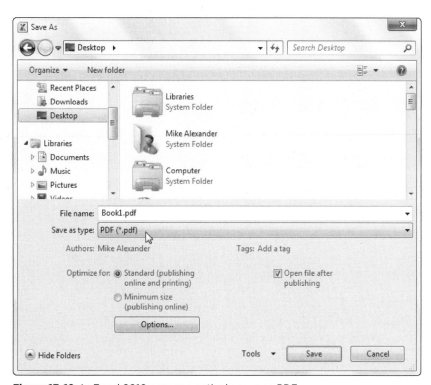

Figure 17-19: In Excel 2010, you can natively save as PDF.

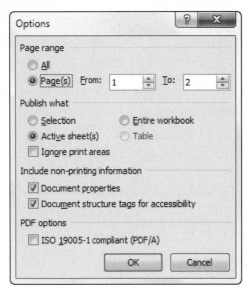

Figure 17-20: Excel allows you to define what gets sent to PDF.

▶ Index

F

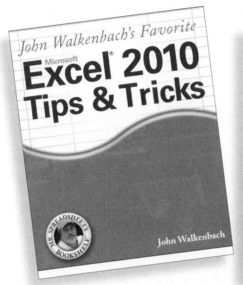
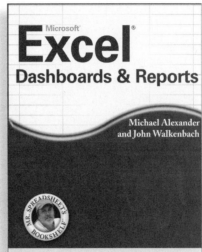

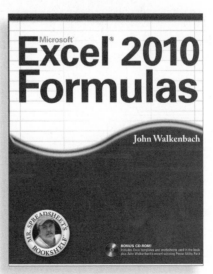